THE
SHARP
END

THE SHARP END

The fight against organized crime

FRANK CATER
AND TOM TULLETT

THE BODLEY HEAD
LONDON

To Bridget

A CIP catalogue record for this book is available
from the British Library.

ISBN 0-370-30789-5

© Frank Cater and Tom Tullett 1988
Typeset by Computape (Pickering) Ltd, North Yorkshire
Printed in Great Britain for
The Bodley Head Ltd,
32 Bedford Square, London WC1B 3EL
by
Mackays of Chatham PLC

First published in 1988

CONTENTS

LIST OF PHOTOGRAPHS

I

1952: BEGINNINGS

There comes a time in the lives of most young men – even if, as I was, they're of little education and no evident skills – when they start looking for some sort of steady, reliable, worthwhile employment. And in my case the pattern was familiar enough. I was twenty-three years old, and since leaving the Royal Marines I'd been working in the Lyons' confectionery factory at Cadby Hall in London, alongside Olympia, processing the chocolate fondant that went on the tops of their famous cup cakes. It was an undemanding job, and pretty boring, but at least it was well-paid – with overtime I was taking home twelve pounds a week, and this in 1952 when a single pound note would feed a hungry family for two or three days. Even so, I was restless, the job held nil prospects of advancement, and my wife Bridget had just told me she was pregnant.

We'd met back in 1950. Bridget had been working as a cook in domestic service in London, a fine-looking Irish country girl, and we'd married no more than a year later, luckily finding rented furnished accommodation in Shepherd's Bush, convenient for my job at Cadby Hall. But now that we were starting a family we both agreed that some more permanent work was needed for me, a career in which I could take a lasting interest.

My experience in the service turned my thoughts towards the police force. I liked the prospect of being useful which the police would give me. But it occurred to me that my lack of formal education might be a disqualification.

I'd had only very scrappy schooling. Born in Fulham in June 1929, by the time I was nine years old my parents had separated and I was living with my grandfather and my Aunt Alice. My grandfather, Joe Cater, had been something of a romantic figure: a country lad, from Ely up in Cambridgeshire, he'd run away from home in his teens, joining a travelling circus as it passed through town. Eventually he'd ended up in London where he'd settled down, put his skills with horses to work with a London bus company, and married my grandmother. They had five children, of whom my father, Harry, was the youngest.

Harry and his two brothers fought in the 1914–18 war. All three survived, but the oldest boy, John, was gassed in France and never fully recovered, and my father, although never physically wounded, carried mental scars from the nightmare of the trenches that were to cripple him in later years with what was diagnosed at the time as 'neurasthenia'. He became ill, pathologically anxious, and unable to hold down a full-time job. And by that time he was married to my mother and they had four children – with myself the eldest – so life in the depression years of the thirties wasn't easy for any of us.

We lived in Fulham, first in the New King's Road and then in Cornwall Street (now known as Rumbold Road), almost overlooking the grounds of Chelsea Football Club at Stamford Bridge. Grandfather Joe, who'd been looked after by his oldest daughter, my unmarried Aunt Alice, ever since Grandmother had died of influenza in 1918, lived on the other side of Fulham. And when my parents finally split up in 1938, my father, sister and I were taken under Alice and Grandfather's wing, while my two brothers went to stay with our other aunt, Elizabeth, who had a husband and jolly family of her own in nearby West Kensington.

Aunt Alice was a wonder. A woman of very strict Victorian attitudes and values, she was all the same marvellously loving and perceptive. I can't believe that I was an easy nine-year-old to deal with, yet she was always patient and caring. In fact, with her good humour, her gentleness, her sound judgement and her strong moral sense, she was to be the finest single influence in my young life – and when she died many years later, in her eighties, I lost a very dear and precious friend.

But then, back in 1939, the war came. Up until then I'd been in the local elementary school – and managing reasonably well in spite of my unsettled home life – and for a while this continued, even if the bombing meant that lessons were unpredictable and often the school never opened at all. Certainly I did well enough to be offered, at the age of eleven, a place in either a secondary school (the equivalent of a grammar school) or a central school (a technical school), either of which would have continued my formal education at least until I was sixteen. But unfortunately both schools required that pupils' parents provided uniforms and books, and my family was unable to manage this. So I stayed on at elementary school and left at fourteen, which I remember as being a bitter disappointment.

In the meantime the German bombing of London had worsened and I had briefly been evacuated to Guildford, and then to Chertsey. But in 1943 my organised schooling ended and I returned to London, to stay with Aunt Alice again, and found a job as an apprentice fitter and turner in a small engineering factory just off the Fulham Road, close to Putney Bridge. I was working there when the V1 buzz-bomb attacks began on London, and I spent much of my first year up on the factory roof, bomb-watching.

I don't know if I'd ever have made much of a fitter and turner. But in any event I was never to find out, since not only did conscription into the armed services loom over me when I got to be eighteen, even after the end of the war in 1945, but also, only a month after my seventeenth birthday in 1946, my poor father fell seriously ill with leukaemia and very quickly died. He was only forty-seven.

His death shattered me. Suddenly I felt a desperate need to get away from London and all its associations. On impulse, I pre-empted my national service call-up and, on 20 August 1946, I enlisted in Her Majesty's Royal Marines and was posted down to Deal, in Kent, for my basic training.

I served in the Marines for two years and four months, and if the rigorous life didn't exactly make a man of me it certainly broadened both my mind and my shoulders, developed my muscles, and extended my vocabulary of unrepeatables. Thus fortified, and presented upon demob with a blue double-breasted chalk-striped suit and a brown, wide-brimmed trilby, I left the service in December 1948 and returned to Fulham. And it was then, stony broke, sketchily educated and without a trade, that I took the job at Joe Lyons' factory.

By 1951 I was very happily married and now, early in 1952, I was wondering if my lack of schooling would stop me from beginning a new, worthwhile career as a policeman. In the event, of course, I needn't have worried. I hadn't completely wasted my time since leaving school, I was able to pass the necessary entrance tests and written examinations quite easily and, on 5 May 1952, I joined the Metropolitan Police Force.

Incidentally, this meant a drastic cut in our living standards. As I've already said, my weekly take-home wage from Cadby Hall was around twelve pounds. A police constable's weekly pay in those days was in the region of six pounds. Policemen weren't paid for the overtime they worked, promotion was slow, and indeed it was nearly ten years before

I would again be handed a twelve pound pay packet. But Bridget and I didn't mind. I knew right from the beginning of my training at Peel House, the police school in Regency Street off Vauxhall Bridge Road, that I'd taken the right decision. Police life, in one form or another, was the life for me.

And then, in July that year, our first son, Geoffrey, was born.

1952: the year of my first cautious appearance as a constable on the beat was also the year of the last of the great London smogs. This coincidence, if not exactly world-shattering, was at least to have a profound influence upon the course of my entire future career.

After completing my ten weeks' basic training I was sent to the old Shepherd's Bush and Chiswick sub-division, and in due course my first period of night duty came round, three weeks out on the beat on my own. And on the very first night the smog came down.

Conditions were terrible. Visibility was down to a few yards, and I spent most of that first tour of night duty groping my way along the Chiswick High Road and listening to shop windows being smashed all around me. I couldn't see a thing, but the smash-and-grab villains were having a field-day. The situation was the same all over London. And in the mornings, when we went off duty, our faces were thick with soot save for the strip across our mouths and noses where we'd tied our handkerchiefs.

I'd had a lot of time during those three weeks for thinking. I liked police work, and obviously all duty out on the beat wouldn't be as uncomfortable and frustrating as this. But all the same, those nights of the smog sharpened and eventually fixed in my mind the decision that had gradually been forming there over the preceding weeks. I was looking ahead at that moment to at least twenty-five years of service, and I knew quite definitely that I didn't want to carry them through as a uniformed man on the beat. Two years of uniformed probationary service were required, but after that a constable could apply for transfer to specialist duty. So I weighed up the alternatives.

There was traffic patrol work. There was the mounted police branch. There were any number of possibilities. There was the CID, at that time an elite department within the service. And within the CID there were its own specialities – fraud, drugs, violent crime, all sorts . . . That sounded interesting. But first of all I had to do well enough during my probationary period to show that I was CID material. So that was what became my central purpose as I settled down over the coming weeks and months to work and learn.

Bridget and I meanwhile had a housing problem. With the new baby our original furnished accommodation would no longer do. The police service provided unfurnished accommodation for its officers whenever possible, but at that time there was simply nothing available. Our local council authority put us on its list, but that would mean a wait of several years, and when I approached the London County Council (as it then was) I got the same answer.

In desperation I now appealed to my Member of Parliament – and, curiously enough, that worked. Shortly afterwards, in February 1953, we were offered an LCC one-bedroomed flat in Hainault. I took the flat, and the force transferred me to Wanstead, East London. The cycle ride from there to Wanstead was seven miles each way, in uniform and often with cape and leggings as well, but I didn't complain. I had a place of my own at last.

In 1953 Wanstead was still something of a sleepy hollow in policing terms. It had – and indeed still has – a decidedly village atmosphere, cut off as it was from the surrounding, busier areas of Forest Gate, Leyton and Leytonstone by the Wanstead Flats, a large area of common land which is part of Epping Forest. Even so, the Flats provided ideal cover for night thieves, so that it wasn't altogether unusual for Wanstead itself to be visited professionally by these gentry during the hours of darkness. And in fact it was the Flats that gave me my first, first-hand experience of crime detection and prevention. I quickly discovered just how much I still had to learn.

Shortly after I arrived at Wanstead the local cricket club, on the very edge of the Flats, became the victim of a miniature crime wave. There was a bar in the cricket pavilion building, and in those days any premises which offered cigarettes or spirits as a haul were particularly attractive to thieves, especially if – as was the case with the cricket club – the building was in an isolated position. In fact, as I remember it, the pavilion had been raided four times, always at night, somewhere between one and three in the morning, over a period of three weeks.

By now, I'd come to my decision to try for the CID as soon as my two years of probation were over. With my next tour of night duty just starting, therefore, this seemed an excellent opportunity to show my mettle: I would catch the thieves in the act, and arrest them.

I looked the situation over. The club building lay at the end of a long gravel drive, on one side of which was a church and graveyard, and on the other Wanstead Golf Course. The golf club side was bordered by a high thick hedge of laurel and holly, and beyond the pavilion lay

Wanstead Flats, from which direction the thieves might be expected to come. I observed the lie of the land carefully but, as things turned out, not quite carefully enough.

My night duty began. I worked out the beats allotted to me so that I could be in the area of the pavilion at around one-thirty in the morning and waited for Thursday to come round, since that seemed to be the thieves' favourite night. I'd worked out a surprise approach, even to the exact place I'd switch off my bicycle light (no Panda cars in those days) and coast invisibly up to the pavilion door.

Thursday's night was moonless and very dark. At a minute or so before one-thirty I approached the entrance to the drive. I paused, putting my foot down on the ground while I drew my truncheon and switched off my lights. The street was silent. Nothing stirred. I moved forward, speeding up and worried at the crunch my tyres made on the gravel drive as I swung into it at some speed.

Suddenly the most dreadful clanking sound assaulted my ears. I was already tensed up, expecting any second to confront one or more pavilion breakers in the act, and in the pitch darkness the sudden noise startled me and I lurched instinctively. With my truncheon in one hand, I was unable to control the handlebars, and my bicycle went into a fast skid on the loose gravel.

I ended up in the hedge, my helmet knocked off, my uniform smeared with leaf-mould, my knuckles skinned and my face scratched with holly prickles. The noise reached a climax . . . and the clock in the church tower close beside me shuddered to a rusty halt at the very moment of the half-hour. It didn't strike. I found out later that it couldn't – something was wrong with the works, and had been so for months.

My daylight reconnaissance had been thorough, but not quite thorough enough. Just another few minutes and I'd have heard and identified the fearsome crescendo of clanks and wheezes with which the nearby church clock always prepared itself before not quite managing to strike.

I never caught the thieves. They weren't there that night anyway, and in fact they never raided the pavilion again. So maybe, even if crime detection wasn't yet quite my forte, I wasn't so bad at crime prevention after all. But it wasn't exactly an episode I could quote as proof of my CID-worthiness.

Another lesson was soon to follow.

At that time probationers with the Metropolitan Police were the subject of bi-monthly reports to area head office, prepared by a sergeant. With one of these reports coming up for me, my sergeant called me in for a friendly word. He pointed out that some weeks had gone by since I'd last issued a summons in respect of a traffic offence, and he went on to remind me of the importance of traffic regulation enforcement. I took his point. I didn't admit it to him, of course, but he was quite right: dealing with minor traffic offences, unless they also involved an accident or other incident, never did enthuse me.

But back out on to the beat I went, determined to do better.

I was on night duty again, and that same night at about 11.30 p.m. I spotted a bicycle coming towards me without a headlight on Aldersbrook Road, a main thoroughfare on the edge of Wanstead Flats. I'd probably have stopped the cyclist anyway, but with the sergeant's reminder ringing in my ears there was no question of my letting the rider get away with it. I stepped forward off the kerb, waved my torch, and he pulled up.

He turned out to be a very polite and well-spoken young man, and he was sitting astride a smart blue and silver, lightweight sports cycle. I pointed out that his front light wasn't working, and that this was an offence, and I reached into my tunic pocket for a report book so that I could report him for a summons. But then I hesitated, noticing that it was only the headlight that was out – his rear light was working perfectly. The lad saw this and quickly assured me that he couldn't understand why the front light had gone dead on him. It'd been fine earlier in the evening and he could only suppose the bulb had burned out.

I hesitated further. Surely the law had never intended that a prosecution should be launched in such circumstances? If I *did* issue a summons, surely it would only be because the sergeant was chasing me? And surely that wasn't the proper way to do my job as a policeman?

I was wrestling with my conscience, of course, and it won. I asked the young man how much further he had to go and he told me he was only a few hundred yards from his home. So I put my book away again and simply spoke to him sharply, telling him to walk home and warning him that if I ever caught him without a light on a bike again I'd most certainly book him. He was very grateful and walked off, obediently pushing his bicycle.

I went on my way, satisfied that I had done the right thing. The night passed, and by the time dawn showed above the rooftops I'd forgotten the incident.

Then, as I was making my final round at about 5 a.m., the growing daylight gleamed on something lying on the grass very close to the beginning of Aldersbrook Road. I walked over and found the smart blue and silver bicycle dumped there. That polite lad with the quick mind and the glib tongue had obviously got rid of it just as soon as he was out of my sight.

The bike was stolen, of course. At least I had got somebody's lost property back for them. But we never did trace that young man, despite the great deal of work we put in. I had learned another lesson. Once again I'd hardly helped my chances for CID selection.

Still, I had my successes as well, and these must have been noted, for when I applied for trainee CID duties at the end of my two-year probation I was sent for interview. And you can imagine how nervous I was as I waited outside the interview room in the old Woodford police station. I'd been extremely lucky even to get that far – in those days only twenty or so CID vacancies came up throughout the entire London force in any one year – and I realised that this would probably be my only chance. If I muffed it the CID would be closed to me for ever.

My two interviewers were very senior men, a detective chief inspector and his boss, the detective superintendent of the whole division. The superintendent was a thickset, heavy-jowled man with iron-grey hair, his massive neck seeming to strain for release from its crisply starched collar. He was a famous figure in police circles, an officer whose cases had often attracted newspaper headlines.

His colleague's appearance was a complete contrast. The detective chief inspector was thin-faced and lugubrious. He wore a high wing collar, black pin-striped trousers and a black jacket, and he could easily have been mistaken for an undertaker.

'Good morning, Mr Cater,' he said.

For some stupid reason my voice barely functioned, I was so nervous. I stood stiffly to attention. There was a long pause. It seemed like an eternity.

'Cater . . . ' This was the superintendent, and he said my name thoughtfully.

'Yes, sir,' I said and then waited.

'Cater?'

'Yes, sir?'

'Are you related to the grocery people in Romford?'

'No, sir.'

He sighed. 'Just my luck. I thought I was on to a good thing.' Then he laughed encouragingly and I think I laughed too, out of sheer relief.

'Sit down then, Cater. Sit down.'

He pointed to a chair in front of the desk and I took it. The ice was broken, I relaxed, and now the questioning began. I had a good interview and the next day I was told that I'd been selected for trainee CID duties. From now on I would work as an 'Aid to CID'.

I was posted first to Barkingside and then to Hackney, in London's East End. Those two areas were totally different to each other and over the next four years I laid the foundations of my long career as a detective. Barkingside in those days was quite rural. Hackney, on the other hand, was a crowded, cosmopolitan East London Borough, with its street markets, its many public houses, its churches, chapels and factories all jumbled together, and its houses and tenements packed with people as loving, hard-working – and sometimes as brutal – as any in the land.

It was here that I was involved in my first murder inquiry. It was a sad, sordid affair, of a young boy who had disappeared after being abducted from outside a pub in Loughton in Essex, on the far side of the police division. A full police investigation was put in hand, and this inevitably began with a systematic search of the area. As an Aid to CID I worked with another trainee, and on this occasion it was the pair of us who found the little boy's body.

It's not a moment I care to think about, even now. The child had been criminally assaulted and strangled, and we found his little naked body jammed head first into a gap between a fence and a wooden builders' hut. He was just seven years of age. His death made a lasting impression on me: I had two small sons of my own by then, and there are times when it's hard to remain detached and professional.

A few days later the murderer was caught. He confessed to the crime, and described how he had got rid of the dead child's clothing over a wide area, even throwing some pieces from a moving train. My partner and I were then despatched to confirm his story. We found the little shorts in a public house urinal in Leyton, the shirt and jersey and some other bits and pieces in a second urinal at Bethnal Green, and then I had to walk the railway line between Bethnal Green and Liverpool Street in order to recover still further items. It was a painstaking operation, and it showed me just how thoroughly a major criminal investigation is carried out. It also reminded me that confession evidence is of little use in court without other strong external corroboration.

And before very long another case involving violence came along. It began when two other Aids to CID, Jim Norman and Bill Warren, spotted a well-known local villain driving an old van. Intending to have a word with him, Jim Norman stepped out into the road to stop the vehicle, but the man had recognised him and in panic drove straight at him. It's hard to know why, since in fact the only stuff in the van was some stolen scrap lead of very little value, but from this one panicky reaction a long trail developed of misery and eventual death.

Jim dodged to one side, and then jumped on the van's running board as it went by. The driver now lost his nerve completely and turned down into a street market where he tried to scrape Jim off the van against the heavy stalls lined up in the roadway. Eventually he succeeded, Jim was knocked off the running board, and the man drove on down the street and got away.

By then the other CID Aid, Bill Warren, had caught up on foot and was able to give the alarm and do what he could for Jim, who was lying injured on the ground between two stalls. Eventually an ambulance arrived, Jim was taken to hospital, and eventually recovered.

Meanwhile, however, even though the van driver had got away he was a local, and known, so we knew where to look. I was one of the officers who went round to his home and when we knocked on the door his wife answered it at once, clearly very upset. She was frantic in fact, sobbing and pointing up the stairs, telling us, 'He's locked himself in with a knife.'

There was a lavatory on the first-floor landing, its door locked on the inside. The woman insisted that her husband was in there so we called to him, telling him to open up. There was no answer. The poor woman was screaming now, so we broke the door down. Her husband was crumpled up on the floor, a large carving knife lying on the floor beside him. It quickly became obvious that he had stabbed himself twice in the stomach, hara-kiri style. They were very serious wounds and there had clearly been a determined attempt at suicide.

We immediately called an ambulance to the house and at the hospital the man underwent major emergency surgery. He survived, stood trial at the Old Bailey for his assault upon Jim Norman, and received a long prison sentence. I gave evidence and for the first time stood in the witness box at the famous No. 1 Court. A few days later the van driver succeeded in committing suicide in his cell, this time by hanging himself. And all, very sadly, for a nearly worthless few pounds of stolen scrap lead.

Some three years later I was selected to become an appointed Detective Constable in the CID and I was posted to the old Commercial Street police station on G Division. The next few months passed swiftly while I felt my way into the job, not that it proved to be a leisurely process. Far from it.

Commercial Street in those days was like nothing I had ever experienced. To say it was cosmopolitan would be a gross understatement, for there, crammed together cheek by jowl, were members of many different nationalities, creeds and colours, all superimposed upon the inner East End of London, just outside the City of London itself. It was the London of Petticoat Lane, Club Row, Tubby Isaacs' jellied eels, Bloom's Restaurant, Spitalfields Market, The Toynbee Trust and Whitechapel, and, historically, the territory of the Huguenots, Jack the Ripper and the rag-trade. It was all there and you could feel it, see it and smell it.

It was even then all decaying away: the overcrowded tenements, the seedy cafés, pubs and gaming clubs of Brick Lane, the prostitutes and their ponces, the destitute and the meths drinkers of Spitalfields and Whitechapel and The Doubles, a hostel for destitute mixed couples, which with its wooden benches and tables was something straight out of the world of Oliver Twist and Fagin. So far as we in the police station were concerned it was, in the main, a world of assaults, prostitution and drunkenness, unlawful gaming in the Sunday markets and the occasional heavy 'breaking' or robbery. The pressures, such as they were, arose simply because of the frequency of offences of petty crime. It was a good place for a young detective to begin to learn his trade.

I spent an exciting, fruitful year at the Commercial Street station, feeling my way and learning from the many helpful and experienced officers around me. Then, after attending a junior CID training course at Hendon, I was transferred to the Drug Squad at New Scotland Yard.

The year was 1959, our squad strength was a detective sergeant and three detective constables. The only unit of its type in the country we had responsibility for the whole of the metropolitan area of London, and we were about to enter the Swinging Sixties.

2

1959: THE YARD

The name 'Scotland Yard' can be traced back to medieval times, when that area to the east of Whitehall and the old Palace of Westminster had been known as Scotland, probably because it was where visiting Scottish dignitaries stayed while paying their respects at the English court. Later, after the destruction of the old palace, 'Scotland' was developed as three residential closes around narrow courtyards: Great Scotland Yard, Middle Scotland Yard, and Little Scotland Yard. It was a smart district – Inigo Jones and Christopher Wren are both known to have lived there.

Come the nineteenth century and the property speculators got at the area. Middle and Little Scotland Yards were demolished, and at the end of Great Scotland Yard a row of houses was built, known as Whitehall Place. In July 1829, when Sir Robert Peel was looking for a home for his new 'peelers', No. 4 Whitehall Place happened to come vacant. It was central, not too expensive, just what he was looking for. He installed one of his two first Police Commissioners, Rowan, in furnished bachelor quarters on the top floor – living over the shop with a vengeance! – and where the rear of the building backed on to Great Scotland Yard he extended it to provide a local station house. And this was the hotch-potch of ancient and not quite so ancient buildings that accommodated the Metropolitan Police Headquarters for the next fifty years or so. In 1890 the headquarters then moved to the Victoria Embankment and became known as New Scotland Yard.

By the time I arrived at Scotland Yard the task it was being asked to perform had far outgrown the accommodation. It was undeniably a handsome building, with a picturesque roofline, turrets, gables, archways and narrow, pointed-topped windows, all set round an attractive cobbled central courtyard, but it was nevertheless grossly over-crowded, its rooms were small and dark and connected by a maze of confusing passages and stairways, and much of its equipment was seriously out of date.

The C (Central) 1 Branch communications room, for example, still used sealed tube canisters and compressed air to distribute messages from one part of the organisation to another. This system must have dated back to Crippen's day – even so, no matter how long one worked there, one never learned to suppress the instinctive urge to duck as canisters blasted by along the overhead pressurised pipes that wound across ceilings and through doorways.

But still, it was an exciting place to work, with a grand spirit and always a lot going on, and for all its drawbacks it inspired great affection and loyalty in its hard-working occupants. Although it housed many departments, and literally hundreds of officers, it managed to retain a friendly, village-like atmosphere, and I know I for one was sad when we were moved, in 1966, to the new modern tower block soon packed with the most up-to-date equipment on Broadway, off Victoria Street.

I was posted to the Drug Squad in the old building, a small unit of C1 Branch. In those days the operational detective branches housed in the old building included not only the famous Flying Squad (known via cockney rhyming slang as the 'Sweeney' after Sweeney Todd, the demon barber of Fleet Street), but also C1 Branch which in fact was the senior branch and by far the largest, both in numbers of staff and in the scale and range of its work. It embraced the internationally respected Murder Squad, the Forgery Squad, the Drug Squad that I'd been sent to, and many other specialised units dealing with matters like extradition, blackmail and extortion, corruption, kidnapping, and overseas crime committed in British territories or on board British ships.

In those days Britain's drug problems were still fairly minor. In general, professional criminals regarded dealing in drugs as 'dirty', and shunned them. It wasn't until the Sixties, with the growth of cannabis smoking as a socially acceptable activity, that this changed. If the public at large thought cannabis was all right even though it was illegal, then why all the fuss? Why not cocaine? Why not heroin? And besides, increased usage meant huge profits even for the middlemen, and your average villain isn't all *that* high-minded. Business is business, after all, even in the criminal world.

But in 1959 the department I joined was still small. We had a single office up on the second floor of Scotland Yard, in a corner overlooking the Cannon Row police station and the 'Red Lion' Gate, and we had one official CID car at our disposal providing we'd booked it well in advance from the transport pool. I remember it well. It was an old Hillman with a steering column gear change that didn't exactly make for snappy acceleration, and a tendency to overheat that ruined several important drug squad operations.

Still, we did our best, and often investigations required perseverance and ingenuity rather than mere speed off the mark. There was one occasion when I went with a team of officers and a search warrant to the basement flat of a suspected drug dealer in the Westbourne Park area of West London. We were certain there was cannabis there somewhere, and we finally narrowed the search down to the kitchen. We searched that kitchen three times. We lifted the carpet and the linoleum and looked three times for an accessible cavity beneath the floor. We examined the cooker three times, and the chimney, and even the walls, since it wasn't unknown for a dealer to remove bricks from a wall and then repaper over the cavity each time he went to it. Three times we examined that kitchen and three times we came up with nothing.

But we still believed the cannabis was somewhere there, so we started a fourth search . . . It was one of the other detective constables present who cleared out the kitchen cupboard for the fourth time and thought it odd that there were eight or nine unopened two-pound bags of Tate & Lyle granulated sugar on the shelf. There they stood, quite openly, all full and neatly sealed, as though still in the shop.

The cannabis was in them, of course, a large amount in small brown paper packets, layered between granulated sugar to make the bags feel right. Every single bag was stuffed with it. The detective constable was young Rex Lewis, later to reach senior rank.

Other dealers were just as imaginative. Stop one of them on the street and the first thing we always did was search his underpants. Nine times out of ten the stuff was there.

In case one was tempted to take the job lightly, however, there were also tours of night duty in Piccadilly Circus, where we saw the registered hard drug addicts queueing up outside the all-night opening Boots the Chemists, as midnight approached. The prescriptions given them by their doctors were dated, to stop them selling the drugs or using them all on the first day, so they often waited desperately for midnight, after which the pharmacist would fill the new day's prescriptions.

Many of them would be desperate indeed, having used up the previous day's supply hours ago, and only minutes after midnight we would see them rushing to the public toilets in Leicester Square, only a

few yards away, where they would lock themselves into a toilet cubicle
for the new day's first fix.

Sometimes we had reason to check up on them. It was a pathetic
spectacle. I prayed that whatever might happen to my own three sons
in the future I would be able to help them never to sink as low as this:
the filthy teaspoon, the match held under it in trembling fingers to help
dissolve in God knows what sort of water the tablets given them by the
chemist, the disfigured forearm below the tourniquet, the well-used
hypodermic needle, the hollow-cheeked faces, the despair. We didn't
have AIDS in those days, but what we did have was bad enough.

And yet nothing was learned. In society at large fashions changed:
pot (cannabis) became smart, and even a little cocaine and heroin. And
as a result many professional criminals turned away from other types of
crime – which offered smaller profits and greater risks of detection –
and sacrificed their 'principles' to jump on the bandwagon.

And so profitable a bandwagon brought with it not only greater
greed and violence but also greater social corruption – the taint of
which inevitably would touch even the police force. The great police
corruption controversy didn't come till later, but even in the early
Sixties we weren't without our accusers. One such case involved me
personally and, although trivial in itself, it will serve to demonstrate
how meticulous the police authorities in fact have always been in
matters of discipline and accountability.

One day the Customs and Excise Investigation Branch contacted our
office to report the seizure of a small packing case which had been
shipped from Africa to Liverpool, with its final destination a supposed
dress agency business in West London. According to the customs
declaration form its contents were African national costumes, but
customs officers had opened the case in Liverpool and found it to
contain a large quantity of cannabis.

I was deputed to help the customs officers uncover the British end of
the shipment. It was decided to remove the cannabis, reseal the case
and deliver it to the West London address as if nothing had happened.

However, since the addressee's name on the case – which I shall say
here was Greene – was almost certainly false, we had to be in a position
to monitor the delivery closely, and also to follow up immediately
afterwards. So we decided to make the delivery ourselves, one of us
posing as a GPO postman.

That role fell to me. I made arrangements to borrow a GPO van,
together with a borrowed postman's uniform and a book of GPO excess
postal charge slips. The idea was to claim that an excess postal charge

was due, for in that case the package could only be released to the addressee himself, Greene, or to somebody claiming to be acting on his behalf and willing to pay the excess charge.

In due course I dressed up as a postman and was driven in the GPO van to the dress agency, with one of the customs and excise officers out of sight in the back. I went to the front door and asked the man who answered it for Mr Greene, giving him the postal charge story we'd agreed. The man told me Greene wasn't there, but said he would accept delivery. I objected that I couldn't do that because Mr Greene had to sign for the package. He then claimed that he was authorised to act for Mr Greene, and when I continued to hesitate, he told me he knew Greene very well. I then allowed him to sign for the parcel and take it. The excess charge was thirty-eight shillings – he handed me two pounds and told me to keep the change.

I went back to the van and handed the two pound notes to the customs officer as we drove off. He gave me a receipt, then we circled the block and returned to the dress agency. I rang the bell again, the same man answered it, and this time the customs officer and I identified ourselves.

My colleague had with him a writ, which provided him with the same powers as a search warrant, and when we entered the house we found that the crate addressed to Mr Greene had already been opened. The customs officer then interviewed the man who had received it. Had this been primarily a police investigation he would then have been arrested and charged, but the customs service works to different rules and my companion simply told the man that the facts would be reported. He then had to refer the matter to his legal branch, and it was up to them to decide whether or not to prosecute.

We therefore left the address, and that normally would have been the end of the matter as far as I was concerned, unless I was called on to give evidence in the event of the man being arrested and charged.

In this case, however, there were complications, for about ten days later an anonymous letter arrived at New Scotland Yard. It described a party held on the Saturday following our visit to the dress agency, at which the man my colleague had interviewed had been bragging about his escape. He told everyone that even though he'd been caught with the packing case he had not been charged, and he was celebrating the police's stupidity. He also told them about the two pounds he'd given me.

Although the letter's basic purpose, therefore, seemed clearly to be to offer information to stop the dress agency man from getting away with anything, there was the inference of a two-pound bribe and accordingly the letter came to be treated as an official complaint. It arrived on the desk of the detective chief superintendent of C1 branch, and a chief inspector and detective sergeant were sent to carry out an investigation. I was interviewed and gave my account of what had happened, exactly as I've described it here. Even so, I was told I must take no further part in that particular investigation.

This worried me. It didn't look well on my record to be taken off a case on account of a public complaint, no matter how unfounded, and for me especially not at that particular moment, for I happened to be hoping for promotion. Interviews for advancement from detective constable to detective sergeant were soon to be held, and I felt I stood a good chance: two of us on the squad had about the same length of service, we'd both passed the necessary exams, and we were both expecting to be called before a selection board.

I heard nothing more about the smuggling case for several days. The customs officer in question didn't contact me, so I had no way of knowing what was going on. I did some thinking. While searching the dress agency I'd picked up the fact that it was in some way connected with a woman who worked as a nurse at a hospital somewhere in Hampstead. Now, I'd seen the anonymous letter, which had been posted up in Hampstead, and its whole style had suggested to me that it was written by a woman. If she were the nurse, therefore, and police were able to contact her, then perhaps she'd be able to confirm the purpose of her letter.

I took this idea to the detective sergeant investigating the complaint, pointing out also that if the woman were traced then what she'd written in her letter might become important evidence. The sergeant made notes, and sent me away.

Again I heard nothing. A further week went by, and then the other detective constable on our squad was told he was to appear before the selection board. I was not. I asked about this but got no satisfactory answers. Clearly, I thought, that was because I was still under suspicion. I confronted the sergeant who was investigating my case and asked him if he had yet traced and interviewed the nurse. He hadn't. And, with the day of the selection board coming closer and closer, time was running out.

I decided to do something about it myself. That evening I went off to the hospital in question, and was lucky enough to find the nurse I was looking for in the nurses' quarters of the Hampstead Hospital. The situation was exactly as I'd suspected. Her reason for writing the letter had been a wish not to see the man get away with drug smuggling, and she'd only mentioned the two pounds handed to me as part of the story.

Next morning I reported what I'd done to the sergeant, and gave him the name and address of the nurse. Later that day I was called in by a much more senior officer and told in no uncertain terms that I'd acted improperly. The rebuke was just – I'd had no right to go off on investigations of my own – and I accepted it. But I was still glad to have set the record straight.

It did me little good, however. Even though the 'complaint' was conclusively cleared up later, when 'Mr Greene' and several others appeared at the Old Bailey and were tried and found guilty, I never did make that year's selection board.

Unfair? Well, maybe. But I must admit that if the police authorities have to err at all, it should certainly be on the side of caution. The public's confidence is our most precious possession: we endanger it at our peril. But you see there is often another side to the story.

Oddly enough, the case did have one rather more lasting consequence. Shortly afterwards a written instruction was circulated throughout the force, ordering that henceforward officers must not borrow or dress in GPO uniform in the course of their duties.

Meanwhile, although I remained a detective constable, at least the cases that came my way were seldom dull. One of them, for example, got me kissed by most of the girls in the chorus at the famous *Moulin Rouge* in Paris.

It all began when the Drugs Squad received a call from a rich elderly widow living in St John's Wood. She told us she had a grandson, aged about twenty-one, who frequently travelled on the Continent. He'd returned from France recently, stayed a few days, and then gone back to Paris. She didn't know his present address there, but since his departure she'd been visited by a frightening stranger, from whom she'd learned that apparently her grandson had taken with him a large quantity of cocaine. Apparently he too was afraid, and was acting under duress as some sort of courier. She told us the cocaine involved was about half a pound in weight.

Clearly the grandmother was calling us out of concern for her grandson, and was telling us the truth as far as she knew it. We had our doubts, however – the amount of cocaine she mentioned was just too large. Cocaine wasn't at that time the fashionable drug it would become later, and although we encountered it from time to time we knew there was no realistic market for it in this country in such a large quantity.

Even so, we obviously followed the matter up, and the following morning we discovered that several months earlier a London hospital had reported thefts of drugs from its dispensary, which had been broken into one night. Included in the stolen drugs was a jar which had contained almost half a pound of highly refined cocaine.

Now of course we believed the grandmother, and a couple of days later we traced her grandson to a plane arriving at Heathrow from Paris. I was at the airport to arrest him on the plane the moment it had landed.

I shall call him 'Michael'. Michael was a tragic mess. Academically brilliant, he was in most other ways a fool. Cursed with too much money, he'd fallen into bad company and was now heavily addicted to drugs. His parents had separated many years before, and his father now lived in Europe, which accounted for the lad's visits. He was therefore an obvious choice as a courier, since his frequent trips made him less likely to attract attention from customs officers.

He admitted receiving the cocaine from some men he'd got to know in a London club. There was indeed little market for the drug in Britain, so the men had asked him to take it abroad, and had given him instructions for its disposal there. He'd been afraid to refuse. But once in Paris he'd panicked, and instead of obeying his instructions he'd tried to get in touch with his father for advice.

He'd hoped to find his father in the bar of a hotel he frequented but the barman – who knew them both – told him his father was away on business. Desperately anxious to get rid of the briefcase containing the cocaine, Michael then asked the barman to look after it, together with a note he scribbled for his father. The barman agreed, took the briefcase and the note, and put them behind the bar.

And there – unless the father had already got to them, in which case he'd have been landed with a difficult problem – presumably they still were.

Clearly a trip to Paris was called for. And as I was the investigating officer I found myself on the following morning, a Saturday, sitting on a plane en route from Heathrow to Paris. This in itself was highly unusual, since back in those days it was very rare for a London policeman to go abroad on duty.

During the flight I remember reading one of our national dailies: in it was a story about a police raid on a farm in the Home Counties which had revealed a whole field of cannabis openly under cultivation. We'd come a long way, I thought, in the two years or so I'd been with the London Drugs Squad – from five-grain packets of cannabis hidden in dealers' underpants to whole fields of the stuff being grown just outside London. And as long as people in general remained ambivalent towards the situation it could only get worse.

I was met at Orly airport by two officers from the Paris Prefecture Police. Their names were Souchon and Voitot, and luckily for me Voitot spoke excellent English – my French was very limited indeed. They settled me into a comfortable hotel in the centre of Paris, and then took me to their headquarters on the Quai d'Orsay, where I was warmly welcomed. Apparently Paris had a drugs squad very similar to ours in London, except that it was also responsible for the city's licensed clubs.

Then we went out to a splendid meal in a restaurant on the Champs Elysées.

They told me we couldn't go to the hotel where the briefcase was until the coming Monday morning: French law required the authority of an examining magistrate, and that wouldn't be available until then. Instead, Voitot and Souchon proposed to show me round their city, beginning with a tour of their evening round of duty.

I was a broad-minded young fellow, but I have to admit that some of the clubs we inspected that night made me blink a bit. But we ended up in all the style and luxury of the *Moulin Rouge*, where I was introduced to the manager and again given the warmest possible welcome. Perhaps he was only being diplomatic, but it seemed like more than that to me. Certainly the Yard's reputation abroad was very high in those days.

Anyway, Voitot and Souchon had work to do, so they left me in the manager's hands. The cabaret was just starting. He found me a ringside table and sat with me through the show, explaining the jokes and helping me through two excellent bottles of wine. I was still there at closing time, waiting for Voitot and Souchon, so the manager then escorted me to a pavement café next door where we had coffee and his staff reported to him before going home. It was then that the showgirls, together with their very proper chaperons, came individually to the table to say goodnight. I was introduced to each, and kissed – chastely, I hasten to say, in the French fashion – on both cheeks.

It all seemed a long long way from Hackney and Commercial Street and the Wanstead Flats.

On the following Monday morning Souchon, Voitot and I got to work. I met the head barman at the hotel in question, and he handed over the briefcase and provided a written statement which exactly confirmed Michael's story. We followed up another couple of leads and then, next day, with a sample of the cocaine in my pocket, I returned to London.

It went on to become a rather more complicated investigation, but eventually we arrested three other men, two of whom had been responsible for breaking into the hospital and stealing the drugs, and for many burglaries in and around London. The drug theft was in fact only a sideline, but it required Souchon's and the barman's presence in London as witnesses at the trial at the Old Bailey, so I was able to return the hospitality they'd given me in Paris. Not that I was able to cap those *Moulin Rouge* girls. Souchon returned to France a few days later with the firm understanding that I'd be back in Paris to see him and Voitot again before very long.

It's sad how seldom these things work out. Not long afterwards, at the time of the French war in Algeria, I opened a newspaper and read that the Moroccan opposition leader, Ben Barka, had been kidnapped while on a secret visit to Paris, it was suggested on the specific orders of General de Gaulle himself, two French secret service agents had kidnapped him, and that he'd been murdered, since he was never seen again. The case resulted in a major political scandal in France, and eventually the director of the French secret service resigned. The two agents' names were given as Souchon and Voitot, both members of the Paris drugs squad. They were brought to trial for the kidnapping, but I never heard what happened in the end. There was a retrial, I think, but by then the British press had lost interest and I was never able to follow the case up.

From *Moulin Rouge* girls to caged birds with gaudy plumage is only a short step, and in that connection I remember another drugs case with its amusing side that I was involved in at about this time. It was cannabis again, and we'd received a tip-off from the Port of London police that it was being smuggled in from Africa on a small merchant ship called the *Winneba*. One of their men, Inspector Jim Tuplin, later to become its Chief Constable, and his officers were waiting on the dockside. The word was that if they found cannabis on board the ship, then we should immediately raid various addresses in London, where the drug smugglers' contacts were believed to live.

The *Winneba* arrived, Tuplin and his officers went on board, and they quickly found that several of the ship's life-jackets were stuffed full of cannabis. He arrested one of the crewmen, passed the word to us, and off we went.

The address I was to deal with was in the East End, off Whitechapel, the top-floor flat in a large four-storeyed house, the home of a woman who in former years had built up a formidable record of convictions for prostitution.

I went with an experienced customs officer, armed with his Writ of Assistance (search warrant). When we arrived we found that the front door to the top-floor flat was on the landing below, with a doorbell there and an enclosed staircase leading up to the flat above. We rang the bell. No response. We hammered on the door. Still no response. Maybe there was no one at home. But then I fancied I heard movements in the flat. Pictures of evidence being destroyed flashed through my mind, drugs being flushed down the toilet, heaven knows what. I glanced at my companion, he nodded, and together we charged the door. In the circumstances it seemed reasonable enough.

We rushed up the stairs. We ran from room to room. The flat was empty. But in the corner of the living room there was a parrot, stamping about in its cage.

We searched the place, and found two deflated ship's life jackets in a wardrobe. Even to our naked eyes there were clear traces of cannabis in those life-jackets and, together with other odds and ends we picked up, this satisfied us that we'd found a link in the smuggling chain. Shortly afterwards the woman came home, I arrested her, and she was charged at the local police station. The case seemed clear, and our action in breaking open the door completely justified.

But life is seldom that simple. In fact the investigation turned out to be widespread, a lot of people were involved, the amounts of drugs were considerable, and accordingly the sentences likely to be handed down at the Old Bailey if the defendants were found guilty were liable to be heavy. In consequence every single aspect of the case would probably be strongly contested, and I anticipated there might be protestations of improper conduct for my forced entry into the premises. If a defending counsel can ever make the police officer in the case look bad, you may be very sure he will.

So the day of the trial came round, and at a fairly early stage I was called to give evidence. Much of it concerned other aspects of the case, but eventually, of course, prosecuting counsel representing the Crown got to my visit with the customs officer to the flat.

Now, up to then that counsel had been 'leading' me. That is to say, he and the defence counsel had agreed that these parts of my evidence would not be challenged, and therefore the court had accepted that he would lead me in my evidence, a quite common practice. It was a way of saving everybody's time, and in that case it went something like this:

Q. Mr Cater, did you go to a flat on the fourth floor of the premises which you understood to be occupied by the defendant, Mrs X?

A. Yes, sir.

Q. Did the customs and excise officer have in his possession a Writ of Assistance?

A. Yes, sir.

Q. And did you find that the front door to that fourth-floor flat was in fact on the third-floor landing, in other words on the floor below?

A. Yes, sir.

And so on, until we reached the moment when I'd knocked on the door and rung the doorbell. This was the stage when I thought the 'leading' would stop and I'd be asked to go on in my own words, indicating that the defence counsel intended to cross examine to challenge my evidence from that point.

But the questions from the prosecuting counsel continued.

Q. Did you then fancy you could hear some movement in the flat above?

A. Yes, sir.

Q. Did you therefore then forcibly enter through the front door?

A. Yes, sir.

Q. How did you do that?

A. I shouldered the door, sir.

I waited for the protest from the defending counsel. None came.

Q. Did you and the customs officer then make your way upstairs into the flat?

A. Yes, sir.

Q. And was there any person present in that flat?

A. No, sir.

I took a deep breath. Again no protest.

Q. Was there however in that flat a parrot in a cage?

A. Yes, sir.

At which point the judge leaned forward quickly and asked, 'And did he ask you in, officer?'

Everyone in the courtroom burst out laughing: jury, counsel, ushers, even the defendants. Obviously it had never been a point the defence wished to challenge – but then, that's the sort of thing the officer in the case never gets told in advance. Counsel like to have their fun, and judges too, and who's to blame them?

But not even they very often get to cruise down the coast of Africa, lounging on the deck under a Spanish sombrero, all in the line of duty.

The year was 1962, and at that time Britain still had a Far East fleet, the flagship of which was the battle cruiser HMS *Belfast*. In fact she was on her last active service cruise and was on her way home to Portsmouth via America's west coast, the Panama Canal, and then New York. She was the last of the Royal Navy's battleships, and their lordships of the Admiralty were determined to make a show of her final, historic voyage.

Early on however, while she was still in mid-Pacific on passage from Singapore, her captain signalled that large quantities of dangerous drugs, opium and heroin, had been found on board and that two Chinese crew members had been taken into custody by the master-at-arms. The ship sailed on, arrived for her courtesy visit to the Californian coast, and FBI agents went aboard to help with the naval investigations.

Unfortunately certain elements in the American press soon began publishing reports accusing the British navy of being used by criminals to exacerbate America's already serious drug problem. At this point mutual confidence broke down, and both the FBI and all American reporters were asked to leave the ship. She sailed shortly afterwards with the investigation not yet completed and, following consultations between the Admiralty, the Foreign and Commonwealth and Home Offices in London, the Yard was asked to send officers of the Metropolitan Police to deal with the matter. By this time the *Belfast* was approaching the Panama Canal, next stop New York.

Here in Britain Detective Chief Inspector Webster and Detective Sergeant Howard of CO.CI branch were put in charge of the enquiry. There wasn't much time, for once *Belfast* reached Portsmouth her crew would be immediately paid off and would leave the ship. Police enquiries therefore had to be completed while the ship was still at sea. Arrangements were made for the two officers to fly out, and since neither of them had specialised knowledge of dangerous drugs or the legislation controlling them, I was nominated to go with them. We flew on Britain's first ever commercial jet airliner, the Comet, from Heathrow to Gibraltar, from whence a ship would take us to intercept the *Belfast* somewhere in mid- Atlantic, after her New York visit.

The weather in England was cold, but it was a warm sunny morning when we touched down in Gibraltar, on a runway that seemed to reach out over the water's edge to receive us. We understood that we were to be met by an admiral's aide, and certainly the resplendent individual waiting for us on the runway could have been nothing less. Wearing immaculately starched whites, gold-braided cap, impressive gaiters and dazzlingly polished boots, he carried a cane complete with a shining silver knob. He handled this cane discreetly, but its smallest movement was like a command from Lord Nelson himself, and we knew at once we were in the care of the Royal Navy.

He was a lieutenant commander, and he ushered us to a vehicle in which we were driven straight to the admiral's offices. Our leader, Inspector Bill Webster, would lunch with the admiral and then pay a courtesy visit to the commissioner of the Gibraltar police, while Arthur Howard and I would be entertained by the admiral's aide. And at three in the afternoon we would report to the docks where a Royal Navy fleet auxiliary tanker would be waiting to take us out across the Atlantic.

The admiral's aide turned out to be only as stiff and starchy as the clothes he was wearing. Once he'd dumped us with a long cool drink at a bar in the officers' mess he went away to change and came back looking entirely human in civilian clothes. Meanwhile we'd been fending off the curiosity of the other officers at the bar, who were astonished to find two CID officers from Scotland Yard in their midst, and this we continued to do all through lunch and the Horses' Necks (brandy and ginger ale, a favourite wardroom drink) that followed. The authorities wanted nobody to know why we were there, and we were careful to give nothing away. But they were great company and the lieutenant commander, by now my very good friend, even accompanied us to the dockside and threw a huge sombrero up to me as I was standing on the deck, shouting that I'd probably need it.

Bill Webster was already on board. The ship, the *Wave Barron*, cast off, steamed out of the harbour, past the rock itself, and out into the Atlantic.

For the first day our course took us down the west coast of Africa. And for the whole of that day and the next we had nothing to do but sit on the deck in the sun and watch the porpoises as they played about the ship. It hardly needs saying that those were by far the most leisurely two days I ever spent on duty in my entire thirty-three years with the police service.

The plan was that the *Wave Barron* should alter course out across the Atlantic to intercept HMS *Belfast* in time to give us two or three days on board in which to complete our enquiries, while the ship maintained her unhurried way to Portsmouth. The tanker had to rendezvous with her anyway, so our passage and transfer were entirely incidental as far as her captain and crew were concerned. We were simply going along for the ride, and they looked after us magnificently.

But then, on the second evening, the *Wave Barron*'s captain received an urgent radio message from the battle cruiser. One of her crew had been taken dangerously ill with peritonitis, and she was now making full speed for Plymouth, in order to get the sick man to hospital as soon as possible. This changed everything. Now, if we were to intercept her, we must immediately turn to the north-west and make all possible speed, and I doubt if the tanker had often been called upon for such a sustained effort.

We steamed for the whole of that night at full speed. It was almost impossible to sleep, so violent was the noise and the buffeting and pitching of the ship, and I bet there were quite a few loose fittings on board her afterwards. But we made it, and at about six the following morning, just after dawn on a drizzly grey misty day in the middle of the Atlantic, HMS *Belfast* suddenly appeared out of a bank of fog ahead of us.

She seemed huge. I have never seen anything more impressive than her great grey bulk as she loomed before us.

Her Captain manoeuvred to bring her on a course parallel with ours, with about thirty yards separating the two ships. Lines were rigged across the gap, and then we three police officers were sent across, Bill Webster going first, by what the Navy called 'Jackstay transfer'. All I remember is a loop to put one foot in, and another loop round my waist – I did not feel at all secure. As I was swung aloft sailors on the deck below me were keeping the line taut, but the two ships were still moving, and the sea appeared to rush past just beneath my feet and those dangling bits of string at a terrible speed. It was not, frankly, my favourite experience.

Once on board the *Belfast*, after we'd reported to the captain, we went straight to work, having only a day or so in hand. In fact the master-at-arms had already carried out an excellent investigation, on the basis of which we were able to recover still more drugs, confirm his arrests of the two Chinese hands already in custody, and to arrest one more. Between us we had assembled a huge hoard of opium and heroin, and three prisoners who would later plead guilty to serious smuggling charges in London at the Old Bailey.

The following day we steamed into Plymouth. We stayed only long enough for the sick rating to be taken off to hospital, and then we sailed on to Portsmouth. There the *Belfast* was met by a Royal Navy motor fishing vessel which took off the three of us, our three prisoners, and our haul of drugs and other exhibits. We were ferried to Gosport, where we transferred to a Metropolitan police coach and were driven straight to Bow Street police station. There the three prisoners were officially charged. Then, quick as you please, I was off back home to Bridget and the three boys. I hadn't picked up much of a tan. I'd only been away five days.

Today, having retired from the force, my new career sometimes takes me past the Tower of London and the place where HMS *Belfast* is now moored, a reminder of all her past glories and those of the Royal Navy. I always give her a silent salute in fond memory. I was with her on her last active service voyage.

At last, in 1963, my selection board came up, and in the April of that year I was promoted to Detective Sergeant (Second Class). The different ranks of sergeant, first and second class, have disappeared since then, but in those days the one was a necessary step to the other. Bridget and I were delighted. The promotion brought with it an automatic transfer, in this case back to general duties on G division and dear old Commercial Street. We now had police housing in Hackney, so the move actually meant I had less distance to travel to work each day.

Nothing much had changed in the four years I'd been away. There were familiar faces on the streets, and the area still represented all the worst, and all the best, of crowded city living – all the crime and squalor, and all the cheerful energy and sense of community as well.

One Saturday lunchtime, for example, I was called to the Ten Bells, one of the best-known local pubs, situated opposite Spitalfields Market and alongside the churchyard of Spitalfields Church, a great hangout for all the local winos. Apparently two customers, obviously drunk, had jumped over the bar, snatched up a handful of notes from the open till, and then had run off. Other police officers had searched the area but the culprits hadn't been found, so all that was left for me to do was to take down all the details from the licensee and staff and then get back to the station.

Later in the afternoon the licensee sent for me again, urgently: the two thieves had been identified sitting in the churchyard next door. I returned, and the two men were arrested. Needing a statement from the witness who had first identified them in the churchyard, I went into the pub and was directed to the bar cellarman who for some reason was in a room at the very top of the building. Slightly mystified, I climbed the several staircases, and found the man sitting on a wooden chair by the window with a pair of binoculars in his hands, in an otherwise completely bare, dusty room.

When I asked him to explain what he was up to he showed me the view from the window – a magnificent bird's-eye panorama of every secret corner of Spitalfields churchyard. It was one of his jobs, he told me, to spy out the churchyard and its inhabitants every afternoon, and decide which would not be fit to be allowed back into the pub when it reopened. The licensee saved the police a lot of trouble that way. But it was entirely a Commercial Street arrangement. No other licensee would have had quite the same problem, or quite the same sound common-sense way of dealing with it. The police always called the area 'Comical Street'. That was an apt description.

There were less easy-going moments too. One day I was sent to a small flat in a tenement block on Flower and Dean Street to look into the death of a little boy. It turned out to be one of the simplest and most pathetic cases I was ever unlucky enough to meet.

The background was that the child's parents were a young couple, with two children, a boy aged eighteen months and a small baby. They'd had a quarrel the previous night, and the wife had walked out. When she hadn't returned in the morning the husband had been worried. He'd fed the children and then he'd asked a neighbour to look after them while he went out to look for her. The neighbour was a sensible woman, with children of her own.

The man spent the whole day contacting all his wife's relatives and friends, but he failed to find her, and in the evening he returned, very upset, and collected his children from the neighbour. He fed the baby, washed it in the kitchen sink, and put it to bed. The sink was one of those deep Edwardian earthenware affairs, with a wooden draining board on one side and a single brass cold water tap sticking out of the wall above it.

When I arrived the man was in a terrible state. His little boy had been rushed to hospital in an ambulance, but had been found dead on arrival. There was the possibility of foul play, which was why I'd been sent for. I listened to the father's story. It was very simple.

With the baby safely in bed it had been time to wash the older child. He undressed his son, half-filled the kitchen sink with water, warming it from a kettle, and then sat the little boy on the draining board, happily dabbling his feet in the water. The man claimed he'd then had an urgent need to go to the toilet, which was just across the passage from the kitchen door, no more than a couple of yards away.

He told his little son to hold on carefully to the tap while he was away – the boy was a clever lad and had been left like that before – and then he darted across to the toilet, leaving both kitchen and toilet doors open in between. While he was away, which was only for a minute or two, he told me he'd heard his son splashing his feet in the water. But when he returned he found the child head down in the water, apparently unconscious. He tried desperately to revive him. Then he sent for the ambulance.

The poor man seemed wretchedly genuine and everything I found out later confirmed his story. Having listened to him I went straight to the hospital, and later attended the post-mortem examination on the child. The cause of death was drowning. There was just one mark on the boy's body, a tiny bruise on his left temple. The doctor gave his opinion and I agreed with it, as the coroner did later: the child had clearly fallen forward from the draining board, hitting his head on the brass tap and, unconscious, had drowned in the shallow water in the sink. That would obviously have caused the splashing the father had heard.

These accidents happen so easily. I was depressed for days. It hadn't really been a matter for the CID, of course, but it was right that one of us had been sent to investigate. I just wished it hadn't been me.

After six months at Commercial Street I was transferred yet again, this time on a home posting, back to J Division where I'd begun my CID service. This time it was to Leyton police station, which was close to our home in Hackney, just down the road in fact. The men at Leyton told me it was a quiet station, but as things turned out I was to spend a very busy fifteen months there.

When I arrived there were already three CID officers at Leyton, two detective constables and one sergeant and I made a fourth. I was very much the junior sergeant, both there and on the division as a whole. In those days the CID promotion structure was less flexible than it is today, there were far fewer sergeants, and promotions beyond that rank were very rare. In consequence most detective sergeants were mature men with fifteen years or more of CID experience behind them. They were the backbone of the CID, and I myself – who'd been lucky enough to reach the rank in only eleven years – was regarded on the division as something of a 'flyer'.

It wasn't long after my arrival at Leyton that I became involved in a dangerous drugs investigation again. It was a case which was to prove to be extraordinarily useful to me several years later, when the London police were in need of a lucky break.

It all began when the other detective sergeant at Leyton, Wilf Burgess, received a tip-off from one of his informers. The man, who had a criminal record, said he knew of a group of men in the East End who were trying to get rid of a large quantity of dangerous drugs, as much as a 'suitcase full of the stuff', and he mentioned cocaine in large quantities.

Now it all sounded pretty improbable, and one is always cautious about informers' tip-offs anyway, but Wilf told me he thought the man was genuine – and I remembered that I'd been wrongly dubious about large quantities of cocaine before, in Paris. So I asked Wilf if I could have a word with his man in person, and within an hour the three of us were sitting down together.

Wilf's informer told us the men he was talking about weren't normally drug dealers, but they'd somehow come into possession of this suitcase of drugs, and now they wanted to sell it. There was quite a gang of them, and they were expecting a good price. When I questioned him particularly about the cocaine he said he hadn't seen it himself, he was only going on what they'd said.

Like Wilf, I thought there was probably something in the informer's story. But it might still be the sort of 'con' job he wouldn't know about. Quite often in those days men would offer drugs for sale, lure a potential purchaser to a lonely place to complete the deal, and then either rob him of his money or sell him imitation drugs, harmless tablets or powders of one sort or another.

So I asked the man if he could tell his friends that he knew someone who might be interested in doing business, but that he needed a sample just to prove that what they had was genuine. He thought he could manage this and, indeed, later he came back to us with a small glass phial containing some crystals he said he'd got from the men with the suitcase. It was indeed a tiny quantity of cocaine, so now it was time for us to plan our next move.

We needed someone convincing who could pose as the buyer. Now, it may be a well-known joke that you can always tell a policeman, no matter how he's dressed, but I'm afraid there's more than a little truth in it. The ordinary citizen may not be able to, but villains have an uncanny nose for these things. But we on J Division were lucky, for at Hackney police station we had Detective Sergeant Leonard Hopkins. Hopkins was *nobody's* idea of a policeman: small and slim, a natty dresser, his hair far longer than regulation length, and a man of artistic talent. I discussed the case with him, and he agreed to be my 'buyer'.

Our informer then arranged a meeting between Hopkins and the men with the drugs over lunch in a famous East End restaurant. Hopkins obviously did a grand job, presenting himself as the agent of some other, more important man who would buy the drugs if the price was right, for the criminals agreed to meet with him again at seven that evening in a pub in Walthamstow. Hopkins haggled the price for the drugs to £15,000, which he promised to bring with him to Walthamstow, ready to hand over in exchange for the goods.

I now reported to the detective superintendent of our division, asking him to draft in extra CID officers to help me recover the drugs and arrest the criminals. Unfortunately he was even more sceptical than I had been. The whole thing, I suspect, sounded to him a bit far-fetched and he told me there was no question of his bringing in extra men, I'd have to make do with what I could muster at Leyton. I didn't really blame him – whole suitcases full of hard drugs were unheard-of in those days.

So back I went to Leyton. There wasn't much time left, but between us Wilf Burgess and I managed to gather together quite a useful collection of officers who would be on duty that evening. There were fifteen of us in all, including Hopkins, and we had the use of four police cars. With this contingent we planned to mount our ambush.

First of all, Hopkins needed £15,000. This we supplied in the form of typing paper cut to the same size as five-pound notes, made up into bundles with real five-pound notes on the top and bottom of each bundle and enclosed in official clear plastic banknote wrappers supplied by a local bank. Hopkins packed these into a briefcase and somehow had to make sure the criminals didn't try to count the money before the drugs had been produced.

He also needed a car that couldn't possibly be spotted as a police vehicle. Bridget and I had a little red Mini Traveller, an estate car, and time was short, so the Mini was an obvious choice. Hopkins had to arrive at the Walthamstow pub in it, do enough of the deal with the criminals to bring the drugs clearly out into the open, and then depart hurriedly as we moved in to make the arrests. In this way he would look genuine and Wilf's informer wouldn't be placed at risk. The criminals would simply think their buyer had got lucky and escaped.

There was always the chance that they wouldn't have the drugs actually with them, and that they'd want Hopkins to go somewhere else to complete the deal. If that happened he was to insist on going in his own car (mine!), he would drive at a speed that would let us keep him under close observation, and he would refuse point-blank to go into any building with the criminals. We all knew none of this was likely to prove easy, and I wasn't alone in being concerned for his safety.

In fact things went surprisingly well. Wilf Burgess and I drove up to the pub just before seven and parked a short distance away to keep watch. By then the three other police cars were also discreetly waiting in the streets around, in radio contact with Wilf and me. We saw Hopkins arrive in the red Mini, go into the pub, and come out again shortly afterwards, now in the company of a couple of other men. They all got into the car and Hopkins drove off, clearly being directed. We followed, and were immediately baulked at a main road, where a constant stream of traffic intervened, through which we somehow had to push, ruthlessly ignoring the rules of the road and leaving behind us some very angry drivers.

In the event there hadn't been much further to go. Hopkins turned right into a side street within a quarter of a mile, and pulled up outside another pub. We drove past and parked some yards further on. Behind us I could see Sergeant Hopkins in the mirror, standing by the Mini talking to the other men. They seemed to be waiting for something.

I got out of the car, leaving Wilf to keep in touch with the other police cars that were moving up after us, and walked across the road, into an off-licence opposite Hopkins and his companions. One of them set off down the road in a hurry just then, so I nipped out of the shop and followed him. He went on as far as a parked van, and had a word with its driver. The van started up and moved slowly back in Hopkins' direction, the first man now walking beside it. It was my guess that the drugs were now arriving, so I gave the signal to all my waiting men over my personal radio.

Suddenly it seemed there were police officers everywhere. Suspects were running in all directions, swearing and shouting warnings to each other, and an old Ford Consul, parked where neither Wilf nor I had noticed it, roared off down the street – only to be blocked by one of the police cars. Its driver then reversed back, at high speed, very expertly, along the whole length of the street, screamed to a halt at the far end, swung round, and escaped.

Meanwhile individual officers had been grabbing all the suspects they could find – in fact it turned out that seven men, plus the Ford Consul's driver, had been involved in the drug deal.

Not quite everything had worked out according to plan, however. The van in question had ended up parked so close in front of Hopkins' Mini that he hadn't been able to get away in it. But he was able to escape on foot, and then did what any criminal in his position might have done – he jumped onto a London bus that happened to be passing at the end of the street, and disappeared from view. But that left the Mini, and in the back was a brown leather suitcase, which by then had somehow been transferred there. And that was a pity, for the Mini would now become part of the evidence, and inevitably my ownership of it would emerge, Hopkins' true part in things would also become known before the trial, and the defence might well claim incitement, that Hopkins had acted as an *agent provocateur*. We could have dealt with this – the police sometimes have to tread a narrow line in such matters, and in this particular case there'd clearly been an on-going crime long before Hopkins came on the scene – but our informer certainly would be placed in an unenviable position, and at risk of reprisal.

But for the moment there was still the clearing up to be done at the scene of the ambush. 1 opened the brown suitcase: it contained an enormous quantity of dangerous drugs of many different kinds, all in their manufacturers' boxes and wrappers. Clearly they'd been stolen from some wholesale chemist or warehouse . . . At that moment another of our men ran up to tell me he'd seen the suitcase brought from inside a house just round the corner, just a second or so before I'd given the signal to move in.

Wilf and I went to the house, interviewed a woman there, and found in her possession yet another suitcase filled with drugs. She too was taken into custody, and it later emerged that with this second suitcase we had made what was at that time the largest ever seizure of illegal dangerous drugs in the United Kingdom, with a black market value of at least a quarter of a million pounds.

A few weeks before, thieves had broken into a chemist's warehouse in Glasgow, using gelignite to blow the door, and stolen the contents. And now, down in Walthamstow, we'd recovered the drugs and arrested some prisoners, but the stylish driver of the Ford Consul had got away, and as far as he was concerned our prospects didn't look good. We had no other information to assist us, none of the prisoners was showing any willingness to help us either then or later, and Wilf's informer was at a loss as well. But then Monday morning came, and with it one of life's more amazing coincidences.

Sergeant Hopkins, back off the bus and in circulation again, had returned to Hackney to take up his more normal duties – which on that particular morning happened to involve his attendance at the old North London magistrates' court. He went by bus, first from Hackney to Dalston Junction and then, after a change, from Dalston Junction on to the court. He was just settling himself inside this second bus, on the lower deck, when another man got on to the bus and sat down next to him. There was instant mutual recognition, for this man had been the Ford Consul's driver.

Hopkins told us the story well. At first he'd been prepared for a struggle. But then the man simply grinned at him.

'So you got away as well, just like me,' he said. 'I thought you'd all got nicked.'

So Hopkins took his lead, and the two men chatted about this and that for the rest of the bus ride, Hopkins getting enough information from him to establish his name and roughly where he lived. The bus passengers were spared a possibly nasty scene, and the man was arrested that night.

We now had the whole gang in custody and the follow-up enquiries began, always a vital part of any criminal prosecution. This took me back to another discovery I'd made when examining the two suitcases. In the inside pocket of one of them was a luggage label upon which was written a woman's name, and an address in North London. The name belonged to none of the people we had so far arrested, so it needed checking.

At the North London address I identified myself and was admitted by a pleasant middle-aged woman who showed me into the parlour. She seemed a straightforward person, and when I explained what I wanted to know she immediately told me it was her daughter's maiden name that I'd found on the label, and that the young woman was married to one of the men I already had in custody.

The daughter, Carol, arrived shortly afterwards. She was an attractive blonde, fairly tough but willing eventually to take her mother's advice and make a written statement. The suitcase was hers, she said, but she hadn't seen it for months and she knew nothing else about it. I thanked her and wished them both good day.

Her statement was accepted and she wasn't brought to court. I never saw the mother again but, as I hinted at the beginning of this episode, I was to meet the blonde young woman, Carol, later on in my police service.

As far as our worries over the Mini were concerned, and Sergeant Hopkins' impersonation, we needn't have bothered. When the defendants came to trial they tried quite a different line of defence. One by one they claimed, on oath, that they'd never met any of their co-defendants before they'd been arrested, and that they'd simply been passers-by scooped up by the police along with the rest. It wasn't the best defence, and it didn't hold up at all well against Sergeant Hopkins' evidence. In the end they were all found guilty and sentenced.

Incidentally, this was a case in which unusually the Police Commissioner commended all the officers concerned, and Sergeant Hopkins and I were singled out for high commendation, Leonard Hopkins for his courage.

Wilf's informer died some years later. In fact, if I hadn't known that I wouldn't be telling this story even now, for obvious reasons.

There are people even outside the criminal fraternity who clearly think that an informer is someone unclean, akin to a Judas. They also attack the police for using such people in their war against crime, as if it were in some way unfair. Personally, I have never seen it that way. Informers, whatever else they may be, or whatever their motives, serve the public well. And certainly, as far as this particular informer was concerned, literally thousands of London parents should have blessed him for keeping such a massive haul of dangerous drugs off the streets and out of the vulnerable lives of their children.

3

1965: THE RICHARDSON GANG

As the Sixties wore on crime and the ways of villains in Britain were changing, both in kind and in quantity. In less than ten years, although the strength of the CID remained the same, the crime rate in London had doubled, violent crime was beginning to assume serious proportions, and the criminals' mobility – out of which these other changes grew – had increased rapidly with the universal availability of motor vehicles and the ease with which they could be stolen.

At first, within the police force itself and in government, there was little response. But then, in August 1963, an event occurred that woke society to the new situation.

At three minutes past three on the morning of Thursday, 8 August 1963, the Royal Mail train from Glasgow to Euston, London was roaring through the countryside of Buckinghamshire at eighty miles an hour. Driver Jack Mills sat at the controls of his snub-nosed diesel locomotive, and in the thirteen coaches behind him seventy-two men were sorting the mail in the Travelling Post Office. Mills knew he was approaching Sears Crossing. In less than an hour the train would pull into Euston, and by then the mail would be sorted for loading into red GPO vans.

The train had begun its journey stopping at stations along the way to pick up mail and put out sorted bags of local letters. As the green bags containing high-value packages came aboard they were passed forward to the special coach, only two away from the locomotive, that was reserved for valuable cargo. There were many green bags, for August Bank Holiday Monday was only three days ago, a time when tens of thousands of English tourists had been up in Scotland spending their money. Scotland prints its own banknotes, so that English notes, although accepted as legal tender, are not paid out by Scottish banks but are shipped instead down to their London offices for redistribution. By now, therefore, most of the holiday money had been sorted in Scotland, and parcelled up for return. There was in fact probably more money on the train that night than on any night of the year. And as it arrived in the second coach the postal officer in charge there made a record and stowed it in a special cupboard.

Ahead, in the darkness, driver Mills saw an amber light at the distant signal, low over the track, and he applied the brakes. Then his fireman, David Whitby, saw that the next signal down the line was still at green. This made no sense, so as the train slowed and stopped Mills ordered his companion to leave the cab and find out what had gone wrong with the signals.

Whitby scrambled down on to the track. There was a railway telephone nearby. He trotted across to it and picked up the receiver. The line was dead. He shone his torch, and then shouted back to Mills, 'The wires have been cut.'

As he turned he saw a dark figure in overalls approaching. It looked like a railwayman. 'What's wrong, mate?' he asked.

'Just come over here.'

Still unsuspicious, Whitby did as he was told. He was immediately hurled to the ground and pushed down the bank to the bottom, where he was grabbed by two masked men, one brandishing a cosh.

'If you shout I'll kill you,' the man told him.

By then driver Mills had been coshed to the floor of his cab. Surrounded by masked men he was then hauled to his feet and ordered to drive the train on slowly. As the locomotive moved off it took with it only the train's first two carriages. The coupling had been slipped, and the rest of the train stayed still and quiet, the seventy-two postmen still sorting and packing the mail, unaware for the moment that they were marooned. And by the time they did realise their plight the front section of the train was out of sight, half a mile away, and in fact stationary. The night was silent. None of them knew what to do.

Ahead, still attached to the locomotive, there were five postmen in the high-value package coach, knee-deep in green bags stuffed with banknotes. During the first stop they'd carried on working. Then the train stopped for a second time. They looked up, mildly curious. For a moment nothing happened. Suddenly a window shattered and a masked man burst into the coach, swinging an axe. He was closely followed by more men, all masked and wielding coshes. The postmen fell back before the onslaught and were forced to lie down on the floor in the corner, their faces to the boards. A man stood over them, threatening them with an iron bar.

Still more masked robbers entered the coach and began pulling out the mail bags and passing them out to others down on the track. They were well organised and worked quietly. Outside, in the dark, the bags were handed on from man to man down the embankment and on to a lorry that was waiting on the road by Bridego Bridge. The whole operation took less than ten minutes. Then driver Mills, now bleeding heavily, and his fireman were dragged into the coach and the doors were closed from the outside. A muffled voice came to them: 'Don't move for half an hour. We're leaving somebody behind.'

The lorry drove away and silence descended.

Slowly the railway and post-office officials left in the coach pulled themselves together. Two postmen opened the doors, jumped down on to the track, and walked back, seeking help. They also placed warning detonators on the rails to safeguard the abandoned locomotive and its two carriages by warning other approaching trains. The time was still only three-thirty. Half a mile or so down the track the two postmen found the rest of the train and told the guard, Thomas Miller, what had happened. Miller hitched a ride on a passing slow train to Cheddington signal box, from where he telephoned Euston and gave the alarm. The time was now four twenty-four: inside one hour and nineteen minutes the greatest robbery ever recorded in Britain had taken place.

Fifteen men had been involved, and between them they'd netted £2,600,000. Many of the robbers were eventually caught by the police – not all – and at their trial their record crime earned them record sentences, as high as thirty years. Clearly the judiciary recognised – as we did in the police force – that a new scale of crime had been initiated in this country, and they were prepared to meet it with a new scale of penalties.

There are many people who say that jail sentences, long or short, are an admission of failure, and it may well be so. But there have always been villains in this imperfect world of ours; there always will be. Sometimes jail is the only possible remedy we have left against them. Certainly, after the Great Train Robbery it seemed to us that the world of crime detection and prevention had changed almost overnight. A new elite in organised crime had grown up, syndicates of men, not necessarily with criminal records, who specialised. They considered themselves to be in business, and like any other successful business-men, they insisted on their enterprises being properly supplied with advance finance – equipment and, in particular, information had to be bought.

The train robbers were able to buy not only details of the Royal Mail train timings but also of the train likely to be carrying the most money, and its exact route. They put together a large, well-organised and disciplined team. They had hide-outs planned, and outlets for the money. And even after the robbery they were still prepared to spend lavishly. The police were even tipped off at one stage that part proceeds of the robbery had been left in a Bermondsey telephone box, some said as a bribe for them to stop trying so hard in the investigation. They found the money there, too, and returned it to its rightful owners.

But it was a new league we were entering, a different type of crime and on a bigger scale.

I encountered a small, if much less dramatic, example of this during my last few months in Leyton. One night a group of men were seen by railway employees breaking into a line of bonded railway freight wagons containing whisky on which the duty hadn't yet been paid, which had been marshalled at the Temple Mills sidings before joining another train. The thieves were disturbed and ran off, but not before someone had taken down the registration number of a car seen parked suspiciously in the vicinity. We checked out that number and it led us to a house in Hackney which was divided into two flats, in which lived a couple of brothers and their wives and children. We searched the flats: in each we found identical brand new TV sets bearing consecutive serial numbers, identical brand new Hoover vacuum cleaners, and any number of pairs of brand new shoes, all of different sizes. In one of the flats we also found a large sack containing forty brand new shoes, all of the same make, and all for left feet.

Thieves who keep samples of their labours in their homes are a policeman's dream. Obviously these men weren't real professionals – a few years earlier and they wouldn't have aspired to much more than a little local shop-breaking. But now, with the mobility given them by the car, and as part of a gang, they were thinking big and ranging far and wide. We traced the goods we found in those two Hackney flats. The TV sets came from an electrical shop in Tottenham that had been cleared in broad daylight by thieves who had assaulted the manager and tied up his staff. The vacuum cleaners were from a huge trailer-load stolen on the opposite side of London, and the shoes had been cleared out of a shop up in Wood Green – the thieves had even taken the window display, hence all the left-footed shoes.

Because of the stupidity of the two Hackney brothers we were in fact able to clear up a large number of robberies and shop-breakings and make many arrests. But it could easily have been otherwise, for at that time police work was fundamentally organised on the basis that local crime was committed by local criminals, and this was now no longer the case. Suddenly hundreds of vehicles were being stolen off the streets and used for crimes in areas where the criminals knew they were unlikely to be recognised. Suddenly the much-vaunted local knowledge of the man on the beat and his CID colleagues, which had stood the test of time since the formation of the Metropolitan Police in 1829, was no longer all it had been cracked up to be. Local detectives no longer knew where their local thieves were operating.

The use of violence in crime was also increasing – and mostly for the same reason. Previously, any gratuitous rough stuff had been frowned upon among the criminals. It always attracted intense police activity and made things uncomfortable for everybody, and in consequence its perpetrators were often 'grassed' – in secret, of course – to the police. But now the anonymity gained by using a motor vehicle and working away from home removed all such inhibitions – the local villains genuinely didn't have the faintest idea of who was doing what, even on their own patch. And this factor removed one of the most powerful built-in sanctions against violent crime there'd ever been.

I'm also convinced that the abolition of capital punishment, in 1965, did little to help that situation. The majority of murders may well be domestic, and non-professional, and the actual processes of exacting the penalty may well be barbaric. But when all that is said I still wonder if society can afford the luxury of a penal system without an ultimate deterrent. And a deterrent it surely is. Too many criminals, professional and otherwise, and violent or otherwise, have told me so for me to doubt it and thirty years of dealing with crime leaves me totally convinced. Few criminals in this country would pack a firearm in their kit if they knew what might await them if they used it to commit crime and by doing so caused the death of another. The criminal makes the choice, not society.

Drugs I've already dealt with. They have brought in their train violence, torment and death, and I can only repeat that society has paid dearly for its liberalism. I'm thinking of those popular figures of the Sixties who claimed to be 'upholding the rights of the individual' and those who took it upon themselves openly to defy the dangerous drugs law. And also those self-appointed experts who confused the issue by making much of the supposed difference between hard drugs like heroin, which were lethal, and soft drugs like pep pills and cannabis, which they announced were harmless. We now know they are not harmless, because one leads to the other.

Most of all, what we needed in London in the Sixties was an increase in CID strength. But that would have meant spending money, and because the political will was weak, we didn't get it. Instead, with most of our officers already working a thirteen-hour day or more, we got a reorganisation. The first of many.

To lighten the CID work-load, the Commissioner and the Home Office decided that all the so-called 'minor' crime and 'motor vehicle' crime of London – like thefts from a motor vehicle or 'borrowing' one – should cease to be a CID responsibility and should be dealt with by officers of the uniformed branch instead. The authorities seemed to understand neither that the uniformed branch lacked the necessary specialist training, nor that it was the illegal taking and use of motor vehicles that was behind just about all the major crime then being committed – so that by not dealing with minor and motor vehicle crime the CID was missing a host of clues and valuable information.

Frankly, it was a recipe for disaster. And that, sadly, was what we got. The crime rate went up, and the detection rate went down.

And in this connection it's salutary to read the reservations felt by certain members of the Royal Commission on the Police, back in 1962. One of these stated as follows:

In our view the recommendations which the Commission have been able to make do not go far enough to strengthen the police forces in the war against crime. Prevention must be the prime consideration, and a major deterrent to criminal activities is the likelihood of detection either of the crimes themselves or the preparation for them. Crime statistics show that the rate and speed of detection is not high enough to provide this deterrent effect in many fields of criminal activity. It is because we consider there is urgent need to provide for more effective action in this respect that we submit this Reservation and recommend an increase in the strength of the detective establishments of the various police forces and an improvement in the method of recruitment of police for detective duties.

Statistics submitted to the Commission showed that the detective complement of the forces in the Metropolitan area was eight per cent of the regular establishment; in counties eight per cent: in cities and boroughs nine per cent: in Scotland, in counties five per cent, and in cities and burghs seven per cent of the regular establishments. These figures do not suggest an undue diversion of the available manpower and confirm the evidence we have received that the detective forces are undermanned and overworked.

The expert evidence on the allocations of individual policemen within the areas policed was strongly in favour of putting the maximum numbers on the 'beat'. The detective forces are assisted by plain clothes policemen and this indicates the need for augmenting the detective forces. It is possible that the difficulty of recruiting sufficient numbers of constables has been a contributary factor in keeping the establishments of detective forces low. It is our view that serious consideration should be given to increasing the size of the detective establishments within each force.

On 4 January 1965, I was promoted to Detective Sergeant (First Class). This meant another transfer – promotions in the police force usually do – but it wasn't far, back to Hackney in fact, the police station where I'd been serving when I was first selected for the CID. My stay at Hackney police station was brief, and during it two events stick out in my mind.

The first wasn't really anything to do with me at all, but I remember it because of what came later, and partly because it occurred close to Commercial Street where I had recently worked. Police were called out in the middle of the night because somebody had reported hearing gunshots. All they ever found were a cartridge case lying in the street, bloodstains on the pavement, and a pair of spectacles. The spectacles were identified as belonging to a petty criminal known as Ginger Marks. Marks himself had disappeared, and a major crime investigation lasting many years was never, in law, to resolve his fate. But his death proved to be a turning point in London gang warfare.

Meanwhile, however, in Hackney the only gang I became involved with was rather different. In the Fifties there'd been the Teddy Boys, but now in the Sixties it was gangs of Mods and Rockers who were causing the trouble, and in July 1965 two of these rival groups in Hackney decided on battle. The average age was around fifteen, but they set about their plans as if for a full-scale military operation, and assembled a fearsome array of weapons; bicycle chains, coshes, razors and the like. Finally the Mods ambushed the Rockers, led by a character known as Buttons, on foot in an alleyway off Mare Street.

We were soon called. But by then, at the height of the battle, one of the Mods had produced a sawn-off shotgun and shot Buttons in the chest. He'd gained his name on account of the many badges and buttons sewn on to his leather jacket, and fortunately for him he also wore a large and heavy metal medallion round his neck. The full charge of the .410 shotgun cartridge hit this medallion and ricocheted, most of the lead pellets entering his left shoulder. He was seriously injured, but recovered after emergency surgery. He'd been very lucky – a shotgun blast at that range could easily have blown a hole through his body as big as a fist.

But the affray as a whole was a depressing experience. I couldn't help remembering how, in the same area only ten years before, two grown men using an unloaded handgun had held up a wages clerk and stolen the payroll. At that time firearms offences were so rare that the detective superintendent of the whole division had taken personal charge of the investigation. Yet now, in 1965, one of these young lads had blasted off with that most deadly of all weapons, the sawn-off shotgun. How long, I wondered, would it be before we policemen were carrying guns and wearing bullet-proof jackets?

In the autumn of 1965 I was transferred to Scotland Yard's Murder Squad. In those days the policing of Britain was entirely the responsibility of a number of individual town, borough and county police forces, some of them numerically quite small. Consequently, and also because at that time murder was relatively rare, these forces possessed few officers experienced in specialised murder investigations. The London Metropolitan Police, on the other hand, had many such officers, senior, highly experienced men, so over the years the Home Office had asked them to provide a pool of experts who could be called in by other forces to deal with cases of murder. Similarly they could be called upon by government departments such as the Foreign and Commonwealth Office to help with cases overseas.

The Murder Squad's success rate had been impressive, and many successful authors had launched whole series of novels loosely based (*very* loosely based!) on its work. This was a period when murder was still big news, and every real life case was avidly reported in the popular press.

That was still so when I joined the Murder Squad – and the Murder Squad call-out system was still very much in operation. It worked like this. There was a pool of five or six detective superintendents, among them some very famous names. One of these would be deputed to be 'No. 1 in the frame', which meant he would deal with the next case the Yard was called upon to handle, and he would be given a detective sergeant (first class) to work with, so that they became a team. Two reserves were also nominated, so that there'd always be a No. 2 and a No. 3 pair available 'in the frame'. Sometimes all three pairs would be called upon within a week or so.

My first appointment, at No. 3 in the frame, was with Detective Superintendent Cyril Gold, a very senior and experienced investigator. Usually the sergeant's first job, when he reached his team's destination, was to set up a Murder Office, and a 'system' intended to ensure that every piece of evidence or information was meticulously recorded, filed and tabulated in such a way that it could always easily be reached. It was a 'system' that had evolved out of the combined experience of generations of skilled detectives, and it was the envy of police forces around the world. Indeed, it and it alone can be said to have been responsible for solving some of the Yard's most famous cases.

Today a computer does the same job – but a computer is only as good as the information fed into it. It can't think for itself as an experienced detective can, let alone sense things or have hunches. It's still the officer in charge of the investigation who counts.

Inevitably, Murder Squad teams weren't always fully occupied. And while they were waiting they didn't sit around: they were sent off to deal separately with other cases. In theory they could always return if a Murder Squad call came through, but it didn't always work out that way.

One of the cases I worked on separately was what was known in those days as a Sale or Return fraud. Four villains had set themselves up with office premises in Central London and had also hired the forecourts of two car service stations in West London. They then talked to twenty or more owners of expensive cars who were advertising them for sale in London evening newspapers and, by claiming to guarantee them their asking prices, persuaded them to allow their cars to be shown on the forecourts they'd rented for a period of one week, on a sale or return basis. They collected the cars and the Registration Books, leaving businesslike-looking receipts, and by the time the week was up the cars had been spirited away, sold through car auctions in the north of England, and the villains themselves had disappeared.

There'd clearly been four men involved, but they'd done a good smooth job and it was proving very difficult to identify them. Luckily for us, though, the job hadn't been quite smooth enough. A search of the wastepaper basket left in the office attached to one of the service-station forecourts produced a copy of a local newspaper dated some weeks earlier. It was unremarkable in itself, but down the margin of one of its pages the name *Roberts* had been written in a flowing hand more than thirty times. The name and the handwriting matched the signatures on several of the bogus receipts given for the stolen cars – obviously the man had been practising a fake signature. But incredibly, down towards the bottom of the page another name was written in the same hand, and when that was checked at the Yard's Criminal Records Office it was found to be that of a man who already had several convictions for fraud. Hard as it was to believe, he'd absent-mindedly signed his own name on the page in that newspaper, among all the practice forgeries.

He was traced to an address in Manchester, where we found that one of his friends answered to the description of another of the con men. Both men were therefore arrested and brought back to London for identification. At Acton police station all the owners of the stolen cars were assembled, and at eight-thirty the same evening the identification parade began. The law says that suspects can stand wherever they choose in the line of volunteers brought in from the street, and can change their position whenever they choose. Witnesses are brought in one at a time, and are asked to tap on the shoulder anyone they identify.

At this point I was called away to the telephone. My caller was Superintendent Gold: he'd been assigned to a murder up in Stafford-shire and he wanted me to join him immediately. Very reluctantly I had to explain that I'd be busy with identification parades for another couple of hours or so. Mr Gold told me he couldn't wait, he'd have to take another sergeant, and I'd be put back in the frame. And so the chance was lost.

I vividly remember my disappointment. Superintendent Gold's case turned out to be a famous one. It was the first of three murders of young children in Cannock Chase, and the case wasn't resolved until several years later, after the murders of two more young children. The killer was finally arrested in Walsall and the case dealt with by Detective Superintendent Ian Forbes, also from the Yard's Murder Squad.

So I returned to my identification parades. A week or two later I arrested two others who had been involved and they too stood in identification parades in Wandsworth police station. One witness, a man who had lost his car, instead of touching the suspect he recognised on the shoulder, became so incensed he punched him on the nose. We restrained the witness. But there's something about having been conned that really upsets people – and especially when it's something as private, precious and significant as one's own expensive car that's involved.

Anyway, all the thieves were now identified and charged. Later they appeared at the Old Bailey and were sent to prison. But there was a sequel to the case that was far less happy. Tragic, in fact.

I'd had another young officer working with me on that case, a

Detective Constable Christopher Head. While the con men were waiting trial Head was promoted to detective sergeant and was transferred to F Division in South-west London. Soon afterwards he went out on patrol in a Q car with two other officers. In Braybrook Street, near Shepherd's Bush, the three officers in the Q car stopped another car which contained three men, and in the next few seconds Sergeant Head and his men were all shot dead. The killers were tracked down and given long jail sentences, but that doesn't bring back to life three fine policemen. The violence was growing.

After the Sale or Return case I reported back to the Murder Squad and was told to go immediately to the office of Commander John Bliss, CID, who was the national co-ordinator of the then newly formed regional crime squads for the whole of the United Kingdom. When I arrived, mystified, I found three other detective sergeants already waiting, together with Detective Superintendent Adams, who had been my senior sergeant at the Commercial Street police station some years before. None of us had any idea at all why we were there.

Then an Assistant Chief Constable of Hertfordshire, Gerald MacArthur, arrived. He was also a Regional Crime Squad Co-ordinator and he told us we'd be investigating the activities of the Richardson brothers, Charles and Edward, and their associates. But he'd say nothing more, and gave out copies of several long written statements instead. 'Read these,' he said, 'and then we'll talk.'

We'd all heard of the Richardsons, of course. They were powerful gang leaders in South London, and the police had been trying to convict and put them away for years, but they'd always been able to avoid conviction. We knew that they and their thugs were violent, ruthless men, but even so, when we read the statements given us, we were incredulous. They'd been made by several notorious crooks who nevertheless had been treated so badly by the Richardsons that they were now actually turning to the police for help.

There were stories of extended beatings-up, and of torture with burning cigarette ends and acute electric shock. Frankly, I thought it all sounded a bit improbable, copied from accounts of Gestapo methods during the war, and I said so. But MacArthur told us he believed the stories were true, and it was up to us to investigate them and prove if they were. We also had to find other people who might have suffered similarly and to persuade them to come forward. Evidence was going to be difficult to find – the Richardsons it seemed ran a horribly efficient silencing service – but if we had firm evidence he assured us they'd be arrested and charged.

This was the start of a police operation which at that time was unique. Our only way through the Richardsons' defences would be via the very people they'd terrorised. We had no provable offences and only a few allegations. The Richardsons would possibly be able to wriggle out of those crimes, if they were dealt with one by one. Somehow we had to put together a number of offences to be produced as one case before a single jury, offences we didn't even yet know for certain were there. So for once we were starting with suspects then moving on to their probable crimes, rather than the other way round. And so the Murder Squad's 'system', which was one of the reasons why I'd been brought in, would have to cope with a reverse-order investigation, working outwards from the Richardsons themselves to what – potentially at least – was an infinite number of crimes.

The campaign against the Richardsons operated on two fronts. While looking for witnesses willing to give evidence of intimidation and torture, we were also investigating the Richardsons' fraudulent activities, their fake companies and rackets. And almost immediately we had begun those investigations in London information reached Scotland Yard that Charles Richardson was also involved in a business venture far away in South Africa, which he had visited several times recently with one or other of his henchmen, in particular one Lawrence Bradbury from South London.

It seemed that another man in South Africa, Thomas Waldeck, possessed extensive mineral rights upon land in South Africa which was known to contain vast mineral resources, and Richardson had invested a lot of money. Now Waldeck had been shot dead at the front door of his South African home . . . and who should the authorities there be charging for his murder but Lawrence Bradbury, from South London, a known Richardson associate?

Rumour had it, too, that Bradbury was talking. So after a senior South African policeman had consulted with the Yard, Detective Superintendent Gerrard and Detective Chief Inspector Rees went to Johannesburg. Bradbury was claiming he'd been ordered to do the shooting, and he made a detailed statement giving names, dates and places. Interesting as this had been to the South African police, it made even more sense to Gerrard and Rees who knew how it fitted into the London gangland scene. Charging anyone in London was going to be difficult, however, simply on Bradbury's word.

In London, meanwhile, our enquiries were developing with more and more leads to follow, and as a result I got to talk to some expert fraud operators. I remember them as extraordinarily cheerful, extrovert characters. They took professional pride in their expertise and there was intense rivalry between them. They all wanted to be running the most successful fraud of the moment – and were never happier than when able to con a fellow crook. I recall one of them telling me how he'd tricked a friend into paying a five-pounds drinks bill in a bar. He was prouder of that than if he'd conned the Bank of England.

What we learned from these various witnesses was that the Richardsons had become greedy and rather than putting in the hard graft themselves they preferred to intimidate other crooks into working frauds for them, or they demanded shares in other men's on-going rackets. And saying no to the Richardsons wasn't easy – as many crooks said they had discovered to their cost. So what we had now was a remarkable situation in which villains were coming forward and, to protect themselves from the Richardsons, were actually admitting to serious offences which they had committed themselves. No evidence gained in such a manner could stand up in court on its own unless we could corroborate it with other evidence, but at least it pointed us in the right direction. And some of our witnesses were so valuable that they were put under twenty-four-hour police protection.

One of the names that came up more than once in connection with alleged intimidation and torture was that of a man named George Cornell. Cornell was a well-known associate of the Richardson brothers, and we had high hopes of putting together a case against him. We never got the chance.

On the night of 7 March 1966, at the height of our investigation, violence erupted at a night-club, Mr Smith's Club, in Catford, South London. Two gangs clashed in a gunfight and one man, Richard Hart, not a Richardson gang member, was shot dead. Others were injured, including Edward Richardson and a Richardson associate, Frankie Fraser, a South London crook with a reputation for violence. Forty-eight hours later, in the Blind Beggar public house in Whitechapel, George Cornell himself was killed, shot dead with a .45 revolver at point-blank range. There were two gunmen, one of whom fired warning shots to keep onlookers' heads down, and both men escaped.

There was talk in the East End within a few days that it was the Kray gang who'd been responsible for the murder of Cornell. The Kray brothers led the other major London gang, their territory being East London. With the prospect of a full-scale gang war, Detective Superintendent John Cummings took charge of the Mr Smith's Club affray and the Hart killing in Catford, and Detective Superintendent James

Axon, the Cornell killing in Whitechapel. And further, on account of the obvious connection between these two serious crimes, the Commissioner appointed Detective Chief Superintendent Thomas Butler, then in charge of Scotland Yard's Flying Squad, to co-ordinate both investigations.

Shortly afterwards Edward Richardson and Frankie Fraser were arrested and charged in connection with the Mr Smith's Club affray. But Superintendent Axon's investigation into the Cornell murder made little headway. He was convinced that a barmaid in the Blind Beggar had seen the killing, but she couldn't be persuaded to talk to the police. She was too frightened. The Kray twins were detained and questioned, but they denied any part in the murder, and the police had no firm evidence, so they were released. Not for the first time, and certainly not for the last in our dealings with the Krays, a wall of silence had descended.

In due course Frankie Fraser was tried and found guilty of causing an affray at Mr Smith's Club. On the more serious charge of murder Edward Richardson was brought to trial separately at the Old Bailey. During this trial several jurors reported receiving mysterious and threatening telephone calls at their homes: one juror told the court that a bottle had been thrown through his front window with a handwritten note tied to it. The note, clearly intending some sort of double-bluff, demanded that the man on trial be found guilty.

Finally, at the end of Edward Richardson's trial, the jury were unable to agree on their verdict, and a new trial was ordered.

Evidence of assault and torture had been accumulated by our small team meanwhile and, at the end of July 1966, Charles Richardson and eleven members of his gang were arrested and put under lock and key. Now virtually all the Richardson people were off the streets, and at one point seventeen prisoners were appearing together at a magistrates' court, so that a special dock had to be built for the hearings.

The mass nature of the arrest was important. For years London had been troubled by the activities of gangs so violent that witnesses against them were too frightened to talk. Repeatedly their members had been charged and taken before the courts – whereupon witnesses who had sometimes made lengthy written statements to police would then, through fear, refuse to testify, or would even lie, so that the case had to be dismissed. The criminals would then swagger from the courtroom, often sneering openly at the CID officers, and that night there would usually be a celebration party to which certain sections of the press would be invited. And the following day details of the party would be published, complete with arrogant statements from the crooks claiming it had all been a police 'fit up' and they'd always known they'd be 'proved innocent'.

It wasn't simply that this was frustrating for the police. It was also an excellent way for those gangsters to reinforce their status in the underworld as men it wouldn't be wise to speak about let alone testify against.

In the Richardson case, however, we'd taken into custody virtually their entire manpower. Threats against witnesses must therefore now be empty threats. Inevitably our sweep wasn't one hundred per cent, of course – and indeed one major witness was approached soon afterwards by two of Charles Richardson's men and asked to change his testimony, with offers of money, as it happens, rather than dire threats of violence. Anyway, two men were arrested and later convicted for attempting to pervert the course of justice.

And I too, a few weeks later, was involved in preventing the nobbling of one of the major witnesses. A man called Benny Coulston was going to give valuable evidence of a serious assault upon himself, and he was approached with the offer of a bribe to change his evidence. But we had been tipped off that he'd be meeting the three people involved – a sister of Frankie Fraser, Charles Richardson's young secretary, and another man – in a London pub, so I was able to lie in wait and catch them in the act. All three of them were charged and went to prison.

In those days all the witnesses in a criminal case had to give their evidence first in a magistrates' court, and it was up to the magistrate to send the case for trial to a higher court if he thought the evidence was sufficient. In the Richardson case, which came to be known popularly as the 'Torture Trials', the lower court hearing began on 30 August 1966, at Clerkenwell. It went on there until 10 September, and was then moved to Bow Street where it continued until 2 January 1967, when the defendants were finally committed for trial.

The retrial of Edward Richardson in connection with the Mr Smith's Club affray was also heard at this time: now the jury agreed and he was sentenced to five years' imprisonment. The police had also been able to prove that it was his brother Charles Richardson, with another man named Longman, who had thrown the bottle through the juror's window, so both men, now in custody, were further charged with conspiracy to pervert the course of justice, and later convicted. Tommy Butler dealt with that case himself.

At about that time I helped to investigate a particularly intriguing byway of the Richardson case. Someone was supplying money to the relatives of the people accused who were in prison on remand, and we'd been able to trace the source of that money to large-scale thefts of cash from a firm which at that time operated public car parks at Heathrow Airport. Detective Chief Inspector Ashby, in charge of the enquiry, quickly established that members of the garage staff were systematically stealing the takings, so a series of dawn raids were made on their homes. I was sent to the neat semi-detached house where the car-park supervisor, Mr Charles, lived.

It was yet another case when, as in Leyton, the contents of the house were a policeman's dream. Money lay loose about the place everywhere. Bulging bank statements and building-society accounts cluttered the drawers, and in one bedroom there was a tea-chest so full of coins that it was impossible to move. Needless to say, I arrested Mr Charles.

Greed had been his undoing. A couple of years earlier some member of his staff had found a way of manipulating the time-clock mechanism of the machine which issued the tickets for the car park, and for a while they all cashed in on this, stealing a little more each week as the thefts remained undiscovered. Eventually they were taking so much that if they'd stopped the firm employing them would have seen such a leap in the takings that it would have been suspicious. So Mr Charles took the operation over, and organised the thefts in a thoroughly businesslike manner.

He became rich, so much so that he started asking round for ways of investing his cash without fear of discovery. The Richardsons got to hear of this, and they saw Charles simply as a source of easy money. They easily 'persuaded' him to let them have a regular percentage of the take, and from then on he paid a steady income to several of the Richardsons' men. And even when they were arrested he'd continued to pay others for them, terrified out of his wits.

Anyway, now we had him, and he went to prison for many years.

It was in the summer of 1966 that Scotland Yard finally moved out of its cramped accommodation in Whitehall and into its present building. And there was an improvement for me too, for later I was promoted to Detective Inspector. I was meanwhile appointed Court Presentation Officer at the Richardson trial, and our whole team was moved to an office on the eighteenth floor of the new tower block.

The presentation of multiple interlocking charges at the one trial was a new departure and had resulted from the strategy worked out by

Hertfordshire's Gerald MacArthur, in collaboration with another very senior policeman, Deputy Commander John du Rose, under whom I would be fortunate enough to work on another occasion. The criminal trial would present the jury with a picture of criminal behaviour over a period of several years – a picture the defendants would find hard to counter. One witness might be silenced, even two or three, but not a whole legion of witnesses.

Thus it was going to be a trial with organisational difficulties, with many people to be protected, and all of them to be produced in court at the right moment.

It was also a trial in which much of the evidence was likely to be unsavoury and sensational, and therefore given under a demanding spotlight of nationwide publicity.

It began unpromisingly, on the morning of 4 April 1967, with a series of noisy interruptions from some of the prisoners. It was a trial upon a total of twenty-six counts, and in the dock stood Charles and Edward Richardson, Frankie Fraser, and many others. Had he been alive, George Cornell would have been with them. But he was dead, murdered, a crime that possibly would remain unsolved for as long as the barmaid at the Blind Beggar was afraid to speak. And whoever was putting the frighteners on her it certainly wasn't the Richardsons, for Cornell had been one of their men.

Now the witnesses for the prosecution began to appear. Collectively they told a terrible and horrible story, of mock trials before the Richardson brothers and their associates for trifling offences against the gang's 'rules', and of vicious punishments. Men were stripped naked and doused with cold water. Beatings with sticks and other weapons were common. Cigarettes were stubbed out on bare flesh, men were stabbed, one man was transfixed to the floor, teeth were pulled out and gums were torn with pliers. And for the worst 'offenders' there was a hand generator from which wires could be attached by crocodile clips to their genitals so that violent electric shocks could be administered.

Most of the tortures took place in Charles Richardson's offices in South London, where he ran a scrap metal business. It was there that the generator was kept, the notorious Black Box, a replica of which is now in Scotland Yard's famous Black Museum. In one case we reproduced the whole of one office wall at the court to show the jury the blood splashes caused by violence.

When the Richardson brothers gave evidence in their own defence they denied the charges. They didn't have a lot of evidence going for them, but whenever possible they put forward alibis. One charge concerned a serious assault on a man named Taggart at about eight-thirty on the evening of 15 July 1965. Charles Richardson denied it: he'd been at Heathrow Airport at the time, meeting his brother off an incoming flight from South Africa, and certainly Edward had arrived that night. But fortunately for us the 'system' came up with a telegram from Edward that had been found among Charles's papers. Edward had sent the telegram from Johannesburg to his brother on 15 July giving him the time of his plane's arrival.

Prosecuting Counsel, Mr Sebag Shaw, passed the telegram to Charles Richardson and insisted that he read it aloud to the court. It said that Edward's plane would be arriving at ten-twenty – in other words, a full two hours after the assault.

Edward Richardson, too, produced an alibi. Charged with assaulting Bennie Coulston in London on a night in January 1965, he claimed to have been staying at a hotel in Eire at the time, and his counsel had the hotel register to prove it. In this case we were able to trace the other guests at the hotel that night, in particular the woman whose name appeared above his in the register. She'd been travelling with her daughter and the daughter's married name appeared *below* his. The mother was able to tell the court on oath that she had the habit of using only every other line on lined paper. Thus she'd left the line between herself and her daughter's name blank, and Richardson must have inserted his name on it at a later date.

The lengthy and complicated trial went better than I'd expected. Charles Richardson was found guilty on a number of counts and was sentenced to a total of twenty-five years in jail. His brother Edward, already serving five years for his part in the affray at Mr Smith's Club, was sentenced to a further ten years. Other prisoners were also given long sentences.

And finally Charles Richardson was convicted of conspiracy to pervert the course of justice in the earlier Mr Smith's Club case, and was sentenced to a further twelve years in jail, to run concurrently. So that by the time the case was completed both the courts and we in the police force had given a clear signal to the criminal world that organising a fraud empire, and operating it by extortion and torture would be effectively investigated and firmly punished. It was a lesson that over the next few years other crooks in South London would learn to their cost. We had started to smash the London gangs.

4

1968: THE KRAY BROTHERS

Back in the summer of 1967 I had been promoted to Detective Inspector. This was an important step up the ladder, and I was also transferred from the Murder Squad to the Fraud Squad.

Initially the transfer – a useful broadening of my experience – was on paper only, since I was still heavily involved with the Richardson enquiry. But when that case was concluded, late in 1967, I took up the Fraud Squad posting. It was a small move in physical terms, since I remained based in the New Scotland Yard building and it also proved to be a transfer of short duration for I soon became involved in investigating the Kray brothers, and again found myself dealing with gangs, violent crime, extortion, murder and yet more fraud.

The Kray investigation turned out to be very complex, wide-ranging, and difficult to bring into clear focus. A large number of different criminal activities had to be probed, which needed good police team work and a skilful correlating of apparently disconnected lines of enquiry. Luckily for me I entered the investigation at a highly dramatic stage, after many other police officers had been fruitlessly labouring literally for years.

Like the Richardsons, the Kray brothers – the twins Ronald and Reginald – had been successful gang leaders in London's East End for a considerable period. Calling themselves 'The Firm' and ruling by terror, with a reputation for utter ruthlessness, they controlled a large and diverse crime organisation, including what we called 'long firm fraud' offences: the setting up of phoney companies for the purpose of establishing good credit ratings, running up massive debts, and then decamping with the proceeds.

As well as being merciless, they were cunning and had survived several intensive police investigations. The brutal means of retribution attributed to them laid a cold hand of silence across the network of underworld informers on whom we could otherwise usually rely. Thus they were not only feared but also in a perverse way admired in the criminal fraternity in London's East End. Celebrities sought to be photographed with them and stories about them were legion. At one time two senior police officers, Detective Chief Superintendent Gerrard and Detective Inspector Read, had probed their activities to no avail, and shortly afterwards the Krays had bought two pet snakes at Harrods, South American boa constrictors with their fangs removed, which they'd mockingly christened Gerrard and Read. They'd then given a party at which they'd fed white mice to the two fangless snakes. It was a joke their friends hugely appreciated.

More recently the Kray brothers had extended their activities and it was strongly rumoured that they'd masterminded the escape of Frank Mitchell, known as the 'Mad Axeman', from Dartmoor Prison in December 1966. Mitchell had subsequently disappeared completely, and the Krays were believed also to be responsible for that. And there was a further disappearance, in October 1967, attributed to the Krays: that of Jack 'The Hat' McVitie, a bookie's clerk so-called because of the hat he always wore to cover his bald patch. And in criminal circles it was also accepted that it was Ronald Kray who had shot a member of the Richardsons' gang, one George Cornell, in a public house, the Blind Beggar, back in March 1966. There was even believed to be a witness to this shooting, the pub's barmaid, but 'the frighteners' had been put on her and she wasn't talking.

My own introduction to the Kray enquiry came about unexpectedly when I was sent by Deputy Commander du Rose to interview a man I shall call here Freddie in order to preserve his anonymity. Freddie, a one-time employee of the Krays, was an accountant who had that very day been released from prison after serving a two-year sentence for fraud. The police had arranged to interview him immediately on a quite different matter, and now he was waiting in a solicitor's office in Central London. Freddie was a man with a grievance: he'd already talked to those other officers, as a result of which du Rose had been informed, and he in turn had sent for me.

Freddie was a frail, sparse little chap, and he had a tale to tell. Two years earlier he and another man had been brought to trial for fraud, and just before they went into court his friend told him that his counsel had suggested they both plead guilty as charged: in counsel's opinion if they did this they'd be dealt with more leniently than if they went through with their planned defence, which would likely fail.

Freddie believed this, and the two men apparently agreed between themselves to plead guilty. When they went into the dock together at the Old Bailey the clerk to the court read out the charges and then – as they'd both known he would – put them first to Freddie. He pleaded guilty, as arranged. But when the charges were put to the other man, he pleaded not guilty after all – and in consequence Freddie was taken from the dock to await sentence while the other man's trial proceeded.

Freddie had been tricked, of course. With him no longer in the court, the other man went on to attribute to him the fraud of which they'd both been accused and by so doing secured his own acquittal. Freddie, on the other hand, as a result of his plea had no opportunity to defend himself and was sentenced to imprisonment. He had no complaint against that for he knew he was guilty, but he had been 'conned' and now, having served his term, he was determined not to take the whole blame for others again, even at considerable risk to himself.

He was able to give some very useful information about the Kray brothers, and another man, Leslie Payne, a car dealer who'd done many jobs for the Krays, including managing a club in Chelsea.

Later, in January 1968, I was directed to join the team du Rose had already appointed to look into the Kray brothers' activities: Detective Superintendent Read (who with Gerrard had investigated the Krays before and had since been promoted), Detective Chief Inspector Harry Mooney, and two Detective Sergeants, Algy Hemmingway and Alan Wright.

'Nipper' Read now followed up the Leslie Payne lead while I concentrated on Freddie, who had given us the first lead. He was understandably afraid of being seen with me, and suggested an out-of-the-way church where we might talk. I took Sergeant Wright along with me and we gained a remarkable written statement from Freddie, all whispered to us in the church.

Read was now able to persuade Leslie Payne to help us, and his statement confirmed Freddie's to a significant degree. Even so, these two men would never have agreed to appear in open court as things were, and anyway strong corroborative evidence would also be needed, for they had admitted to criminal offences themselves. And corroborative evidence was something, for the moment, that we just didn't have.

It wasn't going to be easy to get, either. For as long as the Krays were at liberty, silence reigned. And for as long as silence reigned, the Krays would remain at liberty. Thus a frustrating four months of investigations followed, all in secret. We put together a list of all the Krays' known associates (this would prove invaluable later), and correlated all relevant previous police enquiries. Inspector Mooney spent many persuasive hours with the barmaid at the Blind Beggar, in connection with the Cornell shooting, but made no progress at all – except that at least (and this too would help later) they got to know and understand each other.

On the Mitchell prison escape and subsequent disappearance we drew an equal blank. A prison officer in charge of an outside working party on Dartmoor said he'd escaped at around four o'clock on the afternoon of 12 December 1966, and he hadn't been seen since. Reports of sightings in Tangier and other such places had been carefully followed up but then discounted.

His escape had unfortunately come at a time of several other spectacular escapes. In 1964 great train robber Charles Wilson had escaped from Winsom Green Prison in Birmingham. Then another train robber, Ronald Biggs, had got away from Wandsworth Prison in 1965 and fled the country, and then the spy, George Blake, serving a 42-year sentence, had successfully broken out of Wormwood Scrubs, followed two months later in December 1966 by Mitchell's escape from Dartmoor. All this had caused an understandable public outcry, and a Commission of Enquiry had been set up, under the chairmanship of the late Earl Mountbatten. The Commission made recommendations about prison security but had uncovered little fresh evidence, in particular nothing new concerning Mitchell's escape or the identities of those who might have helped him.

Shortly after his escape officers of the Flying Squad had interviewed two men, Garelick and Connolly, both close associates of the Krays, who had visited Mitchell in jail on the day before his get-away, both of them using false names. They had used a powerful Rover car for their journey, which would certainly have been very useful to Mitchell the following day, but the Flying Squad men were never able to prove that he'd actually escaped in it, or that the visit had to do with the escape.

In the case of the apparent disappearance of Jack McVitie, there were persistent rumours that he'd been taken to a party in a basement flat, not far from the Regency Club on Amhurst Road, Dalston, and had not been seen since. It was suggested that the occupant of the flat was a woman known as 'Blonde Carol', but that was as far as the rumours went. Nobody could or would identify the woman Blonde Carol more clearly, and it was a matter that needed delicate handling since if the rumours were true, any open enquiries on our part would simply alert the Krays and, we thought, could almost certainly put Blonde Carol's life in danger.

Then, as so often happens in police work, the long arm of coincidence suddenly made itself felt. Ever since I'd first heard the name Blonde Carol something had been niggling at the back of my mind, and then suddenly I remembered the drugs case in Leyton four years before. At that time there'd been suggestions of a vague connection with the Krays in the case, as so often happened in those days. But I did recall the blonde girl called Carol whose suitcase had been used to transport the drugs. And she'd lived with her husband in a flat on Evering Road in Stoke Newington, which I knew was only a few hundred yards away from the Regency Club. I told Nipper Read about my hunch and then confirmed the address from the papers on the 1964 drugs case. I then sent round a couple of women detectives to try to find out if the Carol I had met was still living at the address. In order to avoid advertising police interest the detectives posed as researchers for a major soap and detergent manufacturer. They spoke at some length to a woman in the basement flat on Evering Road, and from their description afterwards I knew that this was clearly the same girl – and her connection with the Krays was established when we discovered that she'd been recently working at the Green Dragon Club, a known haunt of theirs which we knew was connected with Garelick, the man who'd visited Mitchell under a false name in Dartmoor Prison. We then discovered another interesting fact: also living on Evering Road, and only a few doors away from Blonde Carol, was Connolly, the other man who'd been with Garelick on his Dartmoor visit.

None of this proved anything in connection with Jack McVitie's disappearance, of course, but it was all highly suggestive of a Kray involvement. So we kept an eye on her but, for her own sake, did nothing further. Her information would have to wait until the Krays were safely out of the way.

And then, in April 1968, our patience and perseverance began to pay off. Unobtrusive police activity persuaded another man, an American called Alan Bruce Cooper (we called him ABC), to come forward. He claimed to be associated with the Krays in a fraud involving stolen US Bearer Bonds, and he told us of two murder plots which he said were at that moment being hatched by the Krays. One of these, a man attending the Old Bailey every day, was to be poisoned by means of a spring-loaded hypodermic syringe concealed in the side of an attaché case. The killer would operate it by remote control while standing close to the victim. A second man was to be killed by means of a car bomb, and Cooper gave us detailed information about a man who was about to travel up to Glasgow to collect the necessary explosive.

Improbable as they sounded, both of these tip-offs yielded results. The traveller to Glasgow was followed and arrested there in possession of gelignite, and when his London home was searched an attaché case was found in the garden shed with a hypodermic syringe fitted into it, and a bottle of deadly and fast-acting poison.

That man was charged with conspiracy to murder and illegal possession of explosives. But we could not rely on his word or that of Cooper for they were accomplices. We needed other evidence to prove whether or not the Krays had been involved.

With the help of Alan Cooper we attempted to set up a thoroughly cloak-and-dagger meeting between him and them. At an expensive clinic in Central London, ostensibly there for minor surgery, Cooper telephoned the Krays to invite them for a business discussion, and Nipper Read and I established ourselves in the room next door, complete with audio-surveillance equipment.

Unfortunately the Krays didn't attend the meeting themselves, but sent a henchman named Cowley instead. Also, although Cooper did get this man to admit some knowledge of the car-bomb plot into our tape recorder, their conversation was interrupted by the unexpected arrival of a friend of Cooper, so that all our complicated planning in fact came to nothing. But now a decision had to be taken. Somehow the circle of silence and intimidation had to be broken, for we feared they might be planning other crimes. On 7 May du Rose gathered us all together for a conference at Tintagel House, our headquarters, an office block on the Embankment south of the river near Vauxhall Bridge.

We surveyed the evidence so far accumulated against the Kray brothers. It was less than a water-tight case, but we had a number of charges we could bring and we knew that as long as they were at large we'd be unlikely to improve on it. It was therefore decided that we should commit ourselves, remove them and as many of their principal associates as we could from the streets, on the relatively minor charges we felt we could make stick, and then see what happened.

At six the following morning, on 8 May 1968, after a four-month investigation, in a carefully planned sweep, seventeen men were arrested, including Ronald and Reginald Kray and their older brother Charles. Superintendent Read and I arrested the twins themselves while they were still in bed, and it was Sergeant Hemmingway whose considerable boot secured our entry through their front door. They lived unostentatiously, in a maisonette in council-owned housing on Bunhill Road off City Road in East London, and they and their

associates were all taken to West End Central police station, where
Read and I first questioned them and then charged them with such
offences as we had felt we could best sustain. Appearing at Bow Street
court on 10 May, seven of them were granted bail, but for the other ten,
including the Krays, our appeals for denial of bail were sustained and
they remained safely in custody.

Inevitably the press gave wide publicity to the arrests, and for once
this suited us very well. The more people who knew that the Krays and
their men were out of circulation, the better. Permanent police guards
were now placed on all our major witnesses, just in case other members
of the gang not yet arrested felt like having a go. We sat back and
waited.

Some days later a man walked into West Ham police station in
East London, having tried to commit suicide by taking drugs because
he feared that the Kray gang would kill him because he knew too much.
He was still in possession of dangerous drugs and was arrested. A
doctor treated him and had ruled that he could be detained – which of
course was exactly what the poor man wanted.

I shall call him 'Lennie'. Lennie was a concave chested and shifty
individual, a dealer in dirty books, and he'd been a long-time associate
of the Krays, living in a ground-floor flat on Barking Road in the East
End. Nipper Read and I had hardly sat down at the desk across from
him before he launched into a confession: he'd harboured Frank
Mitchell in his flat for eleven days, right from the time of his Dartmoor
escape, when he'd arrived at the flat at around four-fifteen in the
afternoon.

The Krays, he said, had arranged it all, even sending a rota of guards
to stay in the flat with Mitchell. The name of one of these men had been
Cowley. Mitchell had become troublesome at being so confined,
threatening to take his complaints to the Krays' old mother – they
worshipped her – so a woman called Lisa had been organised to keep
him company. He remained rebellious, however, even though Lisa
stayed with him until 23 December, then he was told he'd be taken to
another address in South London. Another Kray henchman, Albert
Donaghue, then arrived in a van, ostensibly to take him there. We
knew Donaghue by repute. He was a tall man, built like a boxer and
notoriously violent. He was generally feared and, judging by the cold,
forbidding stare from his deep-set eyes, possibly with good reason.

Lennie told us how Mitchell had left the flat with Donaghue that
evening at about 8 p.m., walked to the van parked in a quiet side street,
and climbed into it. Lennie and Lisa, who'd watched him leave,

remained in the flat. They heard gunshots. These seemed to come from within the van, which was immediately driven away. Lennie had never seen Mitchell again.

He described Lisa for us. She had been a night-club hostess working in several London night-clubs, but she'd cooked them all marvellous meals while at the Barking Road flat, and he remembered how often she'd liked to use red peppers. As with Mitchell, he hadn't seen her since the night of 23 December 1966.

He made a long written statement. He also said he'd give evidence in court if we would keep him safe. He was placed in protective custody.

Another person now in urgent need of protection was the woman Lisa. With Lennie known to be in police custody there might well be Kray followers – Albert Donaghue, for instance, was still at liberty – who would be looking to silence her. But we had little to go on. Even the name, Lisa, that we had for her might well be false.

Meanwhile, Lennie had raised a new problem with his account of Mitchell's escape. He was adamant that Mitchell had arrived at the London flat shortly after 4 p.m., yet that was roughly the time the Dartmoor prison officer had reported his escape two hundred miles away. The explanation turned out to be very simple: Mitchell had been a good prisoner and a member of an 'honour' party, trusted not to escape. The prison officer had been rather more easy-going than he afterwards cared to admit. In fact, when he'd been in charge of that outside working party he'd been in the habit of letting Mitchell go off for long periods alone, sometimes even by bus as far as Tavistock and back – and until this final occasion Mitchell had never given him the slightest reason for alarm.

But now, even though the time of Mitchell's escape could be moved forward by six or seven hours, this failed to help us with our enquiries. The Krays it seemed were definitely involved, but we were no nearer to proving it than we had ever been. And since Lennie was an accomplice we had to find some independent evidence in corroboration.

On the principle of pursuing any thread, no matter how slender, and remembering how Garelick and Connolly had visited Mitchell in prison using false names, it now occurred to me that perhaps other Kray gang members might have done the same thing. Prison records at Dartmoor would never reveal this, if false names had been used, so I took a chance and telexed all the police forces responsible for the roads between Dartmoor and London, asking them to search their records for the twelve-month period before Mitchell's escape, to see if they could find any reference to the only established fact we had in all this,

Garelick's Rover car. If he and Connolly had used it once, then maybe he and others had used it before. This was no more than the wildest hunch, but it was to pay off handsomely.

Next morning the example of Lennie was followed by two other men anxious to unburden themselves and gain police protection. While the cats were away the mice were indeed coming out from behind the woodwork. Over the telephone Nipper Read and I agreed a secret meeting with a man named Exley and his friend, a former member of 'The Firm' and now a somewhat faded heavy who'd known Mitchell well: both these men had been arrested with the Krays the previous week and were now out on bail. Read and I met them in Lambeth that same morning, in a sidestreet opposite St Thomas' Hospital.

Exley's friend was actually crying as he urged Exley to tell us all he knew. Both men were clearly very frightened. In fact they had little to reveal about Mitchell that we hadn't already learned from Lennie, except that Exley was also certain the Krays had killed McVitie. He said he must have a talk with his solicitor, and then he'd get in touch with us again.

That same afternoon Superintendent Read had Blonde Carol brought to Tintagel House from her flat on Evering Road. She and I remembered each other well from the Leyton drugs case: she'd been a tough young woman then, and she was tough still. She admitted knowing the Kray brothers but she strenuously denied knowing anything of the 'Jack the Hat' murder. Indeed, her denials were so pointed that she clearly didn't expect them to be believed. I sensed she was letting us know that she was playing safe, and that once the rest of the Kray gang was in custody she'd be far more forthcoming. Meanwhile we asked her to keep our meeting strictly confidential between the three of us, and she agreed. She had every reason to do so – times were dangerous for someone in her position.

The following day, having consulted his solicitor, Exley came back to us. In a written statement he confirmed everything Lennie had told us about Mitchell's stay in the Barking Road flat. He'd been one of the Krays' guards there, and he'd got to know the girl Lisa quite well. When we asked him if he knew where we could find her now he was less helpful – he thought she'd come to London from somewhere up in the north Midlands, he didn't remember her address there, but he thought he might have a note of it at his home, and promised to let us know.

A week had now passed since the arrest of the Krays and their men, and Superintendent Read and I had to attend Bow Street court for the first remand hearing in the case. Other members of our team, headed by Harry Mooney, had been busy out and about in the East End, and we were able to charge several of the men with additional offences. They all took the Krays' lead, however, and put on a great show of confidence that we were whistling in the dark, and that the case against them would soon collapse from lack of evidence.

Now Exley contacted us again. Although he couldn't find an address for Lisa he did remember once giving her a lift in his car to a flat near the Bayswater Road in West London. He didn't recall that address either, but when I took him for a drive in the area he was able to point to the house. I returned later and had a chat with the woman who lived there. She was also a night-club hostess and remembered Lisa well. Lisa had stayed with her for some eighteen months, including the 1966 Christmas period. She remembered Lisa being away for a week or so and refusing to say afterwards where she'd been. The woman didn't know where Lisa was now – except that she'd originally come from 'up north' – and she didn't even know if Lisa was the girl's real name. Apparently she'd been married once but that had broken up, and since then she'd used any number of, as-it-were, 'professional' names.

The trail seemed to have petered out again. But then, as a long shot, I saw the woman next day to ask if she knew who had been Lisa's doctor. She didn't, but she did remember that Lisa had been taken ill on one occasion, some two years earlier, while waiting for a coach at the West London Air Terminal on the Cromwell Road in Kensington, and that an ambulance had whipped her off to hospital for a few days. The woman also gave me a small coloured photograph of Lisa.

These two items of information were just what I needed. Within hours a telephone check on all the hospitals in a five-mile radius of the Air Terminal had produced details of a young woman, first name Lisa, who'd been admitted as an emergency case about two years before. Hospital records gave us her full name and also the name and address of her mother, living up in Leeds. I then sent the coloured photograph up to Leeds on the next fast train, organised a police officer there to collect it from the guard at the station, and provided details of the girl's mother so that she could be asked to identify her daughter from the photograph and tell us where Lisa was now living.

An answer came back the same evening. The mother identified the photograph and provided an address in Battersea where she said Lisa had been living up to two weeks before. But she knew that her daughter was planning to travel overland with her boyfriend to Australia in a motor caravan, and she might already have left.

It was now late evening. I collared two of our police detective sergeants and hurried to the Battersea address. It was a large house, broken up into bedsitters. Lisa wasn't there, but one of the tenants recognised her name and told us she'd left with a young Australian a week or so earlier. They'd been planning to drive to Australia, but they'd been held up because their Dormobile had developed engine trouble. The tenant didn't know where they were now, but Lisa's boyfriend had told him where the motor caravan was being repaired, and he was also able to give us the colour of the vehicle.

The repair shop was in a mews near Paddington, and by the time we got there the time was after midnight. But the Dormobile was parked outside on the cobbles, and when we roused the garage owner from his bed he confirmed that he was working on it for a young Australian. He didn't know the young man's address, except that it was an hotel close to Earl's Court underground station, but he did know that the Australian was temporarily using a hired dark-blue Ford transit van which had a Stuyvesant cigarette advertisement stuck on its windscreen.

It was after one in the morning when the two sergeants and I arrived at Earl's Court station. Working outwards, we began a sweep search of the deserted streets, looking for the blue transit with the Stuyvesant sticker on its windscreen, and within ten minutes we found it, parked outside a small hotel. I rang the doorbell and had a discreet word with the owner. I didn't want any trouble and neither did she. I wasn't arresting Lisa, I simply wanted a quiet chat with her.

The hotel owner pointed to the door of a room on the ground floor, off the hallway, and gave me a pass key. I opened the door quietly. The room was dark, but the light from the door shone in across a man and a woman asleep in bed. I touched the woman's shoulder and she woke instantly. I recognized her from the photograph.

Showing her my warrant card, I whispered, 'Lisa?'

She nodded. 'Yes.'

She was a pretty girl, but it wasn't the first time she'd seen a police warrant card. Her boyfriend was still asleep so I asked her softly to come outside into the corridor for a moment. She came.

Trembling, she asked me what I wanted.

I replied, 'Frank Mitchell?'

Her eyes widened but then she nodded, almost as if she wasn't surprised.

I told her that I was from Scotland Yard, that I knew about her boyfriend, and that there was no reason for him to get involved. She could rejoin him later, but just for the moment I wanted her to come with me to my office. She agreed.

The two plain-clothes officers and I waited while she got dressed, and then I took her out to our unmarked car, leaving one of the detectives to keep an eye on the young Australian. The other detective, Sergeant Trevette, drove, while I sat in the back with Lisa.

Trevette was a cheerful fellow, a real live-wire. Between us we tried to put Lisa at her ease, but she still seemed wary. I was soon to realise why.

All went well as we drove along the deserted Chelsea Embankment in the direction of Westminster and New Scotland Yard. But then Trevette turned right to cross Lambeth Bridge on our way to the Albert Embankment on the south side of the river where my office in Tintagel House was located. Suddenly, halfway across the bridge, Lisa made a lunge for the rear door, pushed it open and tried to throw herself out.

Luckily I was able to grab her coat collar and pull her back in. She was hysterical, obviously terrified.

'You're not from Scotland Yard,' she screamed. 'You're from *them*.'

Then I understood. Lisa knew her London, and as long as she'd thought she was being taken to Scotland Yard (where I'd told her I was from) she'd felt safe. But as far as she was concerned, Trevette's turn across Lambeth Bridge had meant she was being carried off south of the river, towards Kray territory. The poor young woman clearly believed that Trevette and I were Kray henchmen in disguise, perhaps taking her to her death.

Sergeant Trevette had swerved wildly. Now he controlled the car while I tried to convince Lisa that she was safe. At first she wouldn't listen. Then she quietened down.

'Give me your hand,' she said.

I did so, mystified, and she ran her fingers over it. Only then was she satisfied that I really was a policeman. Later I asked her what had convinced her.

'You don't have workman's hands,' she said.

As soon as we arrived at Tintagel House we sat her down with a cup of coffee and she relaxed. Her fear of the Krays had told me a lot, of course, and I was quickly able to convince her that I knew too much about her time with Mitchell – even down to the red peppers she used in her cooking – for her to be able to deny any involvement. I spoke with her for some time and, reassured, she agreed to make a written statement.

After being taken to the Barking Road flat by one of the Kray gang she had stayed there with Mitchell for a week or so. Mitchell and she had got on. She produced from her handbag a page torn from a 1966 pocket diary, a calendar with a number of the dates ringed in ink. Mitchell had bred budgerigars while in Dartmoor, and the ringed dates referred to egg hatchings. He'd given her the page as a memento, and she also produced a comb which she said had belonged to him.

When I asked her why she'd kept these things, she said, 'I wanted something to remind me of him. I'm sure he's dead.'

She described how she'd seen Mitchell leave the flat with a man called Donaghue. She'd seen him climb into the van waiting outside in the street, and then she'd heard shots . . . I asked her if she'd be willing to give her evidence in court, actually in front of the criminals involved, and she began to tremble again. She said she thought she would be too terrified. I suggested that we could withhold her name. She asked if we would let her wear some sort of disguise and eventually she asked if she could wear big plastic Donald Duck sunglasses to disguise her features. I said she could and she then agreed to give evidence.

Later that day, after she'd rested, we established Lisa at a secret address in the country with a twenty-four hour police guard, and her Australian boyfriend was allowed to join her. We were also able to find later an ex-cellmate of Mitchell who confirmed that the diary page and the comb had been Mitchell's property.

Lisa's evidence was golden, for now we had corroboration. One thing leads to another, and as a result Detective Chief Inspector Mooney was able to arrest three more of the Kray gang for their involvement in the Mitchell escape, and two days later Ronald, Reginald and Charles Kray, Cowley, Garelick and two others were further charged with conspiring to effect Mitchell's escape and with harbouring him in Barking. Albert Donaghue was also traced and arrested, and with Reginald Kray was charged with Mitchell's murder.

The Krays and most of their thugs had now been in custody for three weeks. The charges against them were serious, and becoming more serious, and their reputations had been badly dented. Their ship was sinking, and now I received an anonymous tip-off that another of their men was wanting to jump off. Already on remand in prison, and a man of some position in London criminal circles, he was now willing to talk.

A meeting was organised with the prison authorities for that Sunday afternoon. The man's one proviso was that our conversation should be kept secret from the other prisoners – for which we didn't blame him – so the prison governor arranged for Superintendent Read and me to meet him in the prison chapel, in a tiny room behind the altar where the hymn books were kept.

Our informant's evidence turned out to be dramatic, involving two of the Kray brothers and a firearm, with which he said the Krays had threatened to kill him. I took a written statement from him and it took some time. Suddenly there were noises in the chapel on the other side of the thin plywood partition, and the knob rattled on the door to our little room. We had clearly talked for so long that now it was time for Evensong – which represented an hour's extra freedom from their cells to the prison inmates and therefore always played to a packed congregation – and one of them was coming for the hymn books.

Our informant went pale as I grabbed the doorknob and held on, managing to keep the door shut. It was a tense moment, and I frankly wouldn't have given much for our companion's chances later if he'd been discovered in there with us, but fortunately one prison officer, who was in the know, intervened outside and then came in to fetch the hymn books himself.

As soon as the service began we were able to continue our whispered conversation. Outside in the chapel the prisoners lustily sang 'The Lord is my Shepherd . . .' while crouched behind the thin partition I wrote at our informant's dictation, and Superintendent Read watched him as he demonstrated the exact angle at which he said a gun had been held to his head. It was a bizarre occasion.

We left when the service was over and the chapel empty again. Our informant went back to his cell, his secret intact. Weeks later he was to give his evidence again, in court, in the presence of the Krays themselves.

The following morning replies began to come in to my request for sightings of Garelick's Rover on its way to or from Dartmoor in the months before Mitchell's escape. Surprisingly, it had been stopped twice in Surrey in connection with other matters and the occupants questioned, on both occasions with Garelick himself driving, and the police officers concerned had been careful in noting the names and addresses of the people in the car with him. One of these had been Connolly, already in custody, but the others now were all traced and interviewed. Two of them, young women, eventually admitted that the car had been on its way to Dartmoor and that the conversation had all been about plans for Mitchell's escape. One of them, named Clare, later gave evidence in court. Another occupant of the car, a man, also corroborated this, and added further that he and his two brothers knew all about Ronald Kray's killing of Cornell in the Blind Beggar pub.

This was a real gift, and a major breakthrough in the Cornell murder. The witness claimed that one or more of his brothers had been present when Ronald Kray had changed his clothes after the shooting. The family had in fact been 'minding' Kray in a safe flat after the murder, and the witness claimed they'd be able to give exact details of Ronald Kray's movements both before and after the murder, and of conversations that had taken place. His two brothers were quickly picked up, and others of his family, and in due course they confirmed this story in court as witnesses.

The charges which had now been brought, and the publicity they had received had also earned us a further dividend. Inspector Mooney's unwilling witness, the barmaid at the Blind Beggar, had also now changed her mind. With the Krays and so many of their people in custody, and the evidence piling up against them, she decided to tell Harry Mooney all she knew. And she knew a lot.

Now, in connection with the Cornell case, there was yet another group of witnesses needing police protection. Our resources were strained, but somehow we managed it, and on 19 June 1968, Ronald Kray was charged with the murder of George Cornell. He and his brothers had been on remand now for seven weeks, and each time they'd appeared in court we'd had further charges to prefer against them. They still blustered, but their bluster had a hollow ring to it.

We still had a lot of work to do, however.

On 25 June 1968, committal proceedings began at Bow Street magistrates' court in respect of the Mitchell escape plot: nine men stood in the dock charged with conspiracy to effect the escape, and five of them were charged with Mitchell's murder. One of our difficulties was that the motive for his death never became clear. Mitchell had been a hard man all his life. In an era of corporal punishment he had suffered the worst, even the cat-o'-nine-tails, and may well have been hardened still further. He had broken out of every prison in which he'd ever been held, and he was known to be unpredictably violent. The Krays had planned to rescue him much earlier in 1966, some of the witnesses said, in order to enlist him as their principal heavy, a counter to the Richardsons' Frankie Fraser. It was a matter of keeping face.

Admittedly he'd made a nuisance of himself after his release, and admittedly by the time he was sprung the Richardson gang had been smashed by the police, so the Krays no longer had a pressing need of his services.

The charges involving Mitchell were heard eventually at Bow Street magistrates' court, and those charged were committed for trial.

One by one the witnesses were brought from their secret addresses to give evidence. Eventually it was Lisa's turn, and Sergeant Trevette was deputed to pick her up from the country in a car and deliver her sharp at ten-thirty. But there was a general transport strike in London that day and Trevette got no further in than Kingston before he realised the traffic was too bad for him ever to reach Bow Street on time.

Enterprising as ever, he enlisted the help of the Thames Police, who conveyed him and Lisa in a police launch from Kingston to Charing Cross Pier on the Embankment, where they were met by a car for the last short distance. They made it to the court just as the chief magistrate took his seat. But even then our troubles weren't over. The long car and boat journey had taken its toll on Lisa's nerves, and she was desperate to go to the toilet. The court was in session and was waiting for her. Lisa went to the toilet and the chief magistrate grew impatient. After a while the delay became embarrassing, so I sidled out of the court to find out what had happened. Outside the toilets I discovered Lisa, totally distrait. In her hurry she'd dropped her precious Donald Duck sunglasses into the lavatory pan, and now poor Sergeant Trevette was in the cubicle, trying to fish them out.

He managed it eventually, dried them carefully, and order was restored. Lisa was ushered into the courtroom, apologised calmly to the magistrate, and gave her evidence faultlessly. Only Trevette and I really understood the strain she was suffering. In any event, the witnesses all came up to proof and all the accused were sent for trial at the Old Bailey.

Meanwhile, in the Cornell case Inspector Mooney had arrested another man, John Barrie, and charged him with the murder, also. Reginald Kray, too, was further charged with assisting his brother Ronald after the murder.

A few days later another message came from the Kray camp, this time from Albert Donaghue, who asked to see either Superintendent Read or myself. We went together and spent several days with him in a prison cell while he detailed his association with the Krays over many years. His purpose was to establish that he'd had no part in any killing – even without the death penalty I have found the prospect of life imprisonment for murder, possibly with a minimum sentence recommendation, to be a great loosener of tongues.

He dealt with his part in the Mitchell escape – he'd picked Mitchell up in the late morning near the Elephant's Nest pub on Dartmoor, and with another man had driven him to the Barking Road flat – and with his knowledge of the Mitchell, Cornell, and McVitie killings. His account of the McVitie death was vital, for we'd so far made little progress with it.

Mitchell, he said, had been killed in the van outside the flat, shot several times in the head and body. He gave us the names of four men who he said had been waiting inside the van. He himself had witnessed the killing but had taken no part in it. When it was over he'd returned to the flat and the van had been driven away with the four men still sitting in it with the body. He claimed no knowledge of what had been done with Mitchell's remains.

On the McVitie murder, he said he'd taken no part in that either, but he'd been told afterwards what had happened. Jack 'The Hat' McVitie had caused the Krays aggravation, so he'd been lured to Blonde Carol's flat for a party while she was away.

Donaghue admitted to us that he was afterwards detailed to re-decorate Blonde Carol's flat, and to remove all traces of the bloody crime that had been committed there. He went on to emphasise that Blonde Carol hadn't been present at the time of the murder, and although she had seen traces of the blood when she returned to the flat she'd had no knowledge at all of what had actually been done. She'd simply been asked if her flat could be used for a party while she was out.

Meanwhile, a very experienced officer from the Company Frauds Squad, Detective Inspector Holt, had joined our team, and had dealt with all the fraud aspects of the case and he now continued with the case in court. Superintendent Read and I now followed up on Donaghue's story.

Once again we interviewed Blonde Carol. And once again she refused to talk. We spent a long time with her. Clearly her silence was worrying her: there was a lot bottled up behind her apparent toughness, and I sensed that it would only need the right word from us to bring it all pouring out. I remembered that her mother was dead, and I knew that they'd been close, so I asked her how she thought that lady might have advised her.

The façade crumbled. Blonde Carol broke down completely, and in tears told us everything she knew. She had allowed the Kray twins to use her flat for a party in her absence, and when she returned late the same night she found several men cleaning the place. She saw blood on the floor and bloodstained water in a bucket, and the bedspread was missing from her bed. There seemed to have been some kind of struggle, for a pane of glass in the front window had been broken. The men went away after a while, but Donaghue came later in the week and redecorated the room. She'd been warned to keep her mouth shut no matter what.

She now named everyone who had been concerned: they included two other brothers, Christopher and Anthony Lambrianou, Ronald Bender, Donaghue, and men named Hart and Whitehead.

Next morning I went to her flat with an officer from the Yard's science laboratory. In the front room where McVitie was said to have been killed we found signs of redecoration exactly as Donaghue and Blonde Carol had reported. And beneath the wallpaper under the window we found an area of bloodstains and evidence that a pane of glass had recently been replaced. Forensic samples were taken, and the whole room photographed.

Now Read and I traced a man with a smallholding in Kent who we believed had got rid of the Krays' bloody clothing after the McVitie murder. He admitted receiving a suitcase with something in it which he'd burned on this smallholding. Sifting by hand through an enormous pile of compost and rubbish down in Kent revealed the wire frame of a suitcase and its lock, charred but still identifiable.

Slowly the case was coming together with witnesses' accounts, supported by forensic evidence. We still had neither Mitchell's nor McVitie's body, however, and we hadn't yet been able to find the man Hart, mentioned both by Donaghue and Blonde Carol. But the word was out, and on 31 August Superintendent Read and I had a chat with one of Hart's brothers. We pointed out that it was only a matter of time before we caught him. Four days later he surrendered himself.

He confirmed everything we'd already been told about McVitie's killing and – most importantly – exactly where he'd disposed of the gun afterwards, in a canal by Queensbridge Road, Hackney. An underwater search of the canal then led to the gun being found. It was loaded, and had a bullet jammed in its breach.

More arrests followed, including those of the Lambrianou brothers, the proprietor of the Regency Club, Anthony Barry, a South London publican, Freddy Foreman and Whitehead.

When we arrested and interviewed Foreman he casually told us he had tickets for the World Cup in Mexico and had been planning to leave later that day. Read and I suggested that he was going to miss the match.

The Lambrianou brothers and the Kray twins were charged with McVitie's murder, and Charles Kray with assisting them afterwards. Donaghue and Whitehead were charged with aiding and abetting also. In all, by now the police had arrested and charged thirty-eight people, all members of the Kray 'Firm', all these arrests stemming basically from the leads given us by one small man with a grievance, Freddie the accountant.

The Kray trial for the murders of Cornell and McVitie was dealt with as one trial and presided over by Mr Justice Melford Stevenson. It was to be at that time the longest murder trial in the history of the Central Criminal Court, running for a period of forty working days, from 9 January to 5 March 1968. At the end of a mass of evidence, argument and counter-argument, only the club owner, Anthony Barry, was acquitted by the jury and allowed to go free. He attributed his actions to his fear of the Krays. All the other defendants were found guilty.

Ronald Kray, convicted of the murders of both Cornell and McVitie, was first in the dock for sentencing. He was given two sentences of life imprisonment. The judge said to him, 'I'm not going to waste words on you. In my view society has earned a rest from your activities and I recommend that you be detained for a minimum of thirty years.'

Reginald Kray, Ronald's accomplice after the Blind Beggar shooting of Cornell and an active participant in McVitie's killing, was also given life imprisonment, with a similar thirty-year minimum.

John Barrie, who in the Cornell killing had fired shots to prevent people helping Ronald Kray's victim and to frighten witnesses, was also sentenced to life imprisonment, with a recommended minimum of twenty years.

Christopher and Anthony Lambrianou, who'd taken McVitie to the flat of Blonde Carol from the Regency Club and had been present when he died, were sentenced to life imprisonment with a recommended minimum of fifteen years.

Charles Kray was sentenced to ten years in jail for helping his brothers after McVitie's murder. To him the judge said, 'It may be that you were not a member of "The Firm", but I am satisfied that you were an active helper in the dreadful enterprise of concealing traces of the murders your brothers committed.' Frederick Foreman was also sentenced to ten years' imprisonment, accused of disposing of McVitie's body.

Albert Donaghue, who had pleaded guilty to being an accessory after the fact of McVitie's murder, was given a sentence of two years.

Mr Justice Melford Stevenson then paid tribute to the police. He said, 'The debt the public owes to Superintendent Read and the officers serving under him in this case is one that cannot be over-stated and can never be discharged.'

1. The old Police Office *(left)*, in the court of Scotland Yard in 1890. The lower, central, building is the Public Carriage Office.

2. The early days: a group of Scotland Yard detectives in various disguises before setting off on an observation mission that resulted in the capture of a group of thieves, *circa* 1900. An early example of detective undercover work.

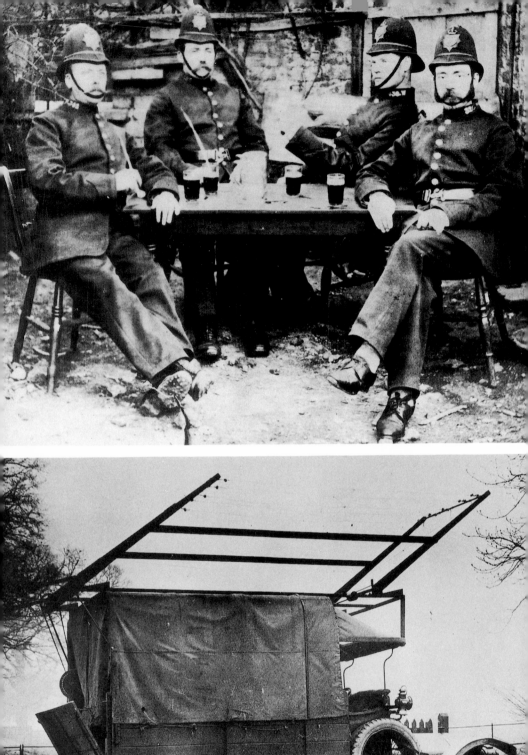

3. *(top left)* The uniform branch: policemen off duty, *circa* 1920.

4. *(bottom left)* The first radio-equipped Flying Squad vehicle.

5. *(above)* HMS *Belfast* approaches *Wave Barron*, to allow Chief Inspector Bill Webster and Frank Cater to board and conduct drug investigations.

6. *(right)* Frank Cater about to jackstay to the *Belfast*.

7. *(above left)* Frank Mitchell, the 'mad axeman', whose escape from Dartmoor was engineered by the Kray twins.

8. *(above right)* George Cornell, murdered at The Blind Beggar public house, Whitechapel, by Ronald Kray.

9. *(left)* Lisa, the night-club hostess chosen by the Kray twins to keep Frank Mitchell company after his escape from Dartmoor.

Much of the Crown's case in the Cornell and McVitie murders had rested upon the evidence of Hart, Blonde Carol, and the barmaid at the Blind Beggar. They had stood up well to examination, and the jury had clearly believed them. For the Mitchell murder trial a month later, however, before a different jury, the Crown's principal witness was Albert Donaghue, and it seems the jury found him less convincing. I accepted his story, but the jury chose not to, and all those charged with any sort of involvement in the murder of Mitchell were acquitted.

The difficulty, of course, was not so much that the police did not have Mitchell's body – McVitie's body, too, had never been found – but rather that the shooting Donaghue said he had witnessed and which Lisa heard had come from *inside* the van so only Donaghue could say what happened in that vehicle. Mitchell's body was never found so we could not obtain evidence from it.

Reginald Kray, Garelick, Cowley, and a fourth man named John Dixon were convicted, however, of conspiracy to effect Mitchell's escape from Dartmoor, and of later harbouring him. Reginald Kray was given a further five years and nine months' imprisonment to run concurrently with his thirty years, Garelick received two years, Cowley and Dixon nine months each, and Donaghue – who had pleaded guilty – received eighteen months' imprisonment on each count.

Donaghue claimed he had taken no direct part in the killing of McVitie or Cornell. In summary, the evidence produced in that trial was that McVitie had in some way caused the Krays 'aggro', so he had been lured to Blonde Carol's flat where the Kray twins, and others, were waiting for him. One of them, Bender, was armed with a carving knife. Reginald Kray had held a gun to McVitie's head and squeezed the trigger repeatedly but the gun would not fire. Then Reginald Kray had taken the carving knife and thrust it into McVitie while Ronald Kray held him. Still McVitie did not die, but he slipped to the floor and then the knife was thrust into his throat and twisted.

When McVitie was dead the Krays went away to clean up at an address in nearby Hackney Road. Bender had been left at the flat to get rid of the body. We never could prove what eventually happened to the body but the evidence given at the trial was that it had been disposed of by Foreman, to whom it was delivered. Another of those present at the murder, the man Hart, then took the gun and later had tossed it into a canal at Queensbridge Road, Dalston, from which we later recovered it. The Krays' clothing was got rid of by the man with the smallholding in Kent.

After that the Krays took a holiday. They went to the house they had bought for their parents at Bildeston, in Suffolk. They were popular there. They even bought a donkey for the local children.

The Mitchell murder trial which followed resulted in acquittals but if Mitchell's death was never resolved by the Court, it did achieve something else, for it was his disappearance which, in my opinion, finally brought the Krays crashing down. That and the courage of four brave women witnesses.

5

1970:
ACCUSATIONS AND APOLOGIES

At the end of the Kray case I was sent to Bramshill, the national police college in Hampshire, for three months to complete what was then styled the 'Intermediate Command Course'. In November 1969, while still at Bramshill, I was promoted to the rank of Detective Chief Inspector.

As a result of the continuing organised crime in London and the success of the methods used against the Richardsons and the Krays, the Home Office had now authorised the Commissioner to establish a new, additional squad of CID officers at the Yard. This was to be called the Organised Crime Squad, and a detective chief superintendent was to be appointed as its head. There were delays in making this appointment, however, and when I returned to London from Bramshill I was asked to take charge of the newly formed squad, on a temporary basis.

I was given six experienced detective officers and authorised to choose my own target criminals, in the manner of the two previous investigations. The first case we successfully tackled in 1970 was complicated and lengthy, involving London night-clubs. Several men were later given prison sentences and subsequently, by twice becoming the subject of a major investigation by the newly formed Organised Crime Squad, one of the men involved in that 1970 case may well have established some sort of record. A record, however, that I don't expect many others will try to beat, for off he went again to prison.

It was during my term as temporary head of the Organised Crime Squad, however, that *The Times* newspaper published the allegations which came to be known as the '*Times* Enquiry'. In a detailed article the *Times*' reporters made accusations of corruption against three police officers in the Metropolitan Criminal Investigation Department. They supplied evidence of corruption and suggested further that as far as the London CID was concerned this was only the 'tip of the iceberg'.

The accusations attracted enormous publicity, and rightly so, and an enquiry was set up, as a result of which two of the three men named were found guilty of serious offences and sent to prison. And I suspect their status in prison as 'bent' coppers cannot have made their time there very pleasant.

As to the allegations, however, that those officers represented only the tip of some vast structure of widespread police corruption in the London force, I would state quite categorically that that simply was not true. And yet, when the then Police Commissioner, Sir John Waldron, retired in 1972 and was replaced by the Deputy Commissioner, later Sir Robert Mark – who had joined the London force only four years earlier as one of its four assistant commissioners, from the small Leicester force of less than five hundred officers – one of the first things the newly appointed commissioner did was to call together representatives of his Criminal Investigation Department and tell them, among other things, that they belonged to what had 'long been the most routinely corrupt organisation in London'.

It was a harsh comment, and I believe totally unjustified. In my opinion it did much to undermine the morale of the London CID and can have done little to sustain the force's reputation for integrity in the minds of the public or the judiciary. I remember wondering at that time what effect it might produce in the minds of the juries who have to decide the outcome of prosecutions.

Years later, following his own retirement in 1977, Sir Robert Mark himself acknowledged in his autobiography that the majority of CID officers in the Metropolitan Police at that time must have been honest. I and many others just wish he had realised that and said it back in 1972, instead of uttering those harsh comments about his CID.

The position in the CID in the Fifties and Sixties should be looked at objectively. In those earlier days, to opt for a CID career within the Metropolitan Police was to choose a decidedly disadvantaged situation within the force. The CID represented a mere eight per cent of the force as a whole and promotion prospects, which were restricted to positions within the CID, were very limited. As I've already said, a CID man would think himself lucky to reach the rank of sergeant within twelve or fourteen years, whereas in the uniformed branch if a man did well in competitive written promotion examinations he could reach the same rank within five years. And so it went on – men who had joined the force with me in the early 1950s and had remained within the uniformed branch were at chief inspector rank before I'd even reached first class sergeant. It hardly needs saying that the salary scales were substantially different.

And yet the CID sergeant with fifteen years' service was an experienced and highly trained officer, with specialised skills most other officers would never have. Not only would he have completed extensive courses at the Metropolitan Detective Training School, with emphasis on the practical application of forensic science, but he would also have studied the considerable intricacies of the criminal law and its administration, for at that time he also had to be capable of preparing and presenting criminal prosecutioning before the courts, often in opposition to highly qualified professional defence solicitors and counsel. Today we have the Crown Prosecution Service, staffed I am sure by very able lawyers, but in the Fifties and Sixties most criminal prosecutions were in the hands of the CID.

No, it was clearly something other than a desire for money or promotion prospects that attracted a young man into the CID. In my opinion he was attracted – and still is – by the very nature of the skills themselves, and the fact that they bring officers into close contact with the challenges presented by major crime and professional criminals, from the beginning of an investigation right through to its end. Much of the most invaluable work of the uniformed branch lies in the keeping of the peace in its more social aspects, interfacing principally with perfectly law-abiding members of the public – so therefore, if it's the closed, specialised world of the criminal that interests you, then your place is probably in the CID. Even if, back in the Fifties and Sixties, there were resulting losses in salary, slow promotion and increases in the hours to be worked.

These, then, were the men who were facing the worst elements in our society.

To some criminals bribery is a way of life. For many of them imprisonment is only part of the punishment, for crime can be most lucrative. And it must be remembered that in the 1950s and early 1960s police pay in London was not simply low – it was humiliating, and during those years the London force lost many fine officers because of it. But corruption and its temptations are insidious and some officers did weaken and disgraced both themselves and the force. They were sought out and dealt with by their fellow officers with rigour and determination. But they represented a very tiny element within the force at that time and, in my opinion, it was shameful that the guilt of those few was allowed to burden the rest for as long as it did. It brought about untold damage to the Criminal Investigation Department. The fact that so few police officers do succumb to temptation is a striking tribute to the collective and individual integrity of the force, and the people of London have always owed a great deal to their dedicated CID officers.

Other results came from the *Times* Enquiry. In particular the structure of the CID within the force was changed. And although some of the changes were said to have brought improved flexibility, it was hard to understand the purpose of many of them.

First of all, 'interchange' between the CID and the uniformed branch became commonplace. Detective constables could now take the uniformed branch's competitive promotion examinations, become sergeants in that branch and return to CID duties later, it was initially proposed twelve months later. This was aimed, it was said, to produce a widening of experience, but it also meant, since a uniformed branch sergeant could similarly make the change to the CID, that men could become CID sergeants whilst their CID experience and training was either nil or very limited, and they often found themselves in charge of detective constables who in effect were obliged to instruct their sergeants in CID work.

The CID constables promoted to sergeant in the uniformed branch, on the other hand, were thus being transferred whilst they were still learning how to be CID officers and whereas it was originally proposed that they should return to the CID after twelve months, that soon became unworkable, and often it was three or four years before they returned to the CID to resume their CID training.

That dearth of in-depth CID experience soon began to permeate up through the various supervisory ranks of the CID so that 'interchange' officers placed in charge and control of operational detectives of twenty years or more of CID experience were quite often either too ill-equipped, or, at worst, totally incapable of giving advice or direction when necessary to those more experienced CID officers and because of that the system soon fell into disrepute.

Other changes which followed were even less desirable in their effects upon the CID. Previously the CID had possessed four detective commanders, one for each of the four geographical areas of the London Metropolitan Police District, each in charge of hundreds of operational detectives. These four men were now relieved of their commands and appointed to purely advisory roles. Similarly, the twenty-five CID detective chief superintendents, who between them had controlled the CID officers of the then twenty-five divisions of the Metropolitan Police, were also relieved of their operational command responsibilities. And finally, so were their detective superintendent deputies.

As a result, it was only at the level of what had been sub-divisional police stations, of which there were several in each of the divisions, that there was a senior CID officer in charge of CID operations – and he was only at a detective chief inspector level. He would now be responsible directly to the uniformed branch chief superintendent, who in many cases would have no CID training or operational experience at all. Above that level there was no CID command structure out upon the twenty-five police divisions of London.

Only at the Yard itself did CID commanders, detective chief superintendents and detective superintendents retain their CID command responsibilities – and then only in respect of the officers of those CID branches at the Yard.

These are organisational matters, of course, technicalities possibly of little interest to general readers. But I make no apologies for airing them, since I believe they are symptomatic of the many, perhaps well-meaning failures and mistakes which bedevilled the police force during my time with it. In addition to all that we were also for the most part under-funded, under-staffed, and increasingly hampered by special-interest legislations. The few measures taken to improve that situation always seemed to me to have been principally cosmetic – a good show in the window but not very much when you really looked at them.

In the January of 1972, after six years of continuous duty at the Yard, I was posted back to an East London division which included my old stamping ground of Hackney not far from Walthamstow, where Bridget and I were now living.

Hackney was now a wilder place. Soon after my arrival on the division I dealt with three major cases in one hectic ten-day period.

First there was a thirty-two-year-old man who lived quietly with his family. Suddenly, clearly deranged, he killed his mother in her kitchen by battering her with a garden spade. Then, when his sister came home from work, he attacked her as well, inflicting the most terrible injuries. Luckily the poor wretch came quietly when he was arrested.

Three days later, at another address in Hackney, a sixty-year-old homosexual was knifed to death by a casual lover. This younger man then attempted suicide, first by swallowing pain-killing tablets, and then by turning on the gas oven and lying down with his head in it. He was saved only because there wasn't enough money in the meter and the gas ran out.

And thirdly, four days after that, a well-built young woman of twenty thrust a long, sharp carving knife through her husband's body as he lay asleep on the bed settee in the one-room flat they lived in with their baby. The knife pinned the man to the bed, its handle protruding from his chest, but miraculously it passed through his body without striking an artery or other vital organ, and he was alive and fully conscious when the police arrived.

Tom Smith, the Hackney Detective Inspector, immediately called an ambulance. Then he got on to me. When the ambulance arrived it brought with it two surgeons from the local hospital and with their expertise, and the help of six policemen, the man was lifted from the bed without further injury and taken down to the ambulance with the knife still in him. He received emergency surgery, and recovered.

I talked with the wife. It was a pitiful, if familiar story. Her husband was unemployed. Mostly he lay in bed while she cooked and cleaned around him and looked after the baby, but sometimes he beat her. And now she was pregnant again. That morning he'd been obliged to get up, in order to go to the nearby social security office so that he'd continue to qualify for unemployment benefit. But then, when he returned, he'd gone back to bed again and had soon begun to snore.

His wife told me that, looking at him lying there, something in her had suddenly 'snapped'. She'd taken the carving knife from the drawer and had stabbed him, just the one blow, with all her strength. She was calm now, obviously in shock, her eyes wide, the baby wriggling on her knee. I had my duty to do. I charged her.

The court at the Old Bailey was merciful. She was tried, and placed on probation for two years. Long before that she had left her husband and returned to live with her parents. But for the skill of the surgeons she might have done so as a widow, after facing a very different trial – for manslaughter if not murder. I believe she has since made a new, good life for herself and her children.

And for me further promotion was in store. At about this time, in response to sharpened public awareness, a new branch was being created at Scotland Yard. Called A10, it was made responsible for investigating all allegations of crime levelled against police officers, and from my division two senior officers were posted to serve on it, a detective chief inspector and a detective chief superintendent. Two such senior vacancies caused much shuffling round on the division, and I ended up being transferred and promoted to Detective Superintendent. And only nine months later, in September 1973, I was boosted upwards yet again, to Detective Chief Superintendent, and put in charge of J Division.

My start there wasn't a happy one. Within a very few weeks I was twice reminded that unfortunately police officers, like other mortals, do sometimes have their domestic problems. Called out in the early hours of the morning to the scene of a murder in Walthamstow, I discovered that the victim was a woman police constable. One of the first Asian women to join the force, she was in plain clothes and had just finished a tour of duty. Then, on her return home, someone had attacked her outside her front door, slashing her carotid artery with a knife. While she lay dying a man had been seen running away.

It was a sad case, but simply solved. She was a married woman with two children, but she had separated from her husband some time before. Her husband was a Sikh, and bitterly resentful. When we traced him he confessed to her murder.

But then, only a few weeks later, another police officer was on the receiving end of a major enquiry, a male police constable this time, with some three years' service. His wife hadn't been seen around their Loughton home and, knowing that there'd been frequent domestic quarrels, neighbours had reported the matter to the local police station. The constable claimed that she'd left him and gone home to her parents, but this story didn't hold up and a search uncovered her body buried in his garden. She had been strangled and the man now admitted that he had killed her. It had been during a worse than usual quarrel, he said, and afterwards he'd panicked, burying her body and making up the story about her leaving him.

Following his conviction for manslaughter at Chelmsford assizes he was sentenced to ten years' imprisonment.

On the day of his conviction, a Monday, while I was still in the court I was called away to another case. Our information was that a woman cashier at a bank in Barkingside had disappeared during her lunch break, and that her bank's manager had since been telephoned by a man claiming she had been kidnapped and demanding a £75,000 ransom for her safe return.

By the time I arrived at Barkingside police station, shortly after five o'clock, a suitable parcel of fake money had been made up. The kidnapper's instruction was that the money should be placed in a certain isolated spot in the Romford area, so the parcel was left as instructed. A careful watch was maintained, however, but possibly it wasn't careful enough, for nobody arrived to take away the money.

Then another report came in. The kidnapped woman had been found lying in the dark in a public park in Romford, unconscious, suffering from the effects of drugs. She was taken to hospital under police guard and a day later, when she was sufficiently recovered, she gave us her story. During her lunch break on the Monday, she said, she'd been approached by two men who introduced themselves as policemen. They told her that her husband had been injured in a street accident and offered to take her to him in hospital. She'd gone with them in their car, and during the journey they'd forced her to swallow tablets they claimed would help her to keep calm. After that her recollection of events was hazy and eventually she'd lost consciousness. That was all she knew until waking in hospital, but she was able to give good descriptions of the two men and their car.

I didn't like her story, particularly the part about the tablets she'd been 'forced' to swallow. The hospital reported that her coma had been perfectly genuine, but even so I didn't quite believe in her ordeal. The descriptions of the men and the car had been so very specific and yet other aspects of her story had been curiously vague.

In any case three days later, when the cashier was fully recovered, she was interviewed again. This time, after further questioning, she admitted that she'd lied. The entire episode had been a conspiracy between herself and several men to defraud the bank. In fact she'd been extremely lucky – according to the doctors looking after her the drugs that she'd voluntarily taken as part of the conspiracy were of such strength that they could easily have killed her. It had only been the fortunate chance of her being found unconscious in the park very quickly after she'd been dumped there that had saved her.

She and her fellow conspirators were all arrested and charged and eventually brought for trial.

This was the the time of the early 1970s bombings in this country, which had required a formation of a special Scotland Yard Bomb Squad. Bombs were rare on my patch, fortunately, but on one evening, even so, a large pub on the Leytonstone High Road was rocked by a mighty explosion. By the time I got there the Bomb Squad had already been called.

Clearly the explosion had taken place in the men's toilets, and it had been powerful enough to demolish the internal wall between them and the saloon bar, causing serious structural damage to the entire building. Luckily, because it was early evening, the bar had been empty and nobody was injured, other than the licensee's wife who suffered severe shock. None of the more usual IRA warnings concerning the explosion had been made, and it was indeed hard to see a political motive for attacking a pub in this sort of area.

When the Bomb Squad experts arrived they quickly had the explosion explained – its mechanism if not its purpose. Apparently two balloons had been filled with an explosive mixture of oxygen and acetylene, placed in one of the cubicles in the men's toilet, just inside the pub's front door, and the mixture had been detonated by means of a long newspaper fuse and matches. The whole thing was obviously an amateur lash-up, and not a terrorist bomb at all.

Since the main ingredients of the bomb, oxygen and acetylene, are generally available only in metal-working shops and garages, a line of enquiry immediately suggested itself to me, and a short conversation with the licensee provided us with a probable solution. Three days earlier he'd had a bit of a barney with one of his customers who worked in a garage just round the corner, and when we followed up this lead the man in question admitted that he and a group of his friends had decided to teach the licensee a lesson. Totally ignorant of what they were doing, however, they'd badly underestimated the explosive power of the gas – all they'd intended was to make a bit of a bang.

All the men involved were charged. It was of course nothing short of a miracle that, in spite of their irresponsibility, nobody had been seriously injured or killed.

It was shortly after this that a crime occurred which was to involve me briefly with the subsequently highly controversial George Davis. Quite by chance, two of my officers working in plain clothes stumbled upon a raid being carried out by a gang of armed robbers in Ley Street, Ilford, on offices of the London Electricity Board. One of the men, PC Groves, who was of course unarmed, raced forward to tackle the robbers as they were leaving the building carrying a large amount of stolen cash. His companion meanwhile was busy on his radio, alerting other officers in cars who might be in the Ilford area.

As Groves ran forward he was shot in the leg and fell sideways onto the pavement. One of the gunmen went up to him, stood over him, and threatened to shoot him again. Then the gunman and his companions ran to their getaway van, and although the two policemen pursued them, Groves hobbling painfully on his injured leg, the criminals escaped.

A series of car chases developed as police vehicles converged on the area. At one stage the robbers were cornered by several policemen but, being unarmed, they were obliged to back off at gunpoint, allowing the robbers to flee again. The robbers then changed vehicles several times, hijacking them from members of the public, and finally disappeared.

This was an investigation I took charge of myself. Tip-offs and general background knowledge led us to interview several possible suspects, and some of my men spent some time with George Davis. He presented an alibi for the time of the robbery, however, and was released. But a few days later, after a request from the Flying Squad who were already investigating a case they believed to be related, I passed the enquiry on to them and they later arrested Davis and several other men, charging them with the Ilford robbery.

The case attracted enormous publicity. Allegations were made that George Davis had been falsely accused, and a campaign was mounted to secure his release. The age of trial by TV had arrived, with heated discussions on all three channels. Also, slogans were painted in large letters on just about every available wall-space in East London: *George Davis is innocent OK* appeared overnight on railway bridges, hoardings, telephone boxes, even the sides of buses. Demonstrations and marches in support of Davis were mounted and finally – in a bizarre gesture – the test-match cricket pitch at Headingley was dug up as some sort of protest against his continued arrest.

Ultimately the campaign was successful. But before that, as I've already said, in January 1973 a new department had been set up at Scotland Yard. The main purpose of A10 branch was to investigate serious allegations levelled against police officers, and I was now transferred from J Division to join the three other senior officers heading the new branch. In the wake of the *Times* Enquiry the police force and the Home Office were clearly taking the matter very seriously, for each of us had under us thirty or so superintendents, chief inspectors, and sergeants, and our brief embraced the widest possible terms of reference. Besides which, our work was obviously considered important, for the authorities let it tie up around a hundred and twenty experienced men who otherwise might have been fighting London's ever-growing crime wave.

I value this nation's civil liberties. It's been my duty all my working life to defend them. But I wonder if the more vehement civil libertarians always realise exactly what their agitations accomplish. Given strictly limited manpower – and I emphasise that proviso – I wonder if we can really afford so much self-searching.

When the allegations made by George Davis came to be investigated officers from another police force carried out the enquiry. Unfortunately, when the *Guardian* newspaper discovered this it published on its front page a story to the effect that this was because I, against whom George Davis's complaints were levelled, as a result of the Ilford enquiry, was now serving in A10 branch and therefore that branch couldn't undertake the enquiry concerning those allegations.

In fact I had no personal knowledge of Davis. I had never met him and I had taken no part in his prosecution. The attack on me was unfounded, false and damaging, and I was obliged to serve a writ upon the *Guardian*. Eventually that newspaper published an apology in which they accepted the total inaccuracy of their article. But that sort of damage, the impression created and confirmed in the public's mind, by inference, that policemen are corrupt and scheming, once done, isn't easily undone. How much better if the article had never been written.

I was to serve two years with A10 branch. During that time I investigated many allegations of criminal activities made against police officers, and most of them turned out not only to be false but in many cases also maliciously made. Most – but regrettably not all. One investigation involved the arrest of three police officers and one other person for alleged corruption offences which involved dangerous drugs. The case didn't look good for the police force – especially when the fourth person jumped bail and left the country, thus failing to appear for his trial at the Old Bailey. And although the three police officers were in fact all acquitted, every one of them immediately resigned from the force.

At about this time I met up again with an old friend and colleague, Detective Sergeant Ted Ward, who'd been in charge of the Crime Squad on J Division and was now also in A10 branch. We worked well together and, when towards the end of 1976 I was transferred back to take charge of the Organised Crime Squad again, I was allowed to take Ted with me. Almost immediately a case arrived on my desk that was to take us out and about across the world, to places as far apart as Rome and Miami.

At the centre of the investigation stood one Pierre Luigi Torrie, an apparently wealthy Italian resident in London, a man whose lifestyle and contacts with the Italian film industry had made him something of a celebrity in his own country. But we became interested in him for other reasons.

In London I placed Torrie under surveillance, and my officers established that he frequently visited offices in central London on the door of which was a nameplate for the 'International Commerce Bank'. Little was known of this bank, save that it had declared assets of less than one hundred pounds. Further enquiries revealed that a certain Italian businessman, apparently in good faith, had made arrangements with that bank for it to issue him with promissory notes to a total of a million and a half dollars, so that he could gain a controlling fifty-one per cent interest in a company in Italy. This Italian company was known to owe money, but by showing proof of collateral it could take up substantial development – hence its need, and the businessman's need, for the promissory notes.

The 'International Commerce Bank' duly issued the promissory notes but, unsurprisingly, when the businessman tried to discount them on the Continent they weren't accepted. He then returned to London, presumably to find out what the hell was going on.

Meanwhile, back in London, the premises of the 'International Commerce Bank' had been vacated and its nameplate removed. But my men had maintained the surveillance. They had seen the plate removed and on the day before the businessman's return they saw the nameplate being screwed back on again and the offices reoccupied. The businessman now met Torrie, who told him there'd been some mistake, and another London financial institution, 'Bear Securities', would guarantee the promissory notes instead.

Discreetly kept informed of all developments, we were able to establish that although 'Bear Securities' was ostensibly owned by a Swiss company, that company was in fact controlled by Torrie. On the face of things, however, 'Bear Securities' seemed reasonably sound. It claimed assets of more than a million pounds, most of these made up of some two hundred thousand shares in a Panama-registered company which was involved in gold mining in British Columbia, and these shares were valued in its books at eleven dollars fifty each. If this valuation was correct, then 'Bear Securities' could indeed guarantee the promissory notes the businessman wanted.

But it soon turned out that the activities of the Panama company were, to say the very least, dubious. And on 6 May 1977, Torrie and several others were arrested by officers of the Organised Crime Squad and charges of fraud were brought against them. Although the case went well at first, it was eventually to become an example of a bureaucratic muck-up hard to equal.

Several days after Torrie's arrest four other men were arrested. They'd just arrived in this country and had gone straight to the London offices of 'Bear Securities' hoping to see Torrie – who of course was already in custody. They had with them papers identifying them as principals in the Panama company, together with glossy brochures describing its gold-mining activities in Canada, the availability of its shares, and its glowing future prospects. The company was represented in the USA and in the Cayman Islands, and its shares were being offered for sale 'over the counter' at current market prices upon what is known as the 'off-shore' market.

We soon learned that the four men were in fact in London in order to establish yet another bank in the premises being used by the 'International Commerce Bank'. This new bank was to be called the 'Anglo-American Trade Bank', and its purpose was to distribute information about the Panama company and to promote the sale of its shares. Now, we already had a keen interest in the value of those shares, on account of our investigation into 'Bear Securities', so there were a lot of tough questions that needed answering.

Ted Ward and others in our team took their investigations across to Europe, in particular to Italy and Switzerland, and then back westwards to Canada and the USA. A detective sergeant and I meanwhile carried out a three-week tour of Miami, Nassau, Panama City where the gold-mining company was registered, the Cayman Islands where its agent quoted its shares via a telex machine in the USA, on to other offices in the Virgin Islands, and finally to St Vincent. The representative in the Cayman Islands, a British expatriate accountant, was especially helpful. He gave me a long written statement in which he explained that he personally had no first-hand knowledge of the Panama company; when he quoted the price of their shares it was entirely on the basis of information he received from others, among whom were some of the men already arrested in London. In other words, the entire share operation was very possibly a fraud.

By the time I got back to Britain, however, all of these men had appeared before London magistrates and several of them had been granted bail. The Italians among these, one of them a lawyer, all disappeared, failed to answer their bail in London, and were last heard of in Italy. Others, including Torrie, remained in custody however.

Details of the police enquiry were sent to the Director of Public Prosecutions who then took over the prosecution case and decided to seek the arrest and extradition of the accountant in the Cayman Islands. These islands are well known as a tax haven, and their economy subsists mainly upon the activities of off-shore banking institutions, shipping registrations, insurance agencies and other similar off-shore businesses. Thus their government is very protective towards its businessmen and an extremely careful case had to be prepared and presented to the chief magistrate in London before Bow Street magistrates' court was willing to issue a warrant in support of the extradition application. This warrant was then authenticated with the seal of the court and the Chief Magistrate's signature.

On 22 September 1976, with this warrant in my pocket, I set off from Heathrow for the Cayman Islands, travelling via Miami. But when I touched down for my stopover there, bad news was waiting for me. An old FBI colleague met me in airport reception. 'Frank, you got to call your London office pronto,' he said. 'All your prisoners there have escaped.'

I telephoned Scotland Yard immediately. Four of my prisoners had indeed escaped. For many weeks they had been appearing regularly on remand at Thames Court in Arbour Square, East London, where they'd been held each week in a communal cell in the court which adjoined the police station. The cell had a skylight secured with iron bars and clearly, during the night before this most recent hearing, some accomplice had climbed on to the roof and had cut through one end of two of the bars, so that they could easily be bent back. During the hearing, therefore, when the prisoners were placed in the cell for the lunch recess, they'd been able to get up out on to the roof and make their escape. Luckily officers in the police station next door had spotted the four men running across the roof and had raised the alarm. One prisoner, slower than the rest, was caught but the other three, including Torrie, got away to a waiting car and were driven off.

I was furious. The escape had been easy to plan and execute, and it made the Metropolitan Police look very foolish. And there I was, three thousand miles away, shouting instructions down the telephone but basically powerless. I had ideas as to where the missing prisoners might have gone, of course, but I wasn't particularly hopeful. And the loss of three prime suspects also made my present mission to the Cayman Islands somewhat hollow.

On the following day I arrived on Grand Cayman and presented the Bow Street warrant at the extradition hearing before a coloured magistrate by the name of Mr Hercules. Hercules accepted the warrant, held a full hearing and ordered the accountant's extradition back to Britain. The man now had a fourteen-day period in which to appeal to the Grand Court in Cayman against the extradition order, so I was obliged to wait the necessary fortnight.

While I was waiting some good news came through from London. Ted Ward called to tell me that he had found two of the escaped prisoners hiding above a false ceiling at an address in North London, and that they had been taken back into custody. Ted had also tracked down and arrested several of the men who'd conspired to effect their escape. Only Torrie was still missing, and it was now established that he had flown out to America. Ironically, on the day of his escape he must have passed through Heathrow while I myself was actually sitting in a plane there, waiting for take-off to Miami.

But the bad news was that my accountant in the Cayman Islands now lodged an appeal against his extradition order, which would take some months to be heard, so I had to return to London without him.

In December of that year the appeal finally came to the Grand Court in Cayman. I attended once more, together with a representative of the Director of Public Prosecutions, and after a hearing that dragged on over the Christmas holidays, extradition was again ordered. And again the accountant appealed, this time to the High Court in Kingston, Jamaica.

This second appeal hung around until June 1978. Then, before a tribunal of three judges, with myself again in attendance, counsel appearing on behalf of the British Director of Public Prosecutions presented a large bundle of documents as the evidence which the Chief Magistrate at Bow Street court had authenticated as being the evidence upon which the British accountant's extradition was being sought. And among these documents was a typed copy of the accountant's initial written statement to me.

His counsel picked on this, claiming that the law required a photostat of the statement rather than a typed copy. Now it so happened that I personally had with me the actual statement originally made and signed by the suspect, so our counsel asked the judges to allow me to present it to the court. After some discussion, however, that proposal was for some reason refused.

Furthermore, by a majority of two to one the judges then went on to reverse the previous extradition orders made on the Cayman Islands, and our application for extradition was refused – the grounds being that the evidence in support of this application had not been presented in the proper form.

So finally, after three trips to the Caribbean and a time-lapse of nearly a year, I returned to London without my suspect and prisoner.

The unfortunate effect of that ruling was that much of the evidence which police had wished to introduce at the Old Bailey upon charges of conspiracy concerning the shares of the Panama company could not now be introduced. Even so, other convictions were obtained against the men still in custody – and Torrie himself, traced to America and successfully extradited, was tried for fraud, found guilty, and sentenced to seven years' imprisonment.

It's not only the intricacies of other country's laws that sometimes seem to defy all reason. We in Britain notoriously have more than our share of oddities and anomalies – hence the exhaustive training needed by all those professionals employed by both ordinary citizens and the law enforcement agencies to tread a safe path among them. But every now and then an amateur comes along, with a little learning and a lot of brass neck, who tries to use both to his own criminal ends. Perhaps he's found a little-known quirk he thinks he can capitalise upon. Or perhaps he's just found a perfectly reasonable rule of law that he can take advantage of.

In 1978, shortly after my return from Jamaica, a certain professional criminal, who had been responsible for an audacious theft in London that had netted him some two million pounds-worth of jewellery, was arrested by police on the Continent where he had bolted, and was eventually returned to Britain to stand trial for the crime. He appeared in court here and was remanded in custody to Brixton Prison pending a further hearing at which he would be committed for trial.

A few weeks later, at a further appearance in court, he alleged that police and prison officers dealing with his case were improperly impeding his defence to the charges brought against him by intercepting his correspondence with his solicitor. He claimed that this was being done in collusion with an assistant prison governor at Brixton Prison, and he supported this accusation with a memorandum typed on internal prison memorandum paper, addressed to the security staff at the prison and purporting to come from the assistant governor. The memorandum instructed the security staff to examine and bring to the notice of the police any communication between the prisoner and his solicitor concerning the charges brought against him.

On the basis of this memorandum, which appeared to be genuine, the High Court in London was asked to issue an injunction against the prison governor for his actions in ordering the examination of the prisoner's mail, and to place the governor in contempt of court. This was a serious charge and, if successful, could very well jeopardise the prosecution's entire case.

The matter was passed to the Director of Public Prosecutions, who in turn asked Scotland Yard to carry out enquiries. I was given the task, and my first move was clear enough: to establish the authenticity or otherwise of the memorandum. Although it was typed on genuine prison service stationery the assistant governor flatly denied ever having seen it before, so I asked our forensic experts to examine the typing upon it and find the prison typewriter that it matched. They were unable to do so: the memorandum had not been typed upon any typewriter in official use at Brixton Prison.

The assistant governor was therefore telling the truth so from that point on it was fairly easy to reconstruct the prisoner's actions. In fact he'd been clever, but not quite clever enough. Somehow – we never found out how – he obtained blank sheets of internal prison memorandum paper. Then, taking advantage of his status as a remand prisoner, which allowed him more facilities than he would have as a prisoner serving a sentence, he had organised one of his visitors, a relative, into hiring a typewriter and bringing it into the prison for his use. This was in fact a perfectly legitimate request, allowed to all remand prisoners, and at the time had attracted little attention.

The memorandum was typed, the typewriter was removed at the relative's next visit, and then the memorandum was passed to the prisoner's unsuspecting solicitor for production in court. We interviewed the relative and traced the typewriter hire company in East London, and the very machine upon which the memorandum had been typed.

It was the machine the prisoner had received from his relative, forensic evidence proved that the prison memorandum had been typed upon it, and the whole ingenious attempted fraud was exposed. Subsequently that prisoner was not only convicted and sentenced for the original two million pound theft but he also received a further sentence for his attempt to deceive the court. Certain kinds of people may think it easy to make a fool of the law (which after all, as Dickens said, is 'an ass'), but my experience is that it seldom pays.

By now, late in 1978, I'd been transferred from the Organised Crime Squad back to the Murder Squad. And it was in that connection that I now came to undertake a very unusual investigation on behalf of the United States government which is still, even today, somewhat confidential in its details.

This was a time when the assassinations of John F. Kennedy back in 1963, and of his brother Robert Kennedy and Dr Martin Luther King in April and June of 1968, were the subject of renewed enquiry within the US. The media were very active, and widespread concern was being voiced in North America that at least two of those assassinations, those of President Kennedy and of Martin Luther King, had been linked by some sort of conspiracy.

Speculation grew to such a point that a United States House of Representatives Select Committee was appointed and commissioned to reinvestigate the two cases. Members of that committee then came to Britain, where the killer of Dr King, one James Earl Ray, had fled via Portugal immediately after the shooting, using a false Canadian passport, and I was appointed to be their liaison investigator in this country.

On reaching Britain in April 1968, James Earl Ray had attempted to carry out an armed robbery at a bank in Central London, and he'd been arrested and held in custody. This was in fact two months after the killing of Dr King, and coincidentally took place on 6 June, the very day that the assassination of Robert Kennedy was announced in the USA.

James Earl Ray was later deported back to the USA, where he stood trial for the killing of Dr King and was convicted upon what appeared to be overwhelming evidence.

Now, ten years later in 1978, it was my job, as a result of the conspiracy theory now under investigation, to help establish whether James Earl Ray had indeed acted alone in his killing of Dr King, or whether he had been involved with others who in some way had been linked to President Kennedy's death some five years before.

I did what I could to trace Ray's exact movements and his associations while he was in London in 1968. Certainly, as is widely known, he had carried out the robbery alone, and for the rest I can only say that our contribution helped the House of Representatives Select Committee on Assassinations eventually to accept from the evidence before them that James Earl Ray had indeed acted alone in his killing of Dr Martin Luther King.

As to the assassination of President Kennedy, however, in spite of the impressive investigation carried out at the time by the Warren Commission, the new enquiries mounted in the USA produced fresh expert evidence, in particular acoustic recordings of the fatal shots, that cast doubts on the number of gunmen actually involved in his death, and in some quarters those doubts still linger.

In June 1979 I was sent out from the Yard to Rotherhithe, near Tower Bridge in South-east London, to begin an investigation that I was not destined to finish. It was a gangland shooting in which two men, one armed with a shotgun and the other with a handgun, had burst into the saloon bar of a crowded public house late one evening and shot at a man and a woman standing by the bar. The man had been hit and had fallen to the floor. Then the man with the shotgun had put the twin barrels of his weapon into the injured man's mouth as he lay on the floor, as if to shoot him again.

The injured man had reacted convulsively, pushing the gun away, and in the struggle that followed his assailant had somehow shot himself in the arm with his own weapon's second barrel. With that the second gunman had opened fire, wounding the injured man's woman companion. Then the two men had run off, one of them badly wounded, and had escaped in a car.

The car, which was found later that night abandoned nearby, turned out, as is usually the case in these affairs, to be a stolen vehicle. But then, later still, a man already known to the police as a member of a notorious group in that part of London presented himself reluctantly at the emergency department of a local hospital, clearly given no alternative by the serious nature of the shotgun wound in his right arm.

He was arrested and charged, and in due course so were several others. But at that stage in the investigation I was suddenly recalled to Scotland Yard and sent up to Hertfordshire, and the Rotherhithe case was left in the very able hands of the local detective chief inspector.

6

1979: CHILDS AND MACKENNY

I came now to the case that was probably the most shocking that I worked on in my whole police career. If I go into it at some length and in some detail that's because I feel it shows particularly clearly that confession evidence, no matter how convincing, is only as valuable as the corroborating police investigations that follow. A confession is a starting point, very seldom an end in itself.

Although my personal involvement in the case did not start until I was called in to investigate following upon an entirely unconnected armed robbery in June 1979, the web of crimes that my colleagues and I were able to uncover predated that by a good five years. They began, in fact, back in 1974, when a man called Terence Eve disappeared without trace.

Living in Dagenham, Essex, Eve had gone into business partnership with a man of the same Christian name, one Terence Pinfold. They had started a small business manufacturing soft toys, in particular teddy bears, in a nearby church hall in Dagenham which was known as 'the factory', and which they shared with another firm of Pinfold's making specialist diving equipment. The soft-toy business had done surprisingly well – so much so that Eve became known locally as 'Teddy Bear' Eve. Then, quite without warning, one November night in 1974, after making a delivery of toys to a restaurant in Essex, he had apparently returned the firm's van to the church-hall car park, left its key in the factory and walked off, never to be seen or heard of again.

Police 'missing person' enquiries had turned up nothing. Eve's partner Pinfold told the police he could not assist them further and the police had eventually abandoned their investigations, leaving the file open.

Two months later, in January 1975, some miles away in Upminster, Essex, two more disappearances occurred, those of a transport contractor George Brett and his ten-year-old son Terry. Here the London Metropolitan Police had rather more to go on. Brett's wife Mavis told them that on the morning of his disappearance her husband had been visited by a businessman named Jennings. Jennings, a keen jogger with a neat black beard, had been at the Bretts' house in his track suit two days earlier, seeking to discuss a transport deal with George, and on the Saturday he had arrived in his Jaguar car, this time in a smart business suit, to take George to inspect the goods under discussion. They talked for a few minutes, and Mrs Brett offered Jennings a cup of tea, which he declined. The two men then went out to Jennings's Jaguar but it refused to start. George diagnosed a faulty starter solenoid, and fetched his own Mercedes to give the Jaguar a tow start. His young son Terry excitedly brought a clothes line from the house to be used as a tow rope and helped the two men to attach it, then asked if he could go along for the ride. His father agreed, the Jaguar started easily, and Jennings drove off, father and son following him in the Mercedes.

Neither George Brett nor his son were seen or heard of again.

George's Mercedes was discovered by police two days later near King's Cross Station in London, locked and undamaged save for the theft of some cassette tapes from the glove compartment, including at least one recorded by the French singer Charles Aznavour. However, in spite of Mrs Brett's excellent account and very extensive police enquiries which followed, over a period of years, no trace either of George or of Terry was ever found. The man Jennings, too, had completely disappeared. Furthermore, no clear motive was ever suggested as to why George Brett should have chosen to leave home willingly. Understandably Mrs Brett clung to the belief that they would one day return to her.

About three years earlier, in 1972, a convict by the name of Robert Brown, at one time an all-in wrestler known as 'The White Angel', had escaped from Chelmsford Prison and managed to avoid recapture. In 1975 he also simply disappeared in London, but few noticed this and the matter was not reported to police.

The disappearances continued. Two years later, in August 1978, a nursing-home proprietor in Herne Bay, Frederick Sherwood, was seen leaving his nursing-home premises in the Rover saloon he had been intending to sell at that time. With him in the car was a male passenger, presumably a potential customer, about forty years old, with a thin pointed face, long, dark greasy hair and a goatee beard, looking, as one witness put it, 'just like an undertaker'.

This last comment may well have been the result of hindsight, for by the time the witness offered it to the police in Kent, Mr Sherwood was known to be missing. His car, like George Brett's Mercedes, was discovered near to a London railway station, in this case Waterloo, but of Frederick Sherwood himself – again in spite of the most exhaustive police enquiries – no trace was ever found.

And finally, in October of the same year, 1978, and only two months after Sherwood's disappearance, a self-employed roofing contractor, Ronald Andrews, left his wife and two children in their house in Barkingside, Essex, at seven o'clock one evening, saying he had to go out for about an hour on 'a bit of business'. He too was never seen again. But his big American Lincoln Continental sedan was found on the following day submerged in the River Nene in Lincolnshire. A possible romantic liaison in that part of the country was suggested by a postcard then produced by Mrs Andrews which had been received by her husband some weeks earlier bearing a fond message from a woman signing the card 'Ann' and postmarked Wisbech, Cambridgeshire, a town only a few miles away from where the car had been found, but the local police discounted it. The car's windows were open, a half empty bottle of vodka lay on the back seat, and it seemed to police that its driver – presumably Andrews – had lost control in the dark, had left the road and then plunged into the river, the driver's body being swept out to sea on the deep tidal currents that were notoriously strong in that part of the river.

Six disappearances then, in different areas of the country, under separate police jurisdictions and with nothing apparently linking them save in two cases – one in Upminster in 1975 and one many miles away in Herne Bay, Kent in 1978—a mysterious man, possibly with a black goatee beard, and two cars which subsequently reappeared close to London main line railway termini. The police however had perceived no connection between any of those six cases and there was no reason why they should have done so. No single police officer had worked on all of them and it is a fact that hundreds of men and women disappear in Britain every year, often for reasons of their own and in the most inexplicable circumstances: on the face of things, these cases were not all that different.

But then, in June 1979, a robber over in Hertfordshire made a stupid mistake, got caught, and talked to police about more than just the one robbery. And six previously unconnected disappearances were to become six closely linked cases of alleged murder.

On 20 June 1979, a daring armed robbery was committed in the outskirts of the pleasant county town of Hertford. The summer weather that morning was glorious, and a gang of five enterprising men took advantage of it to commit an armed robbery and steal more than half a million pounds, all in banknotes, from a hijacked Security Express armoured van. They had reliable inside information and their planning was excellent – but their execution was rather less so. They got away with the money but one of them left behind a clue so obvious that within days four of their group were under lock and key. Their plan required that they impersonate Security Express employees. They wore uniform overalls and later removed these and left them in a public toilet in Hertford. The overalls themselves would have been hard to trace, but in the pocket of one of them police found a set of car keys. The keys belonged to an expensive BMW saloon, and the car's owner was quickly traced.

Faced with such unequivocal proof of his connection with the robbery, the BMW's owner decided that his wisest course was to help the police all he could. He not only admitted his own complicity but also gave the names of four other men involved in the crime. Three of these were quickly arrested and the four were remanded in custody. The fifth man he named, Henry MacKenny, described as a London businessman, had gone into hiding.

The deputy head of Hertfordshire CID, Detective Superintendent Dickens, had decided in dealing with the robbery to ask for the help of Scotland Yard Flying Squad. Detective Chief Inspector Lundy of the Flying Squad had gone up to Hertford to work with him, and the two police officers had interviewed the robbers. They were quite unprepared for what was to be uncovered.

One of the robbers, who was also a shrewd businessman, married, with a big house, an expensive car and a sea-going yacht, now talked to them and he spoke of suspected murder.

In brief, his outpourings added up to hints that murder had been committed by one of his fellow robbers, the man still at liberty. He claimed that that man may have been responsible for up to four deaths over the last few years, and the names of the possible victims which he gave to Lundy and Dickens were Ronald Andrews, Terence Eve, George Brett and Brett's young son Terry. At this stage, only two of those names meant anything to either of the policemen. The 1975 Brett enquiry had received enormous national publicity and they remembered it. The two detectives were told that MacKenny, the other robber they were now seeking, had been friendly with Mrs Andrews and her husband before the husband had disappeared, his empty car being found in a river. Talking next of Terence Eve, they were told that Eve had been in partnership with the now missing robber and another man named Pinfold in running some kind of business from a former church hall in Essex, on the outskirts of London, known as 'the factory', and that Eve too had disappeared.

Then the officers were told that the wanted robber had also spoken of other disappearances, those of George Brett and his young son, and another involving a man in Kent, details of whom had been given in a newspaper cutting which the informant had been shown. The two officers were also told of a large industrial mincing machine which was kept at 'the factory'.

By now Lundy and Dickens felt that this account by the robber should be brought to the notice of others.

On the following day, 29 June 1979, a Friday, Lundy personally reported all that he'd so far learned to the head of Scotland Yard's Murder Squad, Commander Howard. He immediately consulted his own chief, Assistant Commissioner Gilbert Kelland, and it was decided that the Yard should now investigate. And this was the point at which I myself became involved.

I had been working at that time, as I have said, on another case down in the Tower Bridge area of London. Now I was called off that case and put in charge of the investigation up in Hertford, and I took with me from the Murder Squad an old friend and colleague, Detective Inspector Foxall. Geoff Foxall was an immensely thorough, unflappable fellow, but outgoing too, and inclining to a cheerful stoutness. We had worked together before, and successfully.

Our first job, after a thorough briefing from Chief Inspector Lundy, was to find out everything we could about the people who had been named as possible victims. Obviously, if they now turned out to be alive and kicking, then someone – for reasons best known to himself – was wasting our time.

We quickly discovered that the missing Hertford robbery suspect, a man named Henry MacKenny, was known to police, and that the man Pinfold – currently serving a ten-year prison sentence for an armed robbery in 1976 – had indeed been MacKenny's business partner for some years, running a small factory producing specialist diving equipment in a hall belonging to St Thomas's church in Haydon Road, Dagenham, Essex. In fact a small bungalow next to the hall was, or had been, MacKenny's home address, but it had already been visited without result in the course of the current robbery hunt for MacKenny.

So far so good – the information was checking out. Furthermore,

1974's records at Chadwell Heath police station showed that a certain Terence Eve had disappeared that year. At that time, as well as the diving equipment factory, the church hall had also accommodated a small firm manufacturing soft toys run by Eve, and on 1 November of that year he had apparently delivered a consignment of soft toys to a Mr Bob Patience at the Barn Restaurant in Braintree, Essex, and hadn't been heard of since.

The information was still holding up. The listing of George Brett and his son was accurate also – both had disappeared without trace in January 1975. Ronald Andrews, too, was on record at Barkingside police station as having disappeared in October 1978 and Andrews's car, a big Lincoln Continental, had been found submerged in the River Nene, near to Wisbech.

That left only the unnamed man from Kent, and he too was then identified. Paying a personal visit to the Criminal Records Office at the Yard, Inspector Foxall took less than an hour to single out a Rover saloon car which had been found abandoned near Waterloo station in August 1978 which had belonged to a nursing-home owner, Frederick Amos Sherwood, who had disappeared only a few days earlier from a nursing home which he owned in Herne Bay on the Kent coast.

So the list, it appeared, was one hundred per cent spot-on.

A further examination of the records in the Brett and the Sherwood cases now also suggested that there was a quite remarkable similarity between Mrs Brett's description of the bearded businessman Mr Jennings, and the Herne Bay witnesses' descriptions of the passenger in the car with Sherwood when he had last been seen. I could no longer doubt that all these disappearances might well be connected, and that the missing people might now all be dead. Five possible murders to investigate, with the additional grisly ingredient of an industrial mincing machine, was not a happy prospect. Even after so many years in the force it never failed to depress me to know that there are people who are capable of such crimes.

I could also not fail to notice that between the dates of the Brett and Sherwood disappearances there was a three and a half year gap, and I wondered what else might be involved.

Foxall and I drove up to Hertford early the next morning to interview the informant who was still in custody there, having been placed on remand for the robbery following an appearance in the local magistrates' court. He was an alert and watchful man and obviously frightened, and by now he'd had time to think. He knew what might happen if what he had told police were known by others so he was clearly anxious to play things very cool, distancing himself as much as possible from our enquiry.

At first, I asked no questions, but simply listened to him as he recounted to us what he had told Lundy and Dickens earlier. This proved a useful tactic, for we soon caught him out about the newspaper cutting he had previously claimed he had seen, as he was now unable to explain to us how he'd come to know about the man in Kent.

This inconsistency was enough. His coolness had been paper thin, and now it broke. There are times when a person needs to talk and this was one of them. We spent the next two days with him.

He warned us that MacKenny was in possession of a firearm. He knew MacKenny well – they'd mixed together for years. MacKenny was a clever engineer; he was an aqualung diver and he had invented a new type of valve for a diving jacket; it was this that he'd been manufacturing in partnership with his friend Pinfold in Dagenham. There'd been a third man in their group, another of the robbers now in custody at Hertford, John Childs, who had a wife and two young children and lived somewhere down in East London.

The informant then moved on to explain about Gwen and Ronald Andrews. MacKenny had introduced him to Mrs Andrews and on one occasion all three had flown together to France in a light aircraft with MacKenny as their pilot.

When Gwen's husband disappeared the informant had read in a newspaper that Ronald Andrews's car had been found in a river. He was never told exactly what had happened, but MacKenny did tell him on a later occasion that the police were looking for someone who had left size eight footprints in mud beside the river.

Throughout this account the informant had repeatedly told us that it was Childs who had been MacKenny's really close friend – far closer than himself – and he was sure the two men would have acted together.

On the subject of the other disappearances, however, the informant was cagey and perhaps unwilling to commit himself. I asked him outright about the Brett case, the man and his ten-year-old son, but he would only say that he remembered being with MacKenny when they saw a newspaper story about police searching a farm for the two bodies.

Questioned about the missing Terence Eve, he was even less helpful. Eve had been making teddy bears at the church hall in Dagenham, he said, and then he'd gone away. Eve had been taught to make soft toys while in prison at Eastchurch, Kent. He did add, however, that he remembered another man who'd been working in the factory at about the same time, and that man had also left the firm very suddenly. He couldn't remember the man's name, though.

Clearly this was all we were going to get.

Nevertheless, I asked the informant to make a written statement containing all he'd told us so far. He was predictably reluctant, but after he'd seen a solicitor he agreed, and a statement was taken from him under caution and signed. It was a useful starting point, but in no way proof. It would need to be investigated every step of the way.

I made our headquarters in Loughton in the Metropolitan Police Area, just a few miles down the road from Hertford, and I intended to drive over there to interview Childs, the man described as MacKenny's closest friend, the next day.

Detective Chief Inspector Heyhurst of Lincolnshire Police visited me the next morning at Loughton and brought with him the case papers of the Ronald Andrews disappearance, which he himself had investigated the year before, in October 1978. MacKenny had been introduced to police at that time as 'a friend of the family', and was remembered as a formidable specimen, some six feet six tall and built to match. MacKenny had made a statement describing how he had travelled up to Wisbech with Mrs Andrews to visit the scene of the accident after her husband's disappearance, to arrange for the collection of the salvaged car. He had even mentioned hearing that the Lincolnshire police had discovered size eight footprints on the river bank not far from where the car had entered the water.

And Garth Heyhurst had brought us the postcard which had been sent to Ronald Andrews from Wisbech, in September 1978, some five weeks before he disappeared. Posted on 5 September 1978, the message on it read: *Dear Ron, When will I see you again? Missing you so much. Remember! Remember! Love, Ann. XXXXXX*, and it had been shown by Mrs Andrews to police in October 1978. It suggested, of course, that her husband might have left her for another woman – even though when he had received it he had denied all knowledge of any woman named 'Ann'. And certainly, unless the intention had been to make trouble, the sending of that postcard to Ronald Andrews, so that his wife could also read it, would have been an odd way of carrying on a clandestine affair.

Nevertheless, I now had a hunch that the postcard might turn out to be very significant, but what I needed more immediately was to talk to Childs. I was not optimistic for I now knew he had a long criminal record, had spent many years in prison, and I couldn't see him talking to me at all.

There was nothing else to go on, however, so that afternoon, with Foxall, I drove over to Hertford to interview Childs. When we arrived there I first asked the police there to let me see his personal effects and any other property which had been brought in with him when he was arrested. These included his van and its contents, the van being that which had been used as one of the get-away vehicles after the robbery.

There'd been all sorts of bits and pieces in the van, all of which had been carefully collected together and itemised by the police. I opened a large envelope containing all the pieces of paper which the officers had found in the van and tipped it out on to a desk. Sorting through it I spotted a screwed-up sheet of flimsy paper which I carefully smoothed out. It was a hand-written shopping list and at first sight of no consequence. But the very first item written on it was *Germolene*, and the initial letter *G* rang a bell. When I compared it side-by-side with the Wisbech postcard which I had received from Heyhurst that morning and now had with me in my briefcase, I could see at once I was right. Other similarities then leapt out at me. Both were clearly written by the same hand.

Looking at the items on the list it seemed more likely to have been written by a woman rather than Childs himself. His wife? That seemed a strong possibility, so I decided to postpone my intended talk with him until I'd had a chance to talk to her first.

As it happened, Childs was due to appear in court again in Hertfordshire on the following morning. Mrs Childs, I discovered, had attended his previous remand hearing the week before, so there was a fair chance she'd do so again. I decided to wait, therefore, and have Inspector Foxall bring her over from the court at Hertford to Loughton after the hearing, and meanwhile I took a team of officers down to the church hall in Dagenham, including two specialists from the Yard's scientific laboratory.

We found nothing of obvious or immediate significance, certainly no mincing machine, but in the bungalow next door – where MacKenny had lived – we found a young man who was there acting as a caretaker. He knew nothing of MacKenny's whereabouts, except that he might be in France. He told us that the manufacturing of soft toys and diving jackets had ceased some time before, but Childs, MacKenny and Pinfold had indeed all worked there – as had Terence Eve and a man he knew only as 'Bob'. Remembering that we had already been told that a second man had also left the factory unexpectedly, I asked for a description of this 'Bob', which he gave me. We then returned to Loughton.

Mrs Childs did attend her husband's court hearing that day and afterwards Inspector Foxall brought her over to Loughton. She seemed out of her depth. She was a wisp of a thing, in her early twenties, with dark hair, and she spoke in scarcely more than a whisper. I didn't ask her about the postcard at once, but asked her to tell me about MacKenny. She said she had first met her husband when he was working with MacKenny and Pinfold at the church hall in Dagenham, which was commonly known as 'the factory'. He and MacKenny had known each other for a long time, but she thought MacKenny had a bad influence on him. She and her husband now had two young children, a boy and a girl. They were living in a council flat in Poplar, in London's East End, and since having the children she had often wished MacKenny would stop visiting them – he often arrived late in the evening and always stayed too long.

I asked her about the man Bob, and she said she did remember him working in 'the factory', but then he'd left.

It was time now to ask her for some samples of her handwriting. She seemed puzzled, but sat in front of us at the table in the office and provided them. Then I showed her the shopping list and the Wisbech postcard. She agreed eventually that she had written both. MacKenny had asked her to write the postcard and had told her what to write. I took a written statement from her.

By then I judged she'd had enough so I let her return to her flat in Poplar and sent two detectives to search the flat then watch it. I warned her to say nothing of our conversation and thought it best to explain that she might possibly be in danger: MacKenny, who was still at liberty, was, I now suspected, clearly involved in something much more sinister than armed robbery, and he might think that she knew too much.

I had meanwhile made arrangements that Childs would be remanded in custody at Oxford Prison rather than with the other robbers in a London prison and on the following day, 6 July, I drove there with Inspector Foxall. That morning I had received a set of photographs from Hertford Police of the defendants in the Security Express robbery case – up until then, of course, I had not seen Childs – and during the drive I leafed through them.

Suddenly I sat up, and told Foxall to pull over and stop the car. Then I showed him the photograph of Childs side-by-side with the photofit pictures of the mysterious 'Mr Jennings' in the Brett case and of the 'undertaker' in the Sherwood case. They were, all three, the most remarkable match we'd ever seen.

We drove on, now even more certain that Childs was the key to the whole unhappy business. When we arrived at the prison there was some delay and it was almost lunchtime at the prison when we were admitted to the visiting room where Childs was waiting.

John Childs was forty-four years old, small and slightly built, with untidy hair and a scruffy brownish beard. He wore steel-rimmed spectacles, and although he spoke in a flat, expressionless voice he was quick-thinking, sharp, and a man who knew exactly what he was doing. He immediately demanded to see our warrant cards and then wanted to know why a detective chief superintendent from Scotland Yard should come all the way to Oxford to talk to him about a robbery which Hertfordshire police were dealing with.

I was equally direct. I told him I had no interest in the robbery – my concern was with a man called MacKenny and his association with a Mr and Mrs Andrews.

Childs replied flatly that he wasn't prepared to discuss MacKenny's business.

I pretended not to have heard him. I'd talked to Mrs Childs, I said, and she'd told me she didn't like MacKenny.

Childs conceded that this was so. I again spoke of MacKenny.

Childs refused to answer. Instead, he said, 'You've wasted your time coming to Oxford to see me. There's nothing I can help you with. I don't have to talk to you anyway.'

I agreed, for what he said was true. Nevertheless, I asked him if he would listen to what I had to say and he nodded his agreement.

The large communal visiting room we were sitting in with Childs was in constant use, with people walking through it all the time, and it wasn't suitable for this type of interview. But I had no choice so I showed him the shopping list taken from his van and asked him if his wife had written it. He said he couldn't say. I told him his wife had told me she had. Then I produced the postcard and asked him if his wife had also written that. Again he said that he couldn't say. I told him his wife had done so and had also made a written statement to me to that effect. I then allowed him to examine his wife's signature on that statement and at that point the prison bell sounded for lunch and Childs was taken away.

By the afternoon I'd managed to get a much quieter room for the interview. I could only hope that Childs would reappear – he would be completely within his rights to refuse to see me. But he came, and in the interval he seemed to have done some thinking. His manner had changed, anxiety lying close beneath the surface.

10. Reginald, Charles and Ronald Kray.

11. The team of detectives that worked on the Kray case. It was led by Detective Superintendent Leonard 'Nipper' Read *(third from right, front row)*. Frank Cater stands second left of second row.

12. The house in Valance Road *(fourth from left)*, Bethnal Green, where the Krays lived. It was known as 'Fort Valance'.

13. The shopping list found in the van of John Childs.

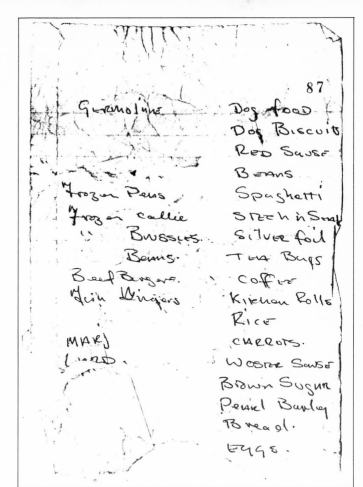

14. The card sent to Ronald Andrews.

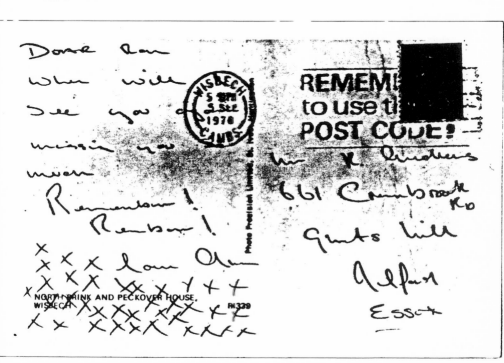

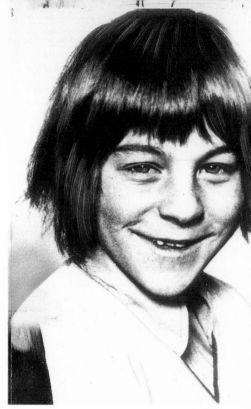

15. and 16. *(above)* George Brett and his son Terry. Both were murdered.

17. *(below left)* John Childs, the killer of six people.

18. *(below right)* Henry MacKenny.

He agreed he remembered what had been said before lunch. 'Let's talk some more,' he said.

It was to be the most incredible and chilling interview of my career.

We began slowly. I asked him again about the postcard, and this time he replied by wanting to know what his wife's situation would be if she had in fact written it. I told him that would depend upon the circumstances. Did his question imply that he knew about the postcard after all?

He fenced, claiming that it had simply been a hypothetical question, and asked me instead if his wife was being held at a police station somewhere.

I told him that so far as I knew she was at home with her children, and then tried to turn the questioning again to MacKenny. But Childs shut down at once, saying he would only discuss matters which concerned him personally. This sort of verbal sparring then went on for some time.

Finally I told him we both knew that he would have to talk sooner or later.

Childs seemed to accept this. But MacKenny was a dangerous man, he said, and if he talked then both he and his wife might be in danger. Did MacKenny know that his wife had been interviewed by the police?

I told him that wasn't possible unless Mrs Childs had revealed this herself.

He sat quietly for a moment, thinking.

Suddenly he appeared to make his mind up. 'Look,' he said, 'if I do open up you'll get more than you bargained for.'

I told him I doubted that, for I thought I already knew what he could talk about if he chose to.

His reaction to that was, 'If I do talk, it will frighten you.'

I told him to try me.

Then: 'Well, what do you want me to talk about, armed robberies?'

'No,' I said.

'Murders?' he asked.

'Yes.'

'But supposing I do tell you, where does that leave me?'

'If you have been concerned in murders yourself and took part in them, you will be charged, there is no doubt about that.'

Childs sat in silence again for a while, looking at me. Then: 'You obviously know something, but I don't know how much.'

'I may know more than you think. Why don't you just start talking.'

There was another long silence. I leaned forward. 'Well, are you going to tell me about these things or not? I get the feeling that you want to, but you can't bring yourself to start.'

'But I've blanked them out . . . it's difficult, you see, will you feel revulsion against me?'

'Mr Childs,' I said, 'I've a great deal of experience as a CID officer. I've been one for over twenty-seven years. I do my job and have to listen to a good many things. Revulsion doesn't come into it.'

Still Childs couldn't bring himself to start. He stared at me, sitting quite motionless.

Then I said, 'Why don't you just start talking?'

'That's it, it's hard.'

I realised Childs could hardly bring himself to speak. I guessed I had to do something so I said, 'Will it help if Mr Foxall leaves us for a minute or two?'

Childs turned to Foxall. 'Do you mind?'

Foxall rose and walked into a toilet cubicle at the end of the room.

The door to the toilet had a gap at the top. He would be able to hear everything that went on.

As soon as Inspector Foxall was in the toilet Childs took the initiative. 'How many are you looking at?'

It was a good question and one I would have least wished. If I said I didn't know, which was the truth, he might simply stop talking. I had information concerning the disappearances of five people over the last four years, with a possible sixth. I took a chance.

'Six,' I said.

Childs nodded. It seemed I had guessed right. But now, he fell silent again.

'Look, if it's difficult to start, you tell me the name of the first one and I'll give you the name of the next one, and so on. Will that help?'

'Well, *you* say.'

'Ronald Andrews.'

'Yes.'

'You name the next one,' I said.

He stayed silent.

'Teddy Bear Eve?' I said.

'Yes.'

'Who else?'

'. . . A fellow from out in the sticks.'

'Do you mean from Kent?'

'Yes.'

'Go on.'

'Another fellow who worked in the factory, Bobbie, and a man and a boy,' he said, almost in a whisper.

'Well, I shall call Mr Foxall back in now and I'll tell him what you've told me.'

I did so and I glanced at the clock. Afternoon prison visiting hours would soon be over, bringing this session to a close. As soon as Foxall was back I asked Childs to tell me more about the murders.

He began with Terence (Teddy Bear) Eve. In his flat voice he told us, 'I was working in the factory at the time. It was a good profitable business with the teddy bears and I was told I'd get a good weekly income for nothing. He was strangled in the alleyway at the factory, but he had a good go for it and I had to help. I hit him with a hammer.'

'What happened to the body?'

'It was burned.'

'Where?'

'At my house. They all were.'

Then I asked him about the man Bobbie.

'Bobbie was shot in the head three times.'

I asked about Andrews.

'Shot in the head at my place.'

I asked him about the man and the boy.

'That was in the factory. I decoyed them there – I used Harry's Jaguar motor car.'

'How were they killed?'

'The man was shot with a Sten gun.'

'The boy?'

Childs hesitated and was showing signs of distress. His eyes were moist as he replied, 'He was shot in the head with the Sten gun as well.'

I asked about the man from Kent.

'I decoyed him as well to the factory. He was shot in the head in the bungalow.'

'Why?' I asked.

'Harry (MacKenny) had a contract and got paid for it. There – I wasn't going to mention names, was I? Well, I've done it now.'

'And the body?'

'They were all burned in my place.'

'Where in your place?'

'In the fireplace.'

'Everything wouldn't burn, surely?'

'No. Some bits were put back on, just little bits of bone like knuckle joints.'

'What happened to the residue, there must be ashes?'

'That was thrown in a river somewhere – in Wanstead Park and other different places. I can show you where.'

Our time was running out – it was almost four o'clock. I asked Childs if all the victims had been shot with a Sten gun and he said that several different guns had been used. Some had been disposed of, but others were in store. I asked him where and he said he would think about it and tell me later.

'How did Andrews's car get into the river?'

'Harry drove it in, where it was found.'

'Did you bring him back from there?'

'In my van.'

Now we had reached the end of prison visiting hours for that day and a prison officer came to take Childs away. I told him Inspector Foxall and I would return in the morning.

It was Friday evening. Foxall and I had been working on the case for exactly a week.

The following morning, Saturday 7 July, we found Childs in a totally different mood. He'd got nothing to add to what he'd already told us.

He attempted to bargain and wanted protection for himself and his family. I told him that we'd do everything we could to protect them.

I could only repeat that if he had committed murder he must expect to be charged.

Childs said he was expecting his wife to visit him that afternoon, and he wanted to talk to her before committing himself any further. I told him I had already listened to her story of how and why she had written the postcard to Ronald Andrews and I suggested that he should give me his account of the Andrews disappearance *before* he saw his wife, so that there could be no collusion in their accounts. He accepted this reasoning and agreed to tell his part – but without naming any other person involved.

As he started to speak I gained the impression that he now genuinely wanted to tell me the story and had probably wanted to do so all along.

Months later Childs was to repeat it all again on oath from the witness box at the Old Bailey. He described how Ronald Andrews's body had been cut up with a saw and a knife and then burned in the living-room fireplace of the Poplar flat whilst Childs's wife and children were away for the weekend. The knife had been thrown away, but the saw was still in the Poplar flat and he described where it could be

found. It had been washed thoroughly. Two steel hooks had been used
to suspend the body over a bath during dismemberment. The dead
man's clothing, including the shoes, had been burned and he described
how 'the other man' had obtained the material to make a fire which
produced sufficient fierce heat. Altogether, the dissection and the
burning had taken sixteen hours.

Tracking back to Andrews's death, Childs told us how he had posed
as a private detective – Andrews wanted his wife watched, as he was
afraid she was being unfaithful – and so had been lured to Childs's flat
in Poplar. There he was shot by 'the other man'.

At that point we were interrupted. Childs's wife had arrived for a
prison visit, and he left to go to her. This gave Foxall and me time to
collect our thoughts. It was hard to talk about what we'd learned –
Childs's composure as he described these events was outside our
experience. We would need to hide our feelings when he returned.

When Childs came back he said he agreed to tell us everything. In
fact Childs's story was to take up the whole of the rest of that day and all
of the next, and those hours were among the most horrific of my entire
police career; and the most taxing, since Foxall and I had to remain
detached and professional in the face of a relentless litany of callousness seldom equalled in criminal history.

The story began in 1972, when Childs was released from Chelmsford Prison after serving a sentence for burglary. He met a man he'd
known in jail called Terence Pinfold, and Pinfold took him to the
church hall in Haydon Road, Dagenham, where he and a third man,
Henry MacKenny, ran a small business manufacturing diving life-
jackets which MacKenny had invented and patented himself.

MacKenny was a huge man, and he lived alone – in a bungalow next
door. They gave Childs employment.

Together the three men frequently discussed schemes for getting
rich. Their plans were interrupted when Childs was sent back to prison
and when he was released from jail in August 1974 he returned to find
that Pinfold and MacKenny had been joined by another man, Terence
Eve, who was now sharing the premises, making soft toys, especially
teddy bears, and doing pretty well. The diving suit business was on
hard times, however, so it was suggested that they get rid of 'Teddy
Bear' Eve and take over his business.

The first idea was to make it appear that Eve had died in a road
accident, or perhaps in a mugging, but they couldn't come up with an
agreed plan. Then they discovered that on a particular Friday evening
Eve had promised to make a delivery of soft toys to a customer over in

Braintree; he wouldn't get back until late, and they saw this as their opportunity. Pinfold owned an ex-prison van which they all used in connection with the two businesses. They offered it to Eve for the Friday evening, but insisted that it must be back at the factory that night. MacKenny was involved in the plot, and they decided he and Childs would be the killers.

Shortly before midnight on 1 November 1974, Eve returned from making his delivery to Robert Patience at the Barn Restaurant in Braintree, parked the van outside the church hall and walked in to leave the keys in the office. MacKenny and Childs were waiting for him. MacKenny hit him with the heavy metal end of a length of industrial hose but failed to knock him out. Childs then felled Eve with a hammer blow to the head, and MacKenny garrotted their victim, using a piece of rope.

Some weeks before, a butcher's industrial-grade mincing machine had been purchased and it had been installed in Childs's flat in Poplar. Childs wasn't yet married and was living there alone. Eve's body was wrapped in polythene sheeting and taken by car to the flat where the bathroom was made ready, with further polythene sheeting covering the floor.

The body was cut into small pieces and fed into the machine. But the machine refused to work, for they discovered its motor required a three-phase supply and the flat was not wired for that. Originally it had been planned that the remains of Eve's body, after mincing, would be small enough to be flushed down the toilet. Now, although Childs and MacKenny tried for a long time to cut the body into small enough pieces, using a pair of shears, the toilet consistently rejected them. Finally MacKenny decided to build a fire in the living-room grate and burn Eve's body, piece by piece, together with every single item of his clothing. It took several days to do so.

Later, after the bones not fully consumed by the fire had been crushed to powder, the resulting ashes were scattered from a moving car driven along the Barking by-pass in East London. Terence Eve had totally disappeared.

Soon afterwards the useless mincing machine was dismantled, carefully washed, and the pieces thrown into a canal.

In due course the police asked questions about Eve's disappearance, when it was reported by his wife, but they got nowhere. Between them, they had apparently committed the perfect crime.

Indeed, they'd been so successful that according to Childs it soon occurred there might well be a good living to be earned from killing by contract. That was discussed, the type of weapons to use and the problem of contacting the sort of people who might be willing to pay for that kind of service. At that time they owned several pump-action shotguns. MacKenny thought the guns were too noisy: he tried to fit a silencer to his but it wasn't satisfactory.

Then, about a month later, around Christmas 1974, their discreet enquiries bore fruit; they were approached by a man who was willing to pay £2,000 to have a man killed. He would supply a Sten gun and ammunition, for which he would charge £200. That was agreed, the contract was accepted, and the gun was handed over, plus three nine-millimetre magazines, two spare barrels and a magazine loader. The intended victim was a man named George Brett, a haulage contractor who lived in Upminster, and apparently the motive for the killing was simply revenge – the client wanted Brett dead.

The Sten gun was now fitted with a silencer, and then MacKenny and Childs drove over to Upminster for a reconnaissance. Brett lived well. He had a nice house and a Mercedes.

The plan was made. Childs, being less easily identifiable than MacKenny, would be used as the front man. Wearing a disguise he would lure Brett to the factory in Dagenham with the promise of a profitable haulage contract. MacKenny would kill him there, and then the body would be cut up and burnt as before, at the flat in Poplar. It all seemed very simple.

To disarm all initial suspicion Childs decided on an unconventional approach. Wearing a blue track suit and running shoes, he got MacKenny to drop him off a short distance from the Bretts' house, and then jogged along the road and up the drive to the front door. By way of disguise he had dyed both his beard and hair with black boot polish. When Mrs Brett answered the doorbell, he introduced himself as Mr Jennings, a company director of a small engineering business. He apologised for his clothes, explained that he went out running every day for exercise and said that he'd called in while passing because he'd heard that her husband was in the transport business and he wanted some work done.

Mrs Brett heard him out, then told Jennings her husband was not at home. It was agreed that he should telephone her husband later for an appointment.

MacKenny picked Childs up half a mile or so down the road, and they returned to Dagenham. Childs later telephoned Brett's home and made an appointment for the Saturday morning, two days later, to discuss the goods he wanted transporting. He made it sound like a large order. Then he and MacKenny arranged the factory for Brett's reception.

The floor was completely covered with soft toys, and the benches were piled high with diving jackets. Two chairs were placed in the only clear area, one on either side of a table. Only one of the chairs was left vacant, however, the other being stacked up with files and documents. The plan was to seat Brett in it while he and Childs discussed business and MacKenny would be behind him.

On Saturday 4 January, his hair and beard dyed again and this time wearing a smart business suit, a dark coat, leather gloves and a homburg hat, Childs drove to the Bretts' house in MacKenny's Jaguar, fitted with false numberplates. He and MacKenny had made sure he had nothing in his pockets which would identify him and he was to keep his gloves on all the time to avoid leaving fingerprints.

He reached the Bretts' house at eleven o'clock. Mr and Mrs Brett were at home and they chatted briefly. She offered him a cup of tea which he declined, and then he and Mr Brett went out to the waiting Jaguar. So far so good – but at that point things started to go wrong. The car refused to start, Brett diagnosed a faulty starter solenoid and offered to give the Jaguar a tow start, using his own Mercedes. Then he shouted for his small son Terry to bring something to use as a tow rope.

By now Childs must have been sweating. Luckily for him, however, the Jaguar started easily on the tow – but now Brett, his own car out on the road, insisted on using it to follow Childs to the factory. Also, at the last moment, his little boy Terry asked if he could go along 'for the ride' and his father agreed. Childs drove off, followed by Brett. The final stage of the plan was in operation. But there were complications. There was an extra car that hadn't been bargained for. And there was a little boy.

MacKenny, as previously arranged, was working at a bench in the factory. As Childs entered, the big man looked up and asked, 'Is everything all right, Mr Jennings?'

It had been arranged that if Childs answered 'Yes', then MacKenny would shoot the man.

Childs was now uncertain, however, and answered, 'Yes and no', indicating the boy who had followed his father in.

Childs then reached down and gave the boy a teddy bear to hold whilst Brett sat down in the one vacant chair. Childs temporised, pointing out to Brett the piles of goods he said he wanted transported.

MacKenny, interrupting him, asked again, 'Is everything all right, Mr Jennings?'

Childs now said, 'Well . . . yes, Harry.'

He held the boy while MacKenny raised the Sten gun and shot Brett with a single round through the back of his head, at a range of a few feet. Brett fell from his chair on to the floor and MacKenny came forward and shot him through the head again. The boy still had the teddy bear in his arms. Childs held him while MacKenny shot him, from one side; a single shot through the head.

Both father and son were dead.

Childs and MacKenny then arranged polythene sheeting and put the bodies on it, ready for removal. They cleaned up the bloodstains, but couldn't find a bullet which had ricocheted, gouging the wood floor, and disappeared.

Childs was now questioned by MacKenny about what he and Mr and Mrs Brett had talked about during their short meeting – to ensure he had said nothing which might lead police to the factory. Childs said all he'd mentioned was light engineering. Then a furious row developed over MacKenny's car having refused to start.

During that day there were visitors to the church hall. The cleaning woman called, and also the St Thomas's vicar, with another man. MacKenny went to the door, and was able to turn them all away.

By now, Brett's Mercedes had been taken from where it was parked outside the factory and dumped near to King's Cross – the conspirators had the vague hope that the police might think Brett and his son had taken a train going up to the north. A number of cassette tapes were removed from the car.

At this point I interrupted Childs. So far, much of what he'd told me could in fact have been the product of a diseased imagination. But I remembered from discussions I had had with the detective officer who had conducted the original missing person investigations undertaken by police that when her husband's car had been returned to her Mrs Brett had indeed reported the loss of several cassette tapes from it, including one made by a certain very famous French singer. This information had never been released. Only the police knew of it, so if this man in front of me got it right then I'd have firm evidence that he was speaking the truth.

'What were they?' I asked him. 'Who was on the tapes?'

'Music.'

'But whose music?'

Childs shrugged. 'I can't remember them all – but there was one or two by that singer Charles Aznavour.'

I glanced at Inspector Foxall. So now we knew.

Childs returned to his story. On the evening of the same day he'd shampooed the black boot polish from his hair and beard. The bodies, the clothing and the plastic sheeting were then loaded into his van. Later the gouge out of the floor of the factory would be filled with wax and stained over. Now, with MacKenny following in his Jaguar, a gun at his side, Childs had driven to his home in Poplar. There the routine used with Terence Eve's body was repeated, and with a large piece of old orange curtain draped round the fireplace to collect any debris which gathered around the fireplace. Then, when MacKenny left the flat briefly and returned, it was to find Childs halfway through a bottle of whisky. There was another row, after which they worked on together. The ashes were put into a bag which was later emptied into a canal.

For days the newspapers had carried big stories about the missing father and son, with pictures of both of them. The killers held a meeting to take stock of the situation. They had been paid £1,800 in cash for the murder of George Brett only. Worried, they decided the man who had paid for the killing of Brett must be told exactly what had happened. Unknown to him, Childs had accepted the job of killing him if he did anything which led to the arrest of either of them.

In fact they'd been very careful. Childs had got rid of the clothes he'd worn on the day of the murders, all the polythene sheeting had been burned, the Jaguar's false numberplates had been thrown away, and the tyres on the car had been changed in case the car had left any prints in the mud at the side of the road outside Brett's house.

This had been a wise move. I didn't tell him, but such prints had been found in 1975 and photographed, and the police had conducted an extensive search for a Jaguar with similar tyres. We now knew why that search had been in vain.

The car still worried them, however, Childs said, and soon afterwards MacKenny sold it. Now, in spite of massive publicity and police activity at that time the killers felt safe . . . until Childs began to wonder about the factory handyman, Robert Brown.

Bob, or Bobbie, Brown was the former all-in wrestler and petty criminal on the run from Chelmsford Prison who'd been given a live-in job working for Pinfold and MacKenny at the factory some months earlier. It was realised he might have his suspicions about Terence Eve's sudden disappearance and if he were to be arrested by police, as an escapee, and questioned, he was capable of making things very difficult. Accordingly, he had to be eliminated.

The first requirement was to get him to leave the factory of his own free will – a second abrupt disappearance connected with the factory would be hard for anyone to swallow. This was managed by pointing out to him that the diving life-jacket business was bad, which it was, and that he'd have to find another job and another place to live. Brown left, got a job working for a roofing contractor, and found lodgings in Ilford. The ground was then laid for him to leave both, by getting word to him that the Chelmsford Prison authorities were on his trail, and when he then phoned asking for advice he was told that a hiding place had been arranged and that he should pack his things and wait to be picked up.

In the event he was taken to Childs's flat, where arrangements had been made for his murder. The wireless was turned on loudly, and a .45 revolver was concealed in a convenient place – it had been modified to take bullets from which some of the charge had been removed in order that their velocity would be reduced and they'd stay within the body. Welcoming Brown in, Childs manoeuvred him to a chair with his back to the door. According to Childs 'another man' came in and shot him in the back of his head. This shot didn't kill him, so he was shot again, now from the front. This shot, too, failed to kill him. He was a powerfully built man, and he fought back. The walls of Childs's living room were decorated with various lethal weapons as ornaments and he and 'the other man' grabbed these to deal with Brown. He was attacked with a fireman's axe, and stabbed repeatedly in the chest with a diver's knife. Childs also used a sword-stick on him and he eventually died, pinned to the floor with the knife.

Childs then went outside the ground-floor flat to make sure the noise hadn't attracted any attention. All seemed quiet so he went back in, turned down the radio and, according to him, the two men then started to get rid of Brown's body, stripping to their underpants and covering the floor and the furniture with plastic sheeting.

At this point in his story Childs complained that he'd been left to do most of the burning himself as 'the other man' claimed he had an urgent appointment somewhere else. Brown had brought a stereo hi-fi set with him, thinking he was going into hiding, so Childs appropriated it. Brown had also brought a TV set, but Childs already had one, so 'the other man' took that.

Brown's ashes were later scattered on Wanstead Flats. The saw and the knife used to dismember him were cleaned while the other weapons, the diver's knife, the fireman's axe and the sword-stick, were all washed and hung back on the walls in the same position as before. The gun, too, was retained.

Childs was unable to put an exact date to that killing, except that it was after the murders of Terence Eve and the two Bretts, and before the date of an armed robbery in December 1976 which he had taken part in, in George Lane, South Woodford. Both MacKenny and Pinfold had been arrested for that crime: MacKenny had been later released, but Pinfold had been convicted and sentenced to ten years' imprisonment. Childs himself was never arrested.

Then Childs told Foxall and me about the fifth murder, that of Frederick Sherwood, the proprietor of the Old Vicarage nursing home in Herne Bay. He claimed it was another contract killing – he never knew the motive – and that the price was £4,000, which had been paid in instalments. That took place in 1978, by which time Childs was married.

The information was that Sherwood had a car for sale privately, a Rover, so a plan was concocted around it. Childs, disguised once more and posing as a potential purchaser, would call at the nursing home and ask for a test drive. He would agree to buy the car, and then persuade Sherwood to drive it, with him in it, to London to collect the money.

He and MacKenny would use MacKenny's bungalow this time, rather than Childs's flat. Sherwood would be set up in a chair at the dining-room table with his back to the adjoining kitchen, and Mac-Kenny would be in the kitchen, a silenced revolver in his hand. There would also be a hammer placed on the floor by the TV set, ready for Childs if he needed it.

MacKenny drove Childs down to Herne Bay on the morning of 1 August 1978. Childs's hair and beard were dyed again, and he wore a dark overcoat, in the pocket of which he carried £500 in cash, to convince Sherwood of his genuine interest in the car. Childs also wore a shoulder holster under his jacket, in which was a loaded revolver. He told us he'd been prepared to shoot Sherwood dead in the car if he'd become suspicious and refused to complete the 'test drive' to London.

Sherwood was out when Childs called at the nursing home at midday, but it was arranged for him to return to look at the car at seven. MacKenny then drove back to the Dagenham bungalow to get everything ready, while Childs spent the afternoon in the sun on the sea front.

At the appointed time he presented himself at the nursing home. All went well. Sherwood and he went for a test drive, they agreed to a price of £1,000 for the Rover, Childs explained that he only had half that on him, but suggested that if they drove to his brother's at an address in

Dagenham he'd be able to hand over the full price immediately. He also offered helpfully to drive Sherwood back to Herne Bay afterwards.

It must have seemed to Sherwood a reasonable arrangement. He drove Childs to Dagenham and went into the bungalow with him. MacKenny was introduced to him as Childs's brother, tea was offered and accepted, and he sat in the bungalow's dining room while Childs handed over a bundle of money. As he started to count it Childs asked him if he'd like a drink, and then fetched a glass of whisky from another room.

It was then that MacKenny came in from the kitchen and shot Frederick Sherwood through the back of the head with the silenced revolver. The bullet went straight through, hit the top of the dining table, ricocheted upwards and smashed the whisky glass in Childs's hand, terrifying him.

Sherwood wasn't yet dead. Incredibly he struggled to his feet, so Childs snatched up the hammer and hit him over the head. Sherwood fell to the floor and MacKenny shot him again where he lay. The two killers stood over him. A small pool of blood spread beneath his head. He was dead.

A piece of cloth was hurriedly wrapped around Sherwood's head to catch the blood. Childs was furious, accusing MacKenny of having tried to shoot him also and the two men had a row, shouting abuse at each other face-to-face across the dead man's body. Eventually they pulled themselves together. They examined their victim's head: there were two entry wounds but only one exit wound, so one bullet was still in Sherwood's skull. They did not find the other and judged it had ricocheted into an adjoining room through an open doorway.

MacKenny left Childs to clean up the blood, and went away to dump Sherwood's car – and chose the neighbourhood of a railway station again, this time Waterloo. Meanwhile Childs started to tidy the bungalow, but soon stopped. He told us he had felt groggy and needed a drink. Apparently he just sat down with what was left of the bottle of whisky.

When MacKenny returned the two of them dumped Sherwood's body into a plastic dustbin and Childs washed the boot polish out of his hair and beard. Before they left to take the body to the flat in Poplar to be cremated, Childs telephoned ahead to make sure there was no one there.

He had sent his wife away to stay with her mother for the weekend and he was afraid she might have returned for some reason. But the telephone rang without being answered so the flat was clearly empty.

The dustbin containing Sherwood's body was carried out to the van. Then Childs drove to Poplar, followed by MacKenny in his own car, the bin was taken in, and the two men started work. They lit the fire and spread plastic sheeting. They dismembered the body and fed it on to the fire, piece by piece. The body took a long time to burn, nearly twenty-four hours, and once it had been dismembered they worked in shifts, one man sleeping.

It was late on Saturday before the body was reduced to ashes. Then MacKenny went home. Childs cleaned up, and the ashes were thrown into a canal at Stratford. By the time his wife had returned from her weekend away the flat was back to normal.

At this point in his remarkable confession Childs broke off to describe exactly where on the floor of the bungalow Sherwood's body had lain, and suggested that we should examine it carefully. He even drew us a plan. He said he was sure we'd find traces of blood there: neither he nor MacKenny had cleaned up properly – the job had normally been his responsibility, but it had been left for MacKenny to deal with.

He also drew us a plan of the dining-room table to show the position of the ricochet mark and another to show the position of the gouge in the floor of the factory, caused by the bullet which had passed through George Brett's body.

He now went back to the Andrews killing. He told us MacKenny had been a friend of the Andrews family for some time. Then he'd wanted to see more of Gwen Andrews, and he'd confided in Childs, discussing how best he could get rid of her husband Ronald. Childs advised him against it, and had pointed out that if Ronald Andrews died suspiciously, MacKenny would be the obvious suspect. If that happened Eve's earlier disappearance might also be brought up again.

MacKenny accepted this and did nothing, but it left him frustrated and very much on edge. Unable to be with Gwen, he took to hanging about the Childs's flat, drinking and watching TV – much to Mrs Childs's annoyance. She didn't like MacKenny and she was afraid of his influence upon her husband.

MacKenny took advantage of this. He told Childs that if he'd help him get rid of Ronald Andrews he'd pay him £500 – and he also pointed out that, with Andrews out of the way, he wouldn't have to sit round in the Poplar flat, upsetting Mrs Childs.

Childs eventually agreed. They discussed several plans. Eventually Childs suggested a road accident, made to look like drunken driving, but it would have to be done so as to account for the fact that his body couldn't be found and without arousing suspicion.

MacKenny thought this was a good idea and he knew how and where that could be accomplished. As a lad during the war he'd been evacuated to Wisbech in Cambridgeshire, and he remembered the strong currents in the River Nene near to Wisbech, in that part of the river used by large sea-going vessels.

A few days later both men drove up to Wisbech to make a reconnaissance, and they found the ideal place where the road had a sharp bend and then ran close alongside the river for some distance. It would be perfectly possible there for a driver to lose control at speed and plunge into the river. If that happened it was also possible that the fierce tidal current would wash the body out to sea, just a few miles down river, particularly on an ebb tide.

Since Andrews never ordinarily visited Cambridgeshire, some reason would have to be invented for his car to be found in the Wisbech area. They decided to send him a postcard from Wisbech, signed by a woman and in obviously affectionate terms. A second trip was made to Wisbech to buy a card with a suitable local scene. MacKenny then approached Childs's wife, asking her to write the message on it. The excuse he gave was that the arrival of such a card would upset Gwen Andrews, and she'd turn to him for comfort, and then he wouldn't need to make a nuisance of himself any more around the Childs's flat.

This was a shrewd move. He thought the idea of seeing less of him would appeal to Mrs Childs and it did. She wrote the postcard, and it was posted up in Wisbech on 5 September 1978. She also agreed to telephone the Andrews's house when they knew Ronald would be out, ask to speak to him when Gwen answered, and then refuse to give her own name.

Childs told us both these tricks worked. For his part though, Andrews too was suspicious, thinking that Gwen was being unfaithful to him. Unaware that he was in fact conspiring in his own death, he asked MacKenny for his advice. MacKenny and Childs immediately saw a chance here of luring Andrews to the flat in Poplar. MacKenny suggested employing a private investigator: Andrews had never met Childs, so he could be taken to Childs's home and introduced to him as the man who would investigate.

Innocently Ronald agreed to have a talk with the private investigator. MacKenny then said he'd fix it. Before the murder could go ahead however there were things he and Childs had to arrange. Most importantly, Childs's wife had to be got away from the flat again for a few days. Weapons had to be got ready. They also knew that on the night of the murder they had to arrive at the river with Andrews's car at high water, just as it was about to ebb. So timing was going to be important.

Finally, on the weekend of 13–15 October 1978, everything was arranged. While MacKenny was fetching Andrews from his home – Andrews, unable to tell his wife the truth about where he was going, would say vaguely that he was going out on 'business' and would be back in an hour or so – Childs positioned the furniture in his flat so that their victim could be placed in a chair with his back towards the kitchen. Remembering the previous occasion, Childs also removed all the ornamental weapons from the walls, to avoid trouble if Ronald didn't die immediately. And as a further precaution he hid a hammer and a second revolver – MacKenny's would be in the kitchen – under a living-room cushion.

MacKenny arrived, brought Andrews in, and introduced him to Childs. They sat him down as planned and Childs began to ask him the sort of questions a private investigator might ask. MacKenny offered to make tea, and as he was going out Childs called after him, 'Take a cup in to the wife, will you? She's watching TV in the bedroom.'

This, he told Foxall and me, was to allay any suspicions Ronald Andrews might have.

Apparently he then brought out some vodka – Andrews's favourite drink – and arranged for him to pour himself some from a bottle that had previously been wiped clean of fingerprints. This was the bottle that would subsequently be found in the car on the river bed, suggesting that the Lincoln's driver had been drunk at the time of the accident.

All this time, while Childs had been asking Andrews more questions about his wife and her movements, MacKenny had been wandering in and out of the kitchen, chatting with the two of them. Now, the next time he came in from the kitchen he carried a revolver fitted with a silencer hidden under a towel, and he shot Andrews once, in the back of the head. His victim fell forward. Childs wrapped a piece of cloth round his head to contain the blood, and MacKenny asked, 'Is he dead?'

Childs had seen instantly that the single shot had been enough. 'Yes,' he answered. 'Stone dead.'

At this point MacKenny apparently became maudlin, saying what a good friend Andrews had been and how sorry he was to have killed him. Childs was irritated, and told him to 'cut the crap'. Once again, as after Sherwood's murder, a quarrel developed between the two men, this time over the order in which they were to carry out the next moves. MacKenny wanted to take the car up to Wisbech immediately, while Childs wanted to get the body out of the way first, in case his wife should return unexpectedly from the friends with whom she was staying. MacKenny told him shortly that if she did they'd simply have to kill her too. Childs shouted that if anything of the sort happened he'd kill MacKenny.

As before, the quarrel died down. MacKenny persuaded Childs that they should get rid of the car first, so they moved Andrews's body temporarily into a spare room, which Childs used as a sort of workshop. The Lincoln's tank was filled with petrol and the vodka bottle was put on the back seat. MacKenny put on a wetsuit, covering it with a big jersey, and the rest of his diving gear was put in Childs's van.

The night had turned out to be foggy, visibility was poor, and they made bad time on the drive north, arriving by the river much later than they'd planned. The tide was now ebbing fast and the water level had dropped, leaving a mud bank beside the road and a drop of some feet to the water below. Even so, MacKenny kitted up with the rest of his diving equipment and drove the Lincoln off the road at such speed that he cleared the mud bank and sank in the deep water beyond. Getting out of the submerged car in the darkness and the strong currents wasn't easy, but he eventually managed it and swam for the shore. The current carried him some distance downstream, and when he reached the bank it was steep and slippery. But he scrambled out somehow, Childs picked him up in the van, and they drove back to London.

They arrived at the Poplar flat in the early hours of the morning, lit the fire in the living room, and began cutting up the body. During the sixteen hours or so that it took them to dispose of the body MacKenny left the flat on a couple of occasions. The first time he left Childs immediately got out the whisky and then fell asleep, letting the fire go out. On his return MacKenny angrily relit the fire, and the burning was resumed. After his second, rather longer absence, however, he returned to find Childs so drunk that he'd fallen over and gashed his forehead. MacKenny cleaned up this new flow of blood and dressed the wound. Childs pulled himself together, and then they removed all traces from the flat of the grisly work that had been done there.

At this point Childs sat back. He'd come to the end of his shocking story. Inspector Foxall and I had been with him in that interview room for three long days and now – apart from a subsequent account of other planned killings which had been abandoned – at last his astounding confession was over. His claim was that six totally callous and calculated murders had been committed. And from that moment the responsibility passed to us: we had to find other firm evidence of those crimes, evidence that would stand up in court quite separately from the confession. In other words we had to prove the confession.

I'd already sent officers to examine the Childs's flat in Poplar. Now, worried for Mrs Childs's safety with MacKenny still at large, I arranged secret alternative accommodation for her and her children. I also had Childs unobtrusively removed from Oxford Prison to Winchester, where at his own request he was placed in solitary confinement pending his trial. Furthermore, to avoid local rumours about police activity in Poplar, before I sent in a specialist team of CID investigators and scientists to the Childs's address I instructed them to pose as council workmen on routine maintenance.

Everything Childs had described was found, including the tools and the diver's knife and fireman's axe on the living-room wall. We also took away a blue track suit, which later helped to establish that Childs had been 'Mr Jennings'.

At the bungalow in Dagenham we found human blood staining in exactly the areas Childs had indicated, not only on the floorboards and skirting but also through three layers of linoleum, and we found the marks on the table and on the parquet flooring in the church hall next door. One astute officer, Sergeant Newell, spotted a small picture on the living-room wall which was surrounded by a faint larger pale oblong outline, suggesting that a larger picture had once hung there. A quick search revealed this other larger picture, with no glass in its frame and a slight tear in its centre which had been carefully repaired with adhesive tape. When Sergeant Newell fitted this picture over the pale outline he found a shallow irregular hole in the wall underneath other wallpaper, exactly behind the tear. Microscopic tests of the plaster produced traces of lead and antimony, evidence which tended to support Childs's story of the bullet that had ricocheted, breaking the glass in his hand and ending up in the room behind him.

Samples of the bloodstains were also examined in the forensic laboratory but unfortunately, although they were found to be of a rare group, found in no more than 0.6 per cent of the population, this proved unhelpful since it was never possible to establish Sherwood's blood group.

Childs, appreciating that we were protecting his family and him as best we could, had also suggested at the end of our interview with him that we would find something of interest at a house in Woodford and gave us a note to the woman who lived there, authorising us to take away two boxes and a kit-bag that she was looking after for him. He emphasised that the containers were padlocked and that she didn't know what he'd hidden in them.

That evening Inspector Foxall and I had gone to the address in Woodford. Our visit was to provide probably the only light moment in the whole unhappy case. I gave the woman Childs's note and she directed us up to the loft, providing a torch and a stepladder. Foxall went first, vanished from sight, and then reappeared in the opening carrying a heavy padlocked box. Not the nimblest of men, he was in serious danger of dropping it as he advanced towards the trap door in the loft and the stepladder, his two feet on separate wooden joists and with the woman watching interestedly from below. He stooped cautiously to pass the box down to me . . . and the seat of his trousers split resoundingly from top to bottom.

Embarrassed at exposing considerable areas of his underwear, and in confusion for he could not move his feet, Foxall was unable to see the funny side of things. Brusquely, but still attempting to retain his dignity, he requested the woman to look the other way. Later, however, she obligingly provided a couple of safety pins with which he made running repairs. We brought the boxes and the kit-bag from the loft and we gratefully departed.

When the padlocks were cut off at Loughton police station a considerable armoury was revealed. We found an Oesterr Waffenfahr sporting rifle with telescopic sight, fifty shotgun cartridges, a Walther automatic pistol, a Webley Mark VI revolver, a Rhoner Sportwaffen pistol, a magazine and magazine loader for a Sten gun, a large quantity of ammunition of various calibres, a rubber mask, gun cleaning equipment, a ski mask, a shoulder holster, a tool for opening cartridges, some twists of paper containing black powder, and a metal template for making vehicle number plates.

We also found four other Webley revolvers, four pump-action sawn-off shotguns, four wooden stocks for use with the shotguns, a Sten gun with two spare barrels and two magazines, an Enfield revolver, a Browning sports rifle, another large quantity of ammunition, another holster, and more than two hundred shotgun cartridges.

Several of the weapons were fully loaded and ready for use, and there were enough firearms there to start a small war. It was, in fact, a unique hoard, and one which ballistics experts at the Yard examined with interest. As well as the murders and the more recent Security Express robbery, Childs had been involved in a large number of other serious offences – and indeed, when he was later brought to trial for the Security Express robbery and pleaded guilty, he asked for twenty-five other offences to be taken into consideration. A number of them were other conspiracies to murder which had not been carried out.

The murder cases, too, were now coming together. Admittedly I still found it hard to believe Childs's description of how he and MacKenny burned the bodies, but there was enough other evidence to establish that we now had six murder cases, spanning four years, to investigate.

Accordingly I asked for more staff and was given six detective inspectors, so that I could now put together six two-man teams. And even though the investigation was still only two weeks old, when the new men arrived for their briefing I was able to give them a remarkable amount of information. Detective Superintendent Dickens's shrewd handling of the robber informant up in Hertfordshire had led us to Childs, and Childs had given us so much that our principal concern now was to find all the corroborating evidence we could – and, of course, to find the missing MacKenny.

From 14 July onwards, Inspector Foxall and I spent a week at Winchester Prison, obtaining a long and detailed written statement from Childs which completely confirmed his earlier confessions. By now officers examining his flat had discovered a roll of polythene sheeting such as he'd described, and upon it were found minute fragments of debris which gave a positive reaction for human blood. Two large plastic dustbins were also found, one smeared with human blood, and a large piece of orange curtaining – also just as Childs had described – upon which were several large and different areas of human blood staining, all of different blood groups, one of which matched the rare group found on the floor of MacKenny's bungalow.

By now Mrs Gwen Andrews had also been interviewed by the Hertfordshire police. Although she made no secret of her friendship with MacKenny, she clearly had no knowledge of her husband's murder, nor of the other, earlier murders. A team of officers from Hertfordshire and the Yard was organised to keep her under surveillance in case MacKenny should try to contact her, but under-manning problems resulted in the watch never being maintained one hundred per cent and a few weeks later we were to learn that she had assisted him after she had been interviewed by police.

Meanwhile the stage was now reached when I had to go out and talk to the close relatives of the victims. It was not a happy task – some of them were still clinging to the hope that the missing people would be found and I had to destroy that hope, telling them I believed they were dead. I also had to ask these poor people not on any account to talk to others about what I was telling them. We particularly didn't want MacKenny warned that we were investigating those possible murders. A man who knows he's wanted for murder has few options and may be correspondingly more dangerous, and Childs had warned us that MacKenny was still in possession of a silenced revolver with plenty of ammunition, and was a crack shot.

Since the press by now had got wind of something big, I had to try to keep them quiet also. The crime reporter of a London newspaper telephoned only two weeks into the enquiry to tell me that his sources in Hertford believed that a number of murders were being investigated by the Metropolitan Police, and he mentioned in particular the 1975 disappearance of George Brett. Inspector Foxall and I met him in a pub and asked him to hold the story until MacKenny was in custody. Reporters never like to sit on a good story but he understood our reasons and agreed to have a word with his editor – who agreed to hold the story back for the time being.

But the word was out in Fleet Street and a week or so later, without telling us, the *Daily Mirror* ran a small piece about a man wanted by the police in connection with the disappearance of Brett, mentioning that the man was believed to be armed, and that he was linked both with the mysterious disappearances of two other men and with a recent big robbery in Hertfordshire.

That same day the newspaper editor I'd originally spoken to telephoned me to say he'd have to go back on our understanding now that the *Daily Mirror* had used the story. This is a time-honoured routine and they printed the story that day. By the next day, 27 July, all the national press had carried the story. Prevented by law from naming Henry MacKenny at this stage for the crimes, they called the killer 'Big H', suggesting that he was responsible for many murders. Intelligent work in their files had enabled some of the papers to carry details of George Brett and his son, Terence Eve and Ronald Andrews, complete with pictures, as people reported missing. MacKenny would have had no doubt as to the identity of 'Big H' nor would others who knew him.

Such publicity, although probably inevitable, placed the police in a difficult position. Usually we would try to avoid issuing the name and description of a wanted suspect because this makes for problems later with witness identifications, and leaves police open to the charge of having prejudiced a fair trial. Now however, with telephone calls pouring in reporting sightings of the mysterious Big H, we felt we had an obligation to identify MacKenny fully, so that the public could be warned that should he be seen he should not be approached since he was armed and dangerous. Accordingly, later on 27 July 1979, we released Henry MacKenny's details for press publication, together with a recent photograph.

Now, of course, police telephones were swamped with calls, most of them bogus. One call, however, claimed that MacKenny would be found between nine o'clock and eleven that night driving a white Volkswagen car in the vicinity of a certain public house in the Ilford area of East London. I took this call seriously. Teams of detectives were deployed to keep watch from unmarked cars, and at ten-thirty two of my officers, Detective Inspector Ted Ward and Detective Ron Peberdy, spotted the white VW in exactly the right area, parked and empty.

They noted down the car's registration number and waited. Soon afterwards MacKenny approached it, got in, and drove off. Instantly Ward and Peberdy gave chase, alerting the other nearby police cars. Within seconds MacKenny became aware that he was being followed, accelerated violently, and crossed a main road against a red light. Two other officers in a car chasing him were forced to stop by traffic crossing the main road, and MacKenny gained a lead which enabled him to escape. The police found his Volkswagen minutes later, half a mile away, abandoned close to the railings of South Park, Ilford.

I was on the scene very shortly. By then the keys of the white VW had been found just inside the park railings, but the night was very dark and I refused to allow a search of the park until morning, by which time specially-trained members of my group would be armed and able to defend themselves against a possibly armed MacKenny. Meanwhile the entire park was surrounded. Inspector Ward then went to interview a woman, a known associate of MacKenny, who we now knew lived in a block of flats near to where he had first been seen that evening. She was taken into custody at Ilford police station.

At dawn I led the search of the park. There was no sign of MacKenny – clearly he'd never been in the park but had simply tossed the car keys over the railings in order to throw police off his track. Once again he'd eluded us.

I went to see the woman detained in Ilford police station. She admitted that MacKenny had visited her the previous evening, and admitted further that her son had a flat in Barking, Essex, where MacKenny had been hiding out ever since the Security Express robbery. He'd left that flat in something of a panic the evening before, after reading about 'Big H' in the newspapers. He'd come to her in Ilford, hoping she could help him, but there'd been nothing she could do, so he had left and she'd no idea at all where he'd gone.

Detectives searched the Barking flat where they found some of MacKenny's belongings, including his passport. An attempt had clearly been made to bleach out the name in the passport, presumably to alter it, but without success. And there was nothing to indicate where he might be now.

The woman in Ilford, her son and his wife were all charged with aiding and harbouring MacKenny in connection with the Hertfordshire robbery, that being the offence for which she had known police had wanted MacKenny at the time.

Meanwhile the white VW had led us back to Mrs Gwen Andrews. Traced through its registration number to a local car dealer, he told us he had sold it to her a few days before. The watch on her house was intensified, and the following day detectives reported that she had returned there with a man in a white van—but the man was not MacKenny.

I ordered them both to be detained. The man turned out to be the van's owner, a Mr 'X', and in the van a television set was found which was later identified as having belonged to Robert Brown, one of the murder victims Childs had told us about. I remembered him mentioning this set. I also knew that we had since traced one of Brown's friends, a woman who sometimes did his washing for him, and that she had described having stood as guarantor for his purchase of this set on hire purchase. Later, after his disappearance, she'd seen the set in MacKenny's bungalow, had asked anxiously about the hire-purchase payments, and been reassured.

The connection thus firmly established between MacKenny and the television set, I questioned Mr 'X' closely about it. He explained that he'd known MacKenny for years – they had been members of the sub-aqua club – and that he'd bought the TV set from MacKenny some time previously. But he claimed he'd only collected it that very day, not from MacKenny himself but from a relative of his, and he produced a receipt that turned out to be genuine. He was allowed to go.

What Mr 'X' didn't know at that time, and what of course I couldn't tell him, was that Childs had told me that 'X' had also been the subject of a murder plot. A man who was apparently seeking vengeance for

some wrong or other had commissioned the killing of 'X', and the plan
had been to entice him to the Poplar flat by offering him a good deal on
the sale of some underwater wrist watches – he ran a shop selling diving
equipment, so he agreed to go to an address at Poplar to take delivery of
the watches. He did not know that the address was Childs's flat at
Poplar.

He was a cautious man, however. He had later picked up Childs in
his car, handed over the money, and they started out for Poplar
together. But he was suspicious so 'X' had asked a friend of his to follow
them in another car, just in case. When Childs spotted this other car
following he was obliged to abandon the plan. He scrambled out of the
car at the first opportunity, hoping at least to make off with the money,
but 'X' and his friend pursued him closely, and eventually Childs took
the only chance he had and threw the money away. His pursuers
stopped to pick it up, and Childs was able to escape.

Mr 'X' knew he'd nearly been robbed, therefore, but he'd never
guessed how close he'd come to death.

Mrs Gwen Andrews was questioned also, particularly in connection
with the white VW purchased by her and then used by MacKenny, and
was taken to Hertford police station where she was charged with aiding
and harbouring MacKenny after the robbery. She was remanded in
custody for a week by magistrates and then, following a plea from her
solicitor, released on bail.

One aspect of the murder case still worried me: the burning of the
bodies in the perfectly ordinary living-room fireplace of the Childs's
council flat. I discussed the problem with Professor James Cameron, a
very distinguished Home Office pathologist whose headquarters were
at the London Hospital in Whitechapel. Despite his vast experience he
too had never before heard of such a disposal method, so he decided to
conduct an experiment.

He obtained a pig's carcass of similar body-weight to a grown man,
cut it up at the Poplar flat with implements such as Childs had
described, and then – in the presence of Home Office scientists and a
trained fireman from the London Hospital – he set about burning it in
Childs's fireplace exactly as Childs claimed he had. For thirteen hours
through the night and in the sweltering heat of that small living room in
Poplar, the pig was fed on to the fire, and finally the animal was
reduced to no more than a pile of powdered bone and ashes.

Once again we'd found that what Childs had told us seemed accurate
and another piece of corroborating evidence was added to the case
against him. Now I was able to charge him formally with the murders

of Andrews and Sherwood. There was still a lot of work to be done, however – and in particular we had to capture the elusive MacKenny.

At this point Gwen Andrews, now on bail, asked for an interview. She arrived at Loughton police station with her solicitor, giving as her reason the fact that she was afraid because someone had written 'Your death is soon' on the door of a lock-up garage her husband had once used. It transpired that the words were in fact not on her husband's garage but on the garage next to it – and I wondered if she also had some other reason for wanting to see me. I asked her if she'd heard from MacKenny, and after a brief consultation with her solicitor in the next room she told me that she had recently received a postcard from him, postmarked 'Jeddah, Saudi Arabia, August 15'. She then showed me the postcard, which was unmistakably written in MacKenny's handwriting.

This seemed to me a ruse. Knowing MacKenny's fondness for fake postcards I felt that Mrs Andrews had been used to produce the card for me in order to persuade me that he was safely out of this country and beyond my reach. That in turn led me to assume that he was still in London, and was worried because the police hunt was getting close.

Just to be certain, however, I ordered time-consuming checks on all recent commercial flights to Jeddah and also, because MacKenny was of course a qualified pilot, of recent movements of private aircraft leaving Britain. Those enquiries tied up far too many of my men and, as I'd suspected, proved a complete waste of time.

Now I was increasingly busy assembling the evidence to corroborate Childs's confession, so I handed over the task of finding MacKenny to a long-time colleague and friend, Detective Superintendent Gibson, who had recently joined my team. Gaining a conviction against Childs wasn't going to be easy; there had never before been a case when six killings without a single body had jointly formed the basis for a murder enquiry, and where the prosecution was not going to be able to produce even a part of a body.

Although Childs had been brought from prison to point out exactly where the ashes of the burned bodies had been scattered, it proved a pointless operation. All the sites except one had either been busy main roads or canals with considerable current flow, and anyway the scatterings had occurred at least four years before. Only one site showed any promise: a small area, three hundred square yards or so, on Wanstead Flats, a piece of common land in East London. Forty police cadets were supplied with scissors and made a minute search of the area on their hands and knees. They found hundreds of small pieces of bone, but all turned out to be animal rather than human.

The woman working in the police store had been amazed when Inspector Foxall went in to ask for forty pairs of large scissors.

'What on earth for?' she demanded.

'For cutting grass with,' he told her patiently.

'Typical CID,' she said. 'Ask a silly question and get a silly answer.'

In September Detective Superintendent Gibson had a breakthrough in his search for MacKenny. Information led him to a maisonette in a quiet close in Plaistow, East London, where the wanted man might be hiding. Detectives kept watch on the property all through 20 September but saw only the people who were known to live there, a Mr and Mrs Woodcraft, and their children. There was no sign of MacKenny.

That evening after dark, on Superintendent Gibson's orders, the house was surrounded by police, including men from D11 branch, the Police specialist firearms unit known today as PT17. Gibson had been in touch with me, and we met that night at Plaistow police station. His plan was to raid the Woodcrafts' maisonette at one o'clock in the morning, when everyone might be assumed to have gone to bed, but to avoid sudden confrontation an officer was to telephone first and try to speak to MacKenny.

Detective Peberdy, who'd been close to catching MacKenny once before, was chosen to make the phone call. He spoke to a woman, identified himself, and asked to speak to her husband. When Mr Woodcraft came to the telephone Peberdy identified himself again and asked if there was a man called Harry in the house. After some hesitation Woodcraft admitted that there was, and said that the man Harry was asleep. Peberdy warned him that Harry might be armed and was dangerous, and advised him to try to get himself and his wife and three children quietly out of the house. Woodcraft seemed to delay.

At this time Superintendent Gibson and I were in position outside the Woodcrafts' maisonette some distance away and Detective Peberdy was communicating with us by radio at the same time as he was talking with Mr Woodcraft. Suddenly he came through on the radio to say that he'd actually talked to MacKenny himself, who'd admitted his identity. Peberdy had told him the house was surrounded by armed police and MacKenny had said he'd come out quietly. He described how he was dressed and told Peberdy he wasn't armed. Peberdy instructed him to walk out of the front door with his hands held high above his head, and to obey the instructions he would then be given from the police outside.

Searchlights were switched on and MacKenny came out through the front door exactly as instructed, his hands above his head. Clearly the lights were dazzling him, but we took no chances.

MacKenny was told through a loudhailer to walk slowly forward into the road and lie down in the middle, face downwards, his arms over his head and spread out.

We wanted no accidents, absolutely no tricks and absolutely no possibility that anything he did might be misunderstood by the police marksmen who stood in the darkness, their guns trained on him.

MacKenny did as he was told. The tension eased as Superintendent Gibson and I walked forward, accompanied by Detective Inspector Breeze. MacKenny was searched, found to be unarmed, and secured with handcuffs. Then he was taken to Plaistow police station and the long three-months' hunt was over.

I went back into the Woodcrafts' house, talked to them, and after a while they admitted that Henry (Harry) MacKenny had been staying with them for the last two or three weeks. They were both subsequently charged with harbouring him.

Later that day MacKenny was moved to Loughton and it was there, in the presence of his solicitor, that I first interviewed him. He was as big as everyone had said, six feet six or seven inches tall, and impressively built. Asked about the murder of Ronald Andrews he claimed an alibi, in that on the night Andrews had disappeared he said he was with a married couple down in Southend. At first he behaved quite reasonably, but soon afterwards he became more difficult. Having offered violence and been forcibly restrained, he then complained of feeling unwell. Next day I charged him with the murder of Ronald Andrews, and he appeared at Bow Street magistrates' court and was remanded in custody.

A few days later Childs was charged with the remaining four murders, those of George Brett and his son, Terence Eve, and Robert Brown. He was committed for trial at the Old Bailey and on 4 December 1979, he pleaded guilty to all six murders and was sentenced to life imprisonment on each count. That same day I saw him in the cells where he signed witness statements and reaffirmed his willingness to give evidence against MacKenny and others in connection with the same murder offences.

This was a vital step in the enquiry. There had been no guarantee that he would admit to the murder charges himself when arraigned for trial and had he pleaded not guilty then he could not have been used as a witness against MacKenny. Equally, having been dealt with himself by the court he was under no obligation to give evidence against others and might have refused to do so. A few days later he appeared at the Old Bailey again, pleaded guilty to the Hertfordshire robbery, and, as I have already said, asked for twenty-five other offences to be taken into consideration, including five other cases of conspiracy to murder. He was sentenced to six years' imprisonment, to run concurrently with the life sentences.

Now, with the conspiracies to murder also admitted, I could return to Mr 'X', who'd been the subject of one of them. Shocked, he and his wife now made written statements detailing their knowledge of Mac-Kenny's movements while he'd been on the run, from June to September, and gave the names and addresses of people who had hidden him. Mrs 'X' also admitted that on one occasion MacKenny had told her that he'd killed Ronald Andrews, and she later gave that evidence on oath at MacKenny's trial.

One point in particular in the case against MacKenny was untidy. Many people, including Childs, had reported him as always carrying a gun, yet he was unarmed when arrested, and we found no gun in the Woodcrafts' house. One of the addresses Mr 'X' gave us did prove useful though. It led us to a tower block in the East End where we interviewed two men, one named Bell, and in the course of our questioning they admitted that they'd helped MacKenny while he was on the run. Furthermore, Bell, who was a builder, was able to solve at least part of the mystery concerning MacKenny's missing revolver. Bell had been doing some work for a teacher at a school on the Isle of Dogs and the teacher had asked him for some solidified mortar he could use as a counter-weight for stage scenery at his school. Bell had provided him with a bucket full of solidified mortar, and when we broke that up we found a silencer for a gun, and a large quantity of ammunition, carefully oiled and wrapped in waterproof cloth. The bucket had been at the school for some months, standing at the side of the stage.

The gun itself was never found, but the silencer became significant evidence and in due course Bell was charged and convicted and was sentenced to two years' imprisonment.

In October 1980, after some sixteen months of concentrated police work, the case against MacKenny was complete and he was brought to trial at the Old Bailey. His trial lasted forty days. John Childs, already serving life imprisonment for six murders, was the chief prosecution witness and his evidence included all the same terrifying details he'd given Foxall and me in his original confession. The jury found Henry

MacKenny guilty of the murders of George Brett and his son Terry, of Frederick Sherwood, and of Ronald Andrews, and he was sentenced to life imprisonment, with a minimum recommended time in jail of twenty-five years. He was at that time forty-eight years old.

Terence Pinfold was tried also, found guilty of Terence Eve's murder, and jailed for life. Two other men, on trial for murder, in that it was alleged they had each paid for a contract killing, were acquitted after the jury had deliberated for almost two full days.

Gwen Andrews was never brought to trial. She had been charged with helping MacKenny while police were hunting him in connection with the Security Express robbery. He was charged with that robbery but he was never tried – the Director of Public Prosecutions decided against it since he was already serving a minimum sentence of twenty-five years. He was never convicted of it and therefore, in law, there was no case against her. The same applied to all the other people who'd been charged with harbouring him or assisting him to evade arrest while he was wanted for that offence – they were all discharged except the man Bell, whose crime related to the illegal possession and handling of the silencer and ammunition found in the bucket.

And so the case was concluded. But a further unhappy twist was still to come. On the day after MacKenny's trial was concluded, 29 November, the *Guardian* newspaper published an article accusing the police of unethical conduct. In an article headed 'Police paper trail that led to the capture of Big H', the writer claimed that back on 26 and 27 July 1979, when we were urgently trying to trace MacKenny, we had 'used the media in an unprecedented way' by feeding the press with information about him that had never been substantiated. One item published at the time and attributed to us reported that 'MacKenny is a psychopath who once killed after having a row with a stranger in a queue. He stalked him and shot him.'

The article concluded that by issuing stories like that the police had acted unethically, and thereby had prejudiced a fair trial for MacKenny.

I must admit that this angered me, for I knew only too well how hard I had tried to avoid any kind of publicity, and the good reasons for this – and furthermore, the particular item quoted had definitely originated not from the police but from some reporter. I therefore took the matter up quite forcibly with the *Guardian* and in due course the newspaper published an apology, making it clear that the original article had not been intended to refer to me or to my handling of the case, and regretting any embarrassment that it might have caused me.

That was not until nearly two years later however and although sometimes the police are accused of being over-sensitive, this did seem to have been a long time to wait to have corrected what was, after all, a major inaccuracy.

7

1983: THE FLYING SQUAD

In 1979, while still working on the Childs and MacKenny case, I had again been promoted, and appointed to the post of Commander of No. 1 Area of the Metropolitan Police. My rank should now have been that of Detective Commander but, as I've already described, that CID rank had now been abolished. So I was now a 'Police Commander'. In fact, during my three years as commander of an area, instead of exercising operational CID command I was reduced to the level of being simply an adviser.

The area I was posted to was very large, very active, and in CID terms, very understaffed. No. 1 Area of the Metropolitan Police at that time comprised one-quarter of the entire Metropolitan Police District, the whole south-west corner of London. It incorporated six of the twenty-five separate police districts within the force area as a whole, and included the London Heathrow Airport district. Yet with all the demands and problems that this sort of area must inevitably make upon its senior officers, my position – as one of four similarly appointed area commanders in the CID at that time – was administrative and advisory and for the most part non-executive.

Like them, I was 'crime adviser' to my area deputy assistant commissioner and to the six district commanders of that area, each of whom had their own district complement of detective officers who were directly and separately responsible to those commanders. Thus the distance between myself and any personal involvement in the direction of CID personnel towards the detection or prevention of crime was enormous, and seemingly insuperable. I have seldom felt so powerless, and those three years were to be the most unproductive and personally unrewarding period in all my thirty-three years of police service.

At that time I was fifty years old and yet retirement, which is compulsory for commanders at fifty-seven, suddenly seemed almost attractive.

One small achievement only in those three years do I claim. This grew out of the greatly increased number of burglaries in London since the early Seventies, so many in fact that detective officers often found themselves able to do little more than record the details at the local station. They had neither the time nor the manpower to do much more, and as a result, I suspect, many of those crimes went unsolved.

One of the main reasons for these increased burglary rates was purely one of definition. Before the introduction of the Theft Act in 1968 which repealed the Larceny Act of 1916, burglary had been a very serious offence. Until then the term 'burglary' had described the crime committed if a dwelling house was broken into by night – between the hours of 9 p.m. and 6 a.m. – for the purpose of committing theft or other serious criminal offences in the premises. To 'break in' meant just that: a forcible entry, such as by breaking open a door or smashing a window. The crime carried with it a possible sentence of life imprisonment.

The offence of 'house-breaking' was similarly defined, save that it took place during the hours of daylight, from 6 a.m. to 9 p.m., and it carried a smaller maximum penalty of fourteen years' imprisonment.

The Theft Act of 1968, however, abolished the offence of house-breaking and redefined burglary to include any act of trespass for the purpose of theft, day or night: it was no longer necessary to break in in order to establish or commit the offence. Thus burglary could now be committed for example simply by walking in through an open kitchen door, or by reaching in through an open window in any part of a house or other building, at any time of the day or night. So the stealing of £1 in cash from a table in the kitchen by stepping through an open door was now burglary.

But although the crime of burglary had been redefined to include many more minor offences, a large number of them petty in nature, it retained its police classification as Major Crime. In consequence it had always to be dealt with by CID officers and these men became so inundated with those investigations that their more serious responsibilities – for which they had received lengthy specialised training – were sometimes sadly neglected.

What was clearly needed was a screening system that would focus the attention of the most skilled officers upon the more serious instances of burglary, leaving those of a more trivial nature to be dealt with by the

19. *(above left)* The entrance (left) to No. 13 Dolphin House where the bodies were burned.

20. *(above right)* The grate in Childs's flat where six bodies were burned. Note the bloodstains on the floor.

21. *(below)* St Thomas's Church Hall, Dagenham, known as 'The Factory', where murders were planned and sometimes executed.

22. David Martin in one of his favourite disguises, as a woman.

23. David Martin, *(centre)* arrested at Belsize Park underground station.

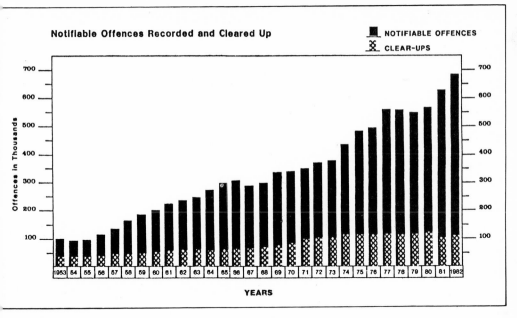

Notifiable Offences Recorded and Cleared Up

■ NOTIFIABLE OFFENCES
✕ CLEAR-UPS

24. Notifiable offences recorded and cleaned up between 1953-83.

25. The Brinks-Mat robbery. The robbers entered the depot through the rear of the building at centre right and left it through the folding doors in the front in a van containing the gold.

26. Masked and armed robbers holding up a London bank. Photographed by an internal TV security camera.

27. A bank raid in London, with customers held at gun-point. Photographed by an internal TV security camera.

uniformed branch as they had been doing in London with 'minor' crime, such as simple theft, for some years. Borrowing from a concept pioneered in the USA by the Stamford Research Institute and now used by several police forces in America, I therefore devised a system in which certain numbers of 'points' would be allocated to reported offences of burglary, using a wide range of criteria to assess the priority offences. This was tried out in 1982 on 'X' district in West London and proved successful. Shortly afterwards, although I had by then been transferred back to the Yard, I was asked by the Police Commissioner, through David Powis, the CID Deputy Assistant Commissioner in charge of CID operations, to form and lead a working party of senior officers with the intention of introducing a Burglary Screening System force-wide. This we did, and our system became accepted practice throughout the force in September 1983.

That screening system of investigation is still used by the Metropolitan Police today, and by other forces in this country, and in London it has now been extended to screen many other types of crime save the most serious.

Early in 1983 I was transferred from my advisory job in No. 1 area of the Metropolitan Police back to Scotland Yard, where I was given overall command of three separate CID branches: the London Regional Crime Squad, the Stolen Vehicle Squad and the world-famous Flying Squad. I was delighted that my period in the wilderness was over – Bridget had never quite got used to seeing me often angry and frustrated.

The Flying Squad, not known at first as such, had been set up back in 1919 as a response to public concern over the wave of crime that swept Britain after the First World War. Gangs of men, trained in the arts of war, were committing widespread crimes often with violence and ruthless determination, and in October of that year a group of twelve detectives of the Metropolitan Police were summoned to Scotland Yard. Their meeting resulted in the formation of a specialised team of officers, all experienced thief-takers, whose job was to tackle the organised crime problems of the day. Their position was new and unique, since for the first time these detectives would not be confined to a particular police area or division; they would be able to go wherever they were needed within the Metropolitan Police District.

The officer placed in charge, and often described as the 'daddy of them all', was Detective Chief Inspector Frederick Wensley, a man of rare distinction in police circles. And his new squad was unusually mobile, using first a covered wagon hired from the Great Western Railway, and later two ex-Royal Flying Corps motor tenders of their own, Crossleys with a top speed of forty miles per hour.

Then, in the *Daily Mail* of 22 September 1920, a crime reporter, W.G.T. Crook, wrote of the achievements of Inspector Wensley's men and referred to them as 'a flying squad of picked detectives'. The expression caught the nation's fancy, and thereafter they became known as the Flying Squad.

In 1921 another innovation was introduced. A telegraph transmitter was fitted into one of the Crossley tenders and, using morse code, two-way communication between the Squad and the Yard was established, the forerunner of all the sophisticated mobile police communication systems in use today.

Next, with the addition of police drivers and radio operators from the uniformed branch, the strength of the Squad was increased from twelve to sixteen. And as their successes mounted and the years passed, so their numbers grew and they were provided with increasingly fast and powerful machines, Bentleys, Invictas, Lagondas, Railtons and Jaguars. Eventually their terms of reference were modified: rather than investigate particular crimes they were to concentrate their efforts upon those responsible, and upon cultivating reliable sources of information. So it was that they built up an impressive network of professional informants and a formidable knowledge of criminal gangs and their activities. This in turn led them in the late Thirties to concentrate upon the racecourse gangs and the specialist ways of professional pickpockets and vehicle thieves.

By the 1960s, under the command of respected senior detectives such as Reginald Spooner, Tommy Butler and others, the Flying Squad had become a major and internationally famous branch of Scotland Yard, even dealing with cases outside London when they were beyond the resources of local forces – cases like the Great Train Robbery in Hertfordshire in 1963. And by the 1970s its strength had grown to about a hundred officers, divided into eight teams, each under the command of a detective inspector and all based at the Yard. Each team had four vehicles and several highly-trained drivers.

By now, various factors had led to a steep increase in armed robberies in London. One was the high level of general affluence: people were earning more, and spending more, and the result was that more money was in circulation, temptingly available in banks, carried in security vans, and in the tills of the humblest of sub-post offices or corner shops. Building societies, betting shops: the list of businesses obliged to hold amounts of ready cash on their premises grew by leaps and bounds. And with it grew the number of armed attacks, now with the sawn-off shotgun a favoured weapon.

To combat this new challenge a specialist Robbery Squad was set up within the Flying Squad itself and it had some notable successes. The Wembley Bank Robbery investigation, for example, in the 1970s resulted in the arrest of twenty-six men for crimes of armed robbery stretching back over a considerable period, and their trial at the Old Bailey produced sentences to a total of 325 years in prison. The total strength of the Flying Squad in the early 1980s now stood at more than 200, including drivers, with only two teams at the Yard doing the original style of work – the rest were all deployed to the Robbery Squad and its four separate offices dispersed around London.

As armed robbery increased in London the fledgling criminals joined in, men who hardly knew one end of a gun from the other and were therefore potentially far more dangerous. Sawn-off shotguns had now begun to give way to automatic weapons, rifles and carbines, as the security companies strengthened their vehicles' armour. The police were catching a lot of robbers, and containing the situation, but only just, for now building societies, post offices, betting shops and even little corner shops were increasingly becoming targets.

And that was the position in January 1983, when I took command of the Flying Squad. And as that first morning, 10 January, began, so my work at the Yard was to continue.

On that first day a team of squad officers were able to ambush four armed men as they attempted to rob a bookmaker's shop on Pimlico Road in Victoria. And the very next morning an armoured van belonging to Security Express was attacked by two coloured robbers while its crew were delivering cash to a bank on the Marylebone High Street in Central London.

In this case, totally by chance, four local policemen, in plain clothes, all unarmed, happened to be passing. One constable, Stephen O'Rourke, raced ahead of the others, charged one of the robbers who was holding a gun on a security guard, knocked him to the ground, and held him there. The second robber then stood over O'Rourke and threatened to shoot him if he didn't release his prisoner. O'Rourke refused, so the gunman coldly shot him at point-blank range, the bullet shattering his right arm.

Now the two coloured men raced off empty-handed, chased by three policemen and a civilian passer-by, John Trevor Green. The robbers reached their escape car. One of the robbers flung himself in and started the engine. When Green and another policeman, Constable Bull, attempted to tackle the second man as he reached the car, the first robber fired his gun at them from inside, the bullet shattering the car's rear window. Broken splinters of glass flew in all directions and Green's arm was badly cut.

Meanwhile the second robber had now gained the car and his accomplice accelerated away in the direction of Baker Street. At this point another civilian, Gerald Leach, on a motorbike, took up the chase. He kept behind the escaping car for half a mile until the robbers spotted him, stopped, and reversed towards him. As he leapt from his motorbike and ran for cover behind some parked cars one of the robbers left their vehicle, took careful aim at him and fired. Luckily Leach was wearing a crash helmet. The bullet struck his helmet at his left temple, penetrated the outer covering, was deflected and traversed the inside of the rim, stopping by his right temple. Dazed from the impact, he could only watch as the two men drove away.

Three years later, in January 1986, O'Rourke and the two civilians were awarded the Queen's Commendation for bravery.

Meanwhile, ballistic examination of the bullets recovered from outside the bank on the Marylebone High Street revealed that the same guns had been used in other robberies on banks, and in some of those cases the pair of robbers had vaulted the counters and fired recklessly at the staff. Clearly these were highly dangerous men, and I chose two very experienced officers, Detective Superintendent Perry and Detective Chief Inspector Farquhar, to direct the investigation. It was to have a sensational climax.

Some three months later, on 6 April, just before eleven in the morning, the same two robbers raided another bank, this time in Bristol. Wearing balaclava helmets and carrying a sawn-off shotgun and a revolver, they held up Lloyds Bank in Bond Street, Bristol, firing a warning shot and clubbing one of the sub-managers to the ground. The terrified staff handed over £30,000. Then one of them managed to sound an alarm and the raiders fled to their waiting car, a big blue Mercedes. As they roared off one of them fired a shotgun blast through the rear window.

Four unarmed mobile policemen chased the Mercedes and cornered it near the city centre. By now armed police had caught up with them and in a short gun battle one policeman and one robber were shot and wounded. That robber was arrested and later charged.

The other criminal had meanwhile escaped, smashing his Mercedes through several cars and driving away. He made it in his damaged vehicle as far as a nearby pub, where he abandoned it in the forecourt. He then forced a woman out of her Austin Marina, and drove off in it in the direction of the M4. A few miles further on he was rammed by a police car driven by an unarmed policeman, but forced him to back off again at gunpoint.

Eventually the robber hi-jacked a sixteen-ton lorry fully loaded with Cow & Gate baby food. It's hard to know what he had in mind, but it was the start of one of the strangest and most dramatic police chases ever seen in Britain. He put his revolver to the head of the driver and told him to make for the M4 motorway. The driver didn't argue: he was a married man with a ten-year-old son. At his best speed of forty-five miles an hour he lumbered up on to the carriageway, while behind him some of the fastest police cars in Britain swung in on to his tail. They didn't intervene, and neither did the two police helicopters clattering overhead: the gunman held a hostage now and they weren't taking any chances.

As the detectives in charge tried to guess the robber's destination other police forces were alerted, Avon and Somerset, Wiltshire, Thames Valley, and London and eventually it was the Thames Valley force that ended the chase. As the strange convoy trundled on they mounted a spectacular road block across the motorway ahead, commandeering a group of heavy lorries and placing them in a taper from the fast lane inwards to the hard shoulder and a final massive barricade. This forced the Cow & Gate lorry across the carriageway until it was obliged to stop where a large posse of armed police waited.

Training their weapons, they ordered the robber to throw out his gun and surrender. After a pause the gun landed on the tarmac. Its chamber was open and six unused rounds were clearly visible – the man had meant business when he'd set out with it that day. He was brought to trial, and his companion with him. They'd been responsible for many other armed robberies and they were put away for a long time.

Police use of firearms is a controversial subject. Sometimes it can go tragically wrong. I'd been faced with the aftermath of just such a case only a few days after taking command of the Flying Squad.

It had all begun some months before, in August 1982, when a man named David Martin came to the notice of the Metropolitan Police. Using the alias David Demain, he had been found posing as a security officer in premises on Portman Close in London's West End. Questioned by one of the policemen on the scene, Police Constable Carr, he had produced an identification card with a photograph of himself and underneath it the legend: A.P.S. Security. The card looked authentic, but PC Carr was still suspicious, so he sent his colleague out to their police car to check over the radio if anything was known either of the security company or of a David Demain. And while he was waiting, he asked Demain/Martin to empty his pockets. At this point, thoroughly nervous, Martin started to edge towards the door, tried to bolt, but was grabbed in the corridor outside by the two constables. A struggle began, in which Martin pulled out a gun, fired three shots and escaped, leaving Constable Carr seriously wounded in the groin.

Enquiries led first to the address Martin (still known to the police at that time only as Demain) had given Carr while he was being questioned. On Old Bond Street, this turned out to be office premises, the occupant of which told police that only a few days before he had disturbed an intruder who claimed to be a security adviser who had been employed by the office's former tenant. The intruder had then given his name as Demain, and left.

The previous tenant was then traced and interviewed. He was a firearms dealer who now had shop premises in Paddington. He knew nobody named Demain and couldn't help the police.

But then, some days later, on 15 September, that same firearms dealer contacted the local police station. Earlier that day a man had walked into his shop in Paddington and had placed an order, to be collected later. Asked for a telephone number at which he could be contacted, he had provided a number and also his name. It was David Demain.

Recognising the name from the earlier police enquiry, the dealer immediately reported the matter. The telephone number led to flat sixteen, on the seventh floor of a block of flats at 3 Crawford Place, in Paddington. Observation was kept upon the door of number sixteen by armed police officers Detective Constable Finch and Police Constable Lucas, both in plain clothes, and at about nine-forty that same evening they saw a figure they took to be that of a woman approach the door. When spoken to, however, the 'woman' turned out to be a man dressed in women's clothes and wearing a blond wig. This man's next action, drawing a 9 mm semi-automatic pistol from his handbag, suggested that he might well be Demain, so Finch and Lucas sprang upon him.

In the struggle that followed the policemen were joined by more officers who arrived on the scene, Detective Sergeant Martin, Detective Constables Francis and Arnold, and an armed policeman, PC Vann-Dee. Demain's pistol was wrested from him, but he then pulled from his waistband another weapon, a Smith and Wesson .38 revolver.

Fearing for the lives of himself and his companions, PC Vann-Dee then used his own police revolver to shoot Demain. The bullet struck Demain's head and glanced off, travelling downwards to fracture his right collar-bone. In fact he was not seriously injured and continued to struggle violently. Eventually he was overpowered, the Smith and Wesson taken from him, and he was arrested and removed to St Mary's hospital in Paddington.

Demain made a rapid recovery and was discharged from hospital exactly a week later. He was taken to Marylebone police station, and over the next few days identification parades were held to establish his connection with the wounding of PC Carr. He was then charged and remanded in custody.

A search of the flat at Crawford Place revealed ownership documents relating to a Volkswagen car and a leaflet describing a safe deposit box service. This last linked in with a set of keys found in Demain's possession at the time of his arrest, and these led to two different safe deposit boxes, rented back in July. In the first of these police found £3,500 in five-pound notes, some jewellery and foreign currency, and seven handguns and ammunition which, along with the two weapons in Demain's possession, proved to be part of the proceeds of a burglary the previous year from a gunsmith's shop in Covent Garden. Yet another gun from this haul had been dropped at the scene of a recent armed robbery upon a Brinks-Mat security van in the City of London, in the course of which a security guard had been shot and twenty-five thousand pounds had been stolen.

In the second safe deposit box four more handguns and ammunition were found, all from the same gunsmith's shop, £200 in five-pound notes, and three plastic identity cards stamped with the legend A.P.S. and bearing photographs of Demain.

The investigation was now being directed by Detective Superintendent Ness of the local 'D' district and a further search of the Crawford Place flat produced evidence that Demain had recently been in Ibiza with a woman from London and a man named Bill, and that on the way back to Britain Demain had left a car – the Volkswagen for which documents had already been found – in a car park in Calais. Further enquiries revealed that this car had been stolen from a manufacturer's car pound in Ramsgate – along with an Audi which had later been recovered while in the possession of two men, Bill Ord and another man called McKenzie. These men had been charged with the Audi's theft and bailed to appear at Ramsgate magistrates' court, but neither had been seen or heard of since.

Bill Ord soon proved to have been the man in Ibiza with Demain, and McKenzie too was established to be a friend of Demain: he was identified in a photograph with Demain, both of them dressed in women's clothing. Superintendent Ness also discovered that the name Demain was an alias, and that the man's true identity was David Ralph Martin, a thirty-five-year-old Londoner born in the borough of Paddington.

By now the Volkswagen left by Demain in Calais had been found by French police, and searched, and in it five more handguns had been discovered, one of which had been actually used to shoot the Brinks-Mat security guard in the City of London.

Clearly a link was emerging between Martin and that Brinks-Mat robbery. This became stronger when a further car key in Martin's possession was traced to a Mercedes stolen from a Heathrow car park – the same car park from which a Ford Granada had been stolen which it was known had been used in the robbery.

The investigation, which had begun back in August, had now dragged on into December and was approaching its unhappy climax. Martin, awaiting trial and on remand in Brixton Prison, had been appearing regularly at Marlborough Street court to have his period of remand extended – and, as in another case already described here, these repeated visits had given the prisoner a chance to study the security arrangements and make plans. Thus, after his court appearance on Christmas Eve, a Friday, Martin managed to escape from his cell and disappear, apparently by means of a duplicate key.

Superintendent Ness and his officers now liaised with the Yard's Criminal Intelligence Branch, and before long they believed that on a certain day and at a certain time Martin would be travelling with other passengers in a yellow Mini through the Earl's Court area of West London. Ness accordingly mounted a surveillance operation, and at about six in the evening of 14 January 1983, officers spotted a yellow Mini and followed it as it turned into Pembroke Street, Earl's Court. They included Detective Constable Finch who was there because he had helped to arrest Martin originally in Crawford Place, and would therefore be able to identify Martin.

The Mini stopped in heavy traffic. Movements of its occupants caused the police to open fire. The Mini's driver, later identified as one Lester Purdy, scrambled out and escaped in the confusion. His male passenger, thought to be Martin by the policemen present, including Detective Constable Finch, stayed behind, seriously wounded. Also in the car was the woman, Susan Stephens, who had been with

Martin in Ibiza.

Unfortunately the injured man was in fact not David Martin – he was a friend of Martin's, Stephen Waldorf. The likeness was remarkable, but nevertheless a terrible mistake had been made. Waldorf had been shot five times: he was taken to hospital, underwent surgery, and survived. But public criticism of the police was harsh and unrelenting. Not only had the wrong man been shot by 'trigger-happy coppers', but the right man was still at liberty.

This, then, was the situation when I was appointed to lead the hunt to find and recapture David Martin, on 17 January, just seven days after taking over the Flying Squad. Waldorf's shooting was to be investigated separately by Commander Taylor of Scotland Yard's Complaints Investigation Branch.

I went at once to see Superintendent George Ness. I knew how he must be feeling. After tracking down and taking Martin into custody he had – through absolutely no fault of his own – not only seen his prisoner escape from the court, but had also seen that result in the mistaken wounding of Stephen Waldorf. But knowing the case inside out as he did, he was able to give considerable assistance to me in my attempts to find Martin. I liaised with him and appointed two Flying Squad teams, working under Detective Chief Superintendent Brown, to help me.

I spoke to Martin's girlfriend, Susan Stephens. She was an attractive girl, a model and a former dancer. Although she'd known Martin for some time she claimed to know very little about him. They'd been together in Ibiza, but had travelled separately. She said she'd no idea where he was now, but if she found out she promised to let me know.

She was in fact not quite as innocent as she wished to appear. After the Waldorf shooting officers had searched the yellow Mini and found in it a receipt from Pickfords storage depot in Fulham. Following this up the Flying Squad discovered that on 15 August, 1982, shortly after the Covent Garden gunsmith's burglary, a warehouse foreman at Pickfords Ltd had received a telephone call from a Mr Demain, wanting arrangements to be made for the storage of four laundry baskets, five tea-chests, a two-drawer filing cabinet and a large cardboard box, all well-filled. And it was a Miss Susan Stephens who had arrived at the warehouse the following day to deliver all these items.

They stayed in store at Pickfords until 6 January 1983, two weeks after Martin's escape from the police court cell, on which day Miss

Susan Stephens again appeared, this time to remove those goods. She brought with her three men to help, subsequently established to have been Stephen Waldorf, Lester Purdy, and a man called Peter Enter. Receipts for the goods they were taking away had been signed by Purdy, using the false name J. Perry.

We were now able to trace some of these goods to a basement flat in Ladbroke Grove jointly leased by Waldorf and Peter Enter. In it we found the four laundry baskets and three of the tea-chests, containing between them a mass of stolen property, including eleven shoulder holsters stolen from the Covent Garden gunsmith, body armour, security and surveillance equipment, and medical goods.

Purdy, Enter and Susan Stephens were arrested on 24 January, and were charged with knowingly and dishonestly handling stolen property. They were all later convicted at the Old Bailey: Purdy and Enter were sentenced to nine months in prison and Susan Stephens was given six months.

Stephen Waldorf, who was seriously ill in hospital, wasn't interviewed about his part in that Pickfords operation. Instead, details were reported to the Director of Public Prosecutions.

Six days after our search of the Ladbroke Grove flat we discovered that Martin might be going that evening to the Milk Churn restaurant in Heath Street, Hampstead. The day was Friday 28 January 1983. A large surveillance team was deployed, some armed. At eight o'clock one of these men, Detective Constable Geraghty, spotted Martin arrive in a Ford Sierra and park. He got out, locked the car, and started to walk along Heath Street towards the restaurant. Now, some criminals seem to possess a sixth sense, and possibly Martin was one of these. At any rate, and for whatever reason, he suddenly stopped, turned, and began to run down the hill.

Detective Geraghty was first to take up the chase. Martin sprinted to the nearby Hampstead underground station, ran down the immensely long stairs to the platform – this is the deepest point in the London Underground Railway system – jumped down on to the electrified railway track and disappeared into the tunnel in the direction of Belsize Park.

Passengers who had seen him were able to direct the police, and Flying Squad men, led by Chief Superintendent Brown, shouted for the electric rail current to be switched off, and then ran after Martin, into the dark tunnel. There was a strong possibility that he was armed, but they stumbled on. Other detectives were meanwhile on their way to Belsize Park station by road, to cut Martin off.

The detectives in the tunnel could hear very little, and see even less. Eventually the first glimmers of light from Belsize Park station came into sight ahead. The tunnel seemed deserted as Superintendent Brown inched his men forward. Martin had left the track and flattened himself into a shallow brick alcove, and it was there that Don Brown and Sergeant Nicky Benwell found him. He surrendered quietly. He wasn't carrying a gun, but he did have a set of pick-locks, a fearsome knife, and a bottle of ammonia. He also had a miniature multi-purpose penknife stuck with chewing gum to the roof of his mouth.

Later a large number of additional charges were preferred against Martin and in October 1983, at the Old Bailey, he was sentenced to a total of twenty-five years' imprisonment.

In prison he became friendly with Donald Neilson, the 'Black Panther', killer of wealthy heiress Lesley Whittle and three sub-postmasters. Martin died as violently as he had lived, committing suicide by hanging himself in his cell.

Later, Stephen Waldorf was awarded £120,000 compensation for his injuries.

Sadly guns continued to feature in our work. Back on 22 January, two days before the arrest of Susan Stephens, another Flying Squad operation had led to the ambush of two armed robbers as they lay in wait for a Securicor armoured van in Chapel Street, North London. Led by Detective Chief Inspector Wilton, the police had pounced just before the armoured van arrived. When one of the gunmen tried to escape, a Flying Squad officer, Detective Sergeant Dave Kelly, chased after him. Kelly was closing on him as the robber half-turned towards him, still running, and fired off both barrels of his shotgun.

Kelly was struck in the face by a pellet, but very fortunately the main blast missed him. He himself was armed with a police revolver but he dared not use it because he and the robber were in a street market crowded with shoppers. He continued the chase on foot, and brought his man down only a few yards further on.

Kelly was awarded the Queen's Commendation for his bravery. This was his second award for bravery in a six-month period, for he had only recently tackled other armed men under very similar circumstances.

Twice in the following month the Flying Squad had to face armed men. First a team arrested two men about to raid a building society in Hatch End, carrying handguns that turned out to be harmless replicas – this operation was followed up so quickly that one of their accomplices was arrested at his home, sitting on his bed, actually counting the proceeds of yet another robbery. Eventually eleven men, all under thirty, were arrested, and between them they'd been responsible for seventy-five armed robberies.

Then on 17 February four more men were arrested in a Flying Squad operation as they were about to attack a security van at a hospital in Enfield. Less than a month later, on 10 March, yet another team of robbers were arrested in the act of attacking another security van, this time at Salford General Hospital in Manchester. The London officers had kept them under surveillance all the way from London.

In all such ambush operations by the Flying Squad the actual arrests are only the culmination of a great deal of earlier, painstaking work, often involving hundreds of hours of surveillance upon possible suspects and known criminals, and equally painstaking collation and analyses of countless snippets of information. A known robber who appears to have dropped out of circulation, a car which has been reported as stolen which might be used as a robbery getaway vehicle, questions which have been asked about a company's security arrangements, or a report that some men have been seen loitering weeks before in the vicinity of a regular wages delivery. These are the things which sooner or later add up, and which bring about the Squad's successes.

Right from my first day with the Flying Squad their work load was prodigious. The total strength of the Squad numbered around 200 detective officers and in the first three months of 1983 alone they investigated and dealt with 343 cases of armed robbery in London. The targets the robbers had chosen were armoured security vehicles, banks, post offices, building society offices, betting shops and other such business premises and in every one of those cases the robbers had either produced or actually used firearms in committing those offences. That was why the Squad had dealt with those cases, for all the other robberies not involving firearms (robbery is theft accompanied by violence, or threats of violence) committed in London during those same three months had been dealt with by the detectives of the local police districts rather than by the Flying Squad.

Quite apart from all that, however, the Squad was also carrying out its other role throughout those three months – that of tracking down, keeping observation upon and mounting countless operations aimed at arresting the armed robbers *before* they could actually carry out their planned raids. And it was in connection with that aspect of their duties that the Squad officers were constantly, almost upon a day-today basis, being brought into direct confrontation with armed criminals.

One inevitable response to such crime had been the increased issue of firearms to those officers. For the officers of the Flying Squad, whose exclusive role it is to deal with such crime and criminals, the issue of firearms was a daily occurrence. Police officers are not obliged to carry police firearms; they have the right to refuse to do so, and only those who volunteer are trained in the use of firearms. As an ex-serviceman myself I can assure you that their training in the use of the type of firearms which they do carry on occasions is excellent, and certainly equals that which I received with Her Majesty's Royal Marines in 1946 and 1947. What is more, they receive regular re-training several times each year.

The carrying of firearms by certain *trained* police officers is I think something which the public now accepts as an unfortunate necessity. But equally the public reacts with great concern whenever mistakes occur, as in the Waldorf shooting, and that concern is shared by all policemen. They do not themselves wish to carry fire-arms. But they realise that some among them must do so, if they are to tackle armed criminals, otherwise they simply would not be able to make arrests.

It is also true to say, however, that for as long as police officers are required to carry firearms then there will also be occasions when they will have to use them, either to protect themselves or others against armed criminals. Yet it has been my experience that whenever a police officer has had to use a firearm in such circumstances the incident invariably attracts immediate public debate and speculation. And all too often, in some quarters, immediate condemnation and vociferous outrage.

Unfortunately, that kind of reaction is also, on many occasions, based upon ill-informed and hasty judgements. I can recall several such occasions when an outcry raised on the day of the incident has died away completely within a few hours, once the true facts have become known. The truth is policemen are *not* trigger-happy coppers – they are simply ordinary, decent men doing their best in what can be a very dangerous job.

Police officers are like any other person. They are human and they can make mistakes. Usually, in dealing with armed men in direct confrontation it is split-second judgement which is required. They are trained for that and trained well, and in my opinion, when one considers the number of occasions when our policemen do come into direct confrontation with armed men, often desperate men, one realises just how effective police training really is.

Whilst we have armed criminals roaming at large and committing armed crime we must also have armed policemen to deal with them. I personally see no alternative and I feel for those present and future policemen who must undertake that dangerous task for society. If those critics who so strongly oppose the carrying of firearms by police could offer some other truly effective alternative then I think every police-man in this country would listen with rapt attention. And if it worked, they would feel great relief.

But I digress. Back in early 1983 and after a rather hectic beginning to my first three months with the Squad, it was, I suppose, too much to hope for that the Easter Bank Holiday would be uninterrupted. All the same, it was a disappointment when, around teatime on Bank Holiday Monday, 4 April 1983, whilst I was off duty at home, the telephone rang.

The vaults of the Security Express Ltd head office in London had been raided by a gang of armed men and emptied. The haul, I discovered later, was £6,375,000 in cash, certainly at that time the biggest ever single cash robbery in the world – and so far as I am aware it still remains so.

It was a meticulously planned crime. Normally the Security Express vaults at Curtain Road in Shoreditch, East London, would have remained closed over the Easter Bank Holiday, protected by sophisti-cated alarm systems. This particular Bank Holiday Monday, however, arrangements had been made for a special collection of moneys from elsewhere to be placed into the vaults and staff had been instructed to report for work in the morning or early afternoon to deal with it.

At first on that Monday all went as usual. At 7 a.m. the night security guard was relieved by the day supervisor. Three hours later this supervisor left the secure building by a back door and walked across the enclosed rear yard to the gatehouse. He wanted to make himself a cup of tea and to open up the gatehouse ready for the security van that would be arriving later.

As he walked across the yard he was attacked by a group of armed and masked men who had come over a wall and hidden behind large rubbish containers in one corner. He was held at gunpoint and blindfolded. Then he was forced to admit the robbers back through the alarm systems into the building that contained the vaults. The doors were then closed behind them and everything was made to look normal. For more than four hours the supervisor was then held at gunpoint and made to let in, as they arrived one by one, the seven other members of staff who were expected that day. The admittance procedure was as laid down by Security Express, and each of the newcomers entered the building totally unsuspectingly. Each was then grabbed by gunmen waiting inside, and tied up. By the time the last of them had arrived, among them personnel bringing with them the vault combinations, it was around 2.30 in the afternoon.

The robbers obtained the vault combinations by the simple expedient of pouring petrol on to the trousers of the men who could reveal them. A match was then struck, which would be applied to the petrol if access to the vaults without activating the alarm systems were not provided. Not surprisingly perhaps, the men capitulated and the vaults were opened without an alarm being raised.

All the staff were tied up and blindfolded. They heard the robbers moving trolleys to and fro, and at 3.30 p.m. the robbers left. Only one young man, who just happened to be passing by the premises, saw anything of their departure. Just as the electronically operated and very heavy rear gates in the yard were closing he saw a man running to avoid being trapped by them as they closed shut and saw him actually trapped momentarily, between the wall and the edge of the shutter, before struggling free to escape in a car which was waiting for him in the road outside.

The robbers had all escaped, however, and when later the alarm was raised and the first Flying Squad officers arrived at the building there was very little in the way of clues. It was an investigation which was destined to last many months and to become a perfect example of how the slow gathering together of apparently disconnected threads of evidence, which is so much a part of detective work, can pay off – with a bit of luck thrown in for good measure.

The robbers had all worn gloves, so there were no fingerprints, and the few footprints which were found suggested cheap rubber-soled shoes of a make and type which were widely available. The Security Express employees agreed that there had been at least five robbers in all, but they'd all been masked, so that facial descriptions could not be given. They'd been heard to speak with Irish brogues, but we knew those could well have been feigned.

When I arrived I arranged to set up an Incident Room at the nearby City Road police station, and decided a team of some fifty detectives of the Squad would take up the investigation. Our best lead at that time was that the criminals had obviously had inside information, so over the next few days searching enquiries were made into all the Security Express employees, in the hope of finding a 'mole'.

It was also of interest that only some four weeks before, on 9 March, an armoured vehicle based in those same Security Express premises and carrying more than one million pounds in cash had been attacked by six armed men while just a few hundred yards from Curtain Road. They'd blocked the roadway with what turned out to be a hired van, and hemmed the security vehicle in from behind with a car driven by one of the gunmen. They'd then fired a number of shots from a high-velocity carbine and a heavy revolver at the vehicle, trying to persuade its crew to open up. Some shots had penetrated the wind-screen, but fortunately had passed between the two men in the cab. The driver had reacted quickly and very bravely, ramming his way out of the trap and escaping with his valuable load intact.

This attack was still being investigated, and it interested me because it too showed all the signs of inside information: the thieves had obviously known about the high-value load and when and where to launch their attack. That attempt had failed and it was quite possible that the same gang, using the same 'mole', had tried again, this time upon the vaults themselves.

Despite the coincidence, however, we never did establish any connection between those two crimes. But a great deal of work was done in following up that possibility and it eventually connected with the seizure, by officers of HM Customs and Excise, of a large haul of cocaine at Heathrow Airport and thence led to the recovery by the Flying Squad of the very guns which had been used by the robbers upon the Security Express vehicle on 9 March.

Yet another possible lead involved the discovery by officers of another police force of a diagram upon which was described the vaults and alarm systems of what transpired to be a quite different high-security complex in another part of this country. A lot of work was done on this aspect of the enquiry and eventually we identified the author of the diagram and he was later convicted of conspiracy.

Later still yet another possible lead was also followed up when officers of the Yard's Drug Squad brought to our notice that on an occasion about a month before the Easter weekend, they had carried out an enquiry during the course of which they had discovered a group of men gathered together at a location in Ridley Road, Dalston. They had never established the purpose of that gathering and thought we should know about it.

That too was pursued by the Flying Squad officers and as a result observations were kept on a public house in Dalston. There, several men were seen to be meeting together on occasions, among them men named Hickson and Horsley, the latter the proprietor of a nearby garage, and connections were established between them and a man named Perkins.

But there was nothing whatsoever which at that time suggested they had anything to do with the Security Express robbery we were investigating.

In short, over a period of weeks and months, dozens of possible leads and lines of enquiry were painstakingly checked out and followed up, but all to no avail, and although a reward of £500,000 had been immediately offered by the insurers for information about the vault robbery, the result, in criminal jargon, was 'not a whisper'.

Meanwhile, of course, all the other work of the Flying Squad went on. In April and May of that year gangs of armed robbers were ambushed in London whilst carrying out armed attacks upon security vehicles and building society offices. In June an ex-policeman, Stephen Rudge, jumped on the back of a robber who was trying to escape with his accomplice on a motorbike after attacking a Security Express van in Old Street in East London. Rudge got his man down on the ground and refused to release him even when another accomplice threatened him with a gun. The gunman fired at him but the breech jammed. He cleared the jam and fired again, but miraculously the shot went wide. That gunman then attempted to ride off, but abandoned his motor bicycle as police officers closed in, and the robbers were both later arrested.

On the same day, in Southwark, there was another robbery with a different outcome, when a security guard was shot in the stomach before the robbers escaped with their haul. And so it went on. Four days later an armed gang stole jewellery worth six million pounds from a shop in Mayfair but this time men were arrested. Another Squad operation that month led to the arrest of an armed gunman, and yet another netted four men armed with knives as they were raiding a petrol filling station. In raids on two different London Post Offices shots were fired at the staff, but luckily the gunmen missed their targets.

The month of July was quieter. Robbery is a business like any other: the criminals were on holiday, some no doubt in Spain or the South of France. At any rate, it provided the Flying Squad with a welcome break since we were seriously over-stretched, with a quarter of our men still engaged on the Shoreditch vault enquiry.

August saw us back on the treadmill. Four robbers attacked a security van and killed one of the crew, blasting him with a shotgun at close range before escaping with more than eight thousand pounds. It happened outside Belsize Park tube station and in this case local police work paid off. Local district detectives had noticed men who were known to them loitering in that vicinity some days before, and this led to all four of them being arrested and charged, one of them with murder. It was a case dealt with by Detective Superintendent Don Brown, the man who'd captured David Martin at the same Belsize Park underground station in January. This time he was able to arrest four for the robbery and killing and five other people for harbouring the robbers after their crime.

What we could not do, however, was relieve the grief of the dead man's family.

Hardly a day passed without armed attacks somewhere in London. In one case an innocent passing witness to a robbery was shot in the leg, and in another four men armed with sawn-off shotguns and sledge-hammers were arrested by the Squad preparing to attack a British Telecom factory in Enfield. Then a jeweller and his wife were shot several times, very seriously wounded and robbed as they left their home in North London, and in another ambush operation a robber was prevented from shooting at the Squad officers arresting him only by the courage of Detective Sergeant Bulger who dived into the getaway car on top of the robber and jammed his thumb into the breech mechanism of the robber's gun to prevent him firing it. Three robbers were arrested.

But it seemed there were always more where those came from. In early October a robbery was planned upon the home in Hyde Park Gate of a director of a major international airline. Flying Squad detectives, alerted, kept watch. Eventually two men arrived, one dressed in police uniform and the other in a smart lounge suit. They walked up to the front door and rang the doorbell. The door was opened by the wife of the director and the two visitors identified themselves as police officers. At this point the Flying Squad officers pounced.

The bogus uniformed policeman had a forged search warrant in his pocket, handcuffs, and a knife. The second man, posing as a CID officer, was carrying a loaded revolver which he attempted to draw from its holster as he was overpowered. Police later found on him a plastic container of ammonia, a reel of masking tape, more handcuffs and another knife, and in his wallet a forged police warrant card.

Meanwhile other detectives had been watching movements in a

garden some fifty yards away down the road, and as the two bogus policemen were arrested two other men broke from cover. One of them was quickly arrested, but tried to throw away a pair of gloves and a loaded revolver. His companion escaped, but was captured later.

The use of a police uniform and false warrant cards to gain admittance was a cunning ploy. We'd been ahead of the criminals on this occasion, but no doubt things wouldn't always be that way.

And all this time our Shoreditch enquiries were coming up against the same blank wall: some men we wanted to interview had disappeared and our information had it that they'd 'gone abroad'. The country most often mentioned was Spain. So it came as a pleasant coincidence when in October I was invited by the principal of the Spanish Forensic Science Institute in Seville to go there to give a lecture on armed robbery and its investigation to a gathering of senior Spanish detectives. It seemed an excellent opportunity to make some contacts and to make some discreet enquiries so I accepted. I took my Flying Squad driver, Keith Banks, along with me so that after giving the lecture I'd be able to travel around a bit.

Question time after giving my lecture through an interpreter was a two-way affair, and produced some intriguing statistics. I asked my hosts how many armed robberies in Madrid they would have in a year. About two thousand, they told me. Ah, I said, about the same as in London. But apparently there'd been a misunderstanding. They shook their heads vigorously. Then the interpreter explained, they'd given me the figure for bank robberies only. I asked, 'What about attacks upon security vehicles?' 'None,' they said. I found that hard to believe, but the answer to them was simple: 'The guards carry guns, señor'.

The following day Keith Banks and I visited Spanish Police Headquarters in Marbella and later were taken on a conducted tour of the opulent waterfront at Puerto Banus. Sitting at a table outside Sinatra's Bar was rather like a trip through the photograph albums of known criminals at the Yard.

A day or so later we returned to London, but the trip had been successful for now I had met the detectives of Marbella and my impression was they were every bit as good at their job as we in London.

8

1984: THE BRINKS-MAT ROBBERY

By now progress in the Security Express vault robbery investigation was losing momentum. Every line of enquiry and every possible lead had been followed up and dozens of likely suspects checked out. The officers still engaged upon the enquiry had worked hard and relentlessly for many months but had simply been unable to get a positive lead or breakthrough. That is often in the nature of things in detective work and sometimes, after months of sustained effort, an enquiry can simply peter out because there is nothing left to follow up and nothing more to go on – that is unless something unexpected happens.

That was the situation with the Security Express vault investigation in November 1983. I had now kept the enquiry going for seven months because it represented a major challenge to the Squad and the force, in many ways similar to the challenges which had been presented by the Great Train Robbery in 1963.

In that case, however, they had at least found some fingerprints to help identify those involved but this time there was nothing – and that after seven months of hard work on the case.

It was clear a decision would soon have to be made whether or not to keep the enquiry going for the drain upon the manpower resources of the Flying Squad as a whole caused by that enquiry had been tremendous for most of 1983, and the officers engaged upon it were most sorely needed for other things.

I decided to keep it going nevertheless and then, as so often happens, other things intervened which served to divert my mind elsewhere.

Towards the end of that month my wife Bridget became unwell with a bout of influenza and took to bed. My sons, now all of course young men, had left home – two of them are now in the force – so Bridget was alone in the house. I decided to take a few days off work to look after her. My 'leave' started on the evening of Friday 25 November, and it was to last less than eighteen hours.

Next morning, just as I was getting ready to go out to do the weekend shopping, the telephone rang: 'It's another big one, Guv,' they told me. Apparently an armed gang had robbed the Brinks-Mat security warehouse at Heathrow, and the losses were likely to run into several millions. Flying Squad officers were already there at the warehouse investigating, but with a major robbery of that scale the responsibility for the investigation would be mine.

I called my driver to pick me up and then had a quick word with Bridget about the shopping and told her I would sort something out.

We drove straight to the Brinks-Mat warehouse in the Heathrow International industrial estate on Green Lane, on the far side of Hounslow.

When I got there men from Scotland Yard's fingerprint, forensic science and photographic branches were already in action – also officials of the Brinks-Mat company, who told me that the haul was mostly in gold, but with other property which altogether would probably be valued at more than £20 million. It was like a rerun of the Shoreditch robbery. My original caller had been right: this *was* another big one.

The gold, about three tons in weight, had been delivered to the warehouse on the previous day, ready to be moved in an armoured vehicle to Gatwick Airport on that Saturday morning. As well as the gold there'd been platinum, diamonds and travellers' cheques, all of which had been stored in the high-security vault together with a large amount of cash in banknotes which were held within three separately locked and alarmed safes within the vault.

To help shift this large amount of high-risk property six Brinks-Mat employees had been deputed to report to the warehouse at 6.30 on the Saturday morning, two of whom would have the information necessary to open the vault. The procedure was detailed and exact: one man with keys would unlock the front door to the warehouse, then switch off one part of the various alarm systems to allow companions to enter the building, and then relock the door and switch all the alarm systems back on again. Only then would he open a Security Control Room on the first floor which housed further alarm systems, then gain access to the vaulting area. Both this area and the vault itself were again alarmed separately from all other alarm systems, and the vault furthermore was fitted with a time lock. If procedures were carried out properly the security systems provided total protection.

However, those systems had been breached and when police arrived they found all six employees had been bound and blindfolded. They were interviewed separately and in great detail. Five of them had followed their reporting instructions exactly and had entered the warehouse together at 6.30 a.m. The sixth had turned up ten minutes late, and had been admitted then. For both entries the employee with the keys had operated the lock and the alarm systems.

The first five to arrive had gone upstairs together to a comfortable room on the first floor, equipped with tables and chairs, a sink unit and a cooker. They'd made tea. Next to this room was the Security Control Room. The man with the keys opened that, and then went down to admit the late arrival who'd announced his arrival at the front door. He relocked the door, switched on the alarm, and then both men went upstairs together to their companions. Within a very few minutes, while they were still chatting and drinking tea, three men – two of them masked and all carrying guns – burst in on them. The Brinks-Mat men were threatened and one of them was pistol-whipped across the head. Then they were all ordered to lie face down on the floor, their arms were tied behind their backs and linen bags were placed over their heads and tied at the neck.

Only two of the six employees possessed, between them, the information necessary to open the vault. These two men then had petrol poured over their upper legs and were threatened with burning if they did not help the robbers. One of them was also stabbed.

Having thus gained entry to the vault, the thieves took the gold, platinum, diamonds and travellers' cheques, but could not get into the separate safes which held the banknotes. The other Brinks-Mat men lay on the first floor, under the threat of a gun, listening to the robbers below moving about as they shifted the loot. Then one of the employees, named Black, had the blindfolding bag briefly removed from his head and was forced to operate the mechanism which opened a heavy metal rear roller shutter door giving access to the vehicle bays in the rear of the warehouse. As he did so Black saw a blue van and a man standing beside it. He was almost immediately blindfolded again and only allowed to see again when he was made to operate the mechanism yet again some minutes later.

At their departure the robbers left the Brinks-Mat staff handcuffed to metal pipes and other parts of the structure in the warehouse. Eventually one man was able to free himself and raise the alarm. The staff put the time of the robbers' departure at about 8 a.m.

Listening to all this my mind went back to the Shoreditch raid only seven months previously. There were remarkable similarities between the two crimes. In both cases staff had been held hostage and made to open vaults under duress by the threat of burning petrol and the production of firearms. In both cases the robbers obviously had detailed knowledge of staff procedures and the security alarm systems. In both cases the robbers had known that the premises would be manned and operating at an unusual time over a weekend period and would contain a huge haul. And in both cases the criminals had left very little in the way of clues – for although we did find a sheet of paper lying on the ground in the Brinks-Mat vehicle area which bore a tyre imprint upon it which didn't match any of the Brinks-Mat vehicles and there were the linen bags which had been used as blindfolds, there was little else to help us.

My first concern of course was to discover how the thieves had gained access to the warehouse. There was no sign of forcible entry and there was no way in other than through the locked front door with its various alarm systems, so the possibility had to be considered that the robbers had somehow got in during the previous day and had concealed themselves in the warehouse overnight. But a thorough search and check gave no indication of this either.

I also needed to see the Brinks-Mat employees myself, but by the time I arrived that morning they had all been taken to hospital for treatment to their injuries and for shock. Petrol can blister delicate skin quite seriously, and two of them were suffering from such burns, one of them badly.

Then, by late afternoon, the television and newspaper reporters were demanding a press conference. I had set up a mobile police station on the industrial estate in order to organise house-to-house enquiries, so I held it there. As I was arranging for this I suddenly remembered Bridget's shopping. I sent my driver out to the shops in Hounslow, which luckily were still open.

There were so many newspaper and television reporters present later that evening that some of them had to eavesdrop from outside. I didn't have very much to tell them. I described the boxes which had contained the gold and made an appeal for anyone who had been in the vicinity at the time of the robbery to come forward – in particular, any motorists who had driven along Green Lane, the road giving access to the warehouse, in the early hours of that Saturday morning. Apart from this I simply gave the media a broad account of the day's events.

It had been a long day. By the time all the officers involved in the investigation had been debriefed and their tasks set for the next morning it was well after midnight. In fact, by the time I arrived home with the shopping it was almost two in the morning.

Next morning, Sunday, the second day of my 'holiday', I left home at seven. Bridget told me she was feeling much better, but I knew that was only for my benefit. I spent that day between Hounslow police station, where I'd set up an Incident Room, and the mobile police station at the scene of the crime. In particular I studied the lengthy statements taken the day before from the men who'd been taken to hospital.

All Brinks-Mat employees are heavily vetted, but it seemed to me that someone must have assisted the robbers or supplied information to help them get into the warehouse. I therefore ordered detailed enquiries into the Brinks-Mat employees' backgrounds, friends, associates, and general lifestyle. I didn't expect any quick results, since those enquiries needed to be conducted with discretion so that we would not alert anyone if we were proved to be right.

The statement of the man called Black, however, was immediately of special interest. He was the man who'd arrived late at the warehouse – he said he'd overslept – and he was the one who'd been chosen to let the van in through the steel shutters. He also admitted something that not all his companions had mentioned – that he'd gone downstairs again to use the toilet almost immediately after he'd arrived, while all the others were still drinking their tea on the first floor. He'd gone down alone, and I now knew that the toilets on the ground floor were at the other end of a short corridor just inside the locked main door, in fact only a few feet from it. This in itself meant very little, since the man with the key to that door had still been upstairs with his keys, but it was at least a point to bear in mind. No other door could have been used by the robbers and there was no other way they could have got in, so only Black and the man who claimed to have relocked the door earlier could possibly have had anything to do with helping the robbers, unless there was some other explanation which we were not yet aware of.

Meanwhile there were other aspects of the enquiry to pursue – in particular, the whereabouts of the gold. That amount of gold, especially when all clearly identifiable as this was, isn't easy to dispose of. There were six thousand gold bars in all, each weighing either a kilo, half a kilo, or slightly less than four ounces, and most of them clearly stamped with a number and other markings. I was no expert in gold marketing or dealing, but the Company Fraud Squad had a man who was, Detective Inspector Smith, so I quickly arranged to have him transferred temporarily to my team. It was clearly of vital importance that, before the robbers could have a chance to get the bullion on to a legitimate gold market, details of it and of the robbery be circulated round all the official gold markets of the world and to all bullion dealers. We did so immediately and that was to pay excellent dividends, but not until much later. And meanwhile, to make it even more difficult for the thieves to dispose of their loot, the insurers also announced a two million pound reward to anyone providing information which led to the recovery of the stolen property and the arrest of those responsible. Such a huge reward, one would think, was bound to bring results and it did, but not the results we were seeking.

In fact it brought a deluge of calls from people wanting to give advice or to give information about robbery teams, but none of it turned out to be useful.

On the Monday morning after the robbery we blanketed the area around the industrial estate and Green Lane, stopping motorists and pedestrians – and in particular tradesmen such as milkmen and postmen – to ask them if they'd seen anything unusual there on the previous Friday night or early Saturday morning. This enquiry lasted forty-eight hours and produced good results. Several witnesses had seen a transit van, either blue or green and possibly with another similar vehicle, parked near the Brinks-Mat warehouse earlier than 6.30 on the Saturday morning, and one passing motorist had seen them being driven in the vicinity at about 6.15 a.m. Another vehicle, 'an old box-type van', had been seen heavily laden, leaving Green Lane at around 8 a.m., the time when the robbers must have been carrying off the stolen gold, and that appeared to marry up with the sighting of a similar vehicle on the industrial estate late on the Friday night.

None of these descriptions were detailed, but the majority of witnesses believed one of the two transit vans to have been blue, and one witness was able to give a partial registration number for the box-van seen in Green Lane. Vague as it was, we now had at least something to go on. We needed to trace those vehicles, either to eliminate them from the enquiry or to establish where they were now. A day or so later we also discovered that Black, the Brinks-Mat employee, had a sister who went around with a man known to the police and this was another matter to be delved into.

But one major robbery, no matter how serious, doesn't bring the rest of London's crime to a halt and on that Monday and Tuesday two other Flying Squad teams had been carrying out quite separate operations.

On the Monday one team tailed and arrested four men in the city of Oxford in possession of three stolen motor vehicles, and on the Tuesday another team followed a man to Oxford where they arrested him in a car with two other people, finding a sawn-off shotgun in the car, ammunition, and a ski mask. Both these operations resulted in charges of conspiracy and neither case had any connection with the other. That they both involved Oxford was pure coincidence.

As a result of those other enquiries and a development in one which suddenly required my personal attention I was obliged at the last minute to put off a second Brinks-Mat press conference, which was to be held on the Monday, until the following day. Understandably this upset the waiting newsmen, but the last-minute postponement had been unavoidable and I could not tell them the reasons for it. Even so, the next day when the conference was held at the Yard some of the reporters present appeared not to accept the apology I made to them, and the situation was not helped by the fact that I had little else I could tell them anyway. What I did know, or suspected, I had to keep back for fear of alerting the robbers. I was able to describe the vehicles we were looking for, however, and I made an appeal for help from the public at that conference. Shortly before the conference was actually held we were suddenly asked to produce a photograph of a transit van for the benefit of the cameramen at the conference, so we hurriedly obtained one from a car showroom nearby. Unfortunately the transit shown was red in colour rather than blue. There simply was no time to obtain another photograph so I used that at the conference, but I explained why and I emphasised that the van involved in the crime had been blue in colour. But somehow there was a muddle and the actual photograph I had produced was shown later that evening on the TV news programme without the presenter telling the viewers that the van we were looking for was blue. So every viewer that evening was left with the belief the police were looking for a red transit. It was to prove a mistake of some importance.

Over that weekend the press had its own problems. Because of an industrial dispute most of the nationals had been off the newsstands, some until the Wednesday – the day after that press conference – so possibly their impatience was understandable. But when they did finally publish the story of the Brinks-Mat robbery in their papers they gave it all they'd got. And not in the friendliest manner.

The *Sun*, for example, hadn't gone to press until the Wednesday. They had been represented at the press conference and on the Wednesday morning they featured this editorial:

SHAME OF OUR MEN AT THE YARD

'Send for the Yard!' in the days of Sherlock Holmes and Bulldog Drummond, that phrase used to chill the hearts of criminals.

Today, the sad truth is that it is more likely to reduce them to helpless laughter.

A harsh verdict? Consider Scotland Yard's hapless, bumbling performance over the £27 million bullion robbery.

Imagine the frenzy of activity there would have been among the guardians of law and order in the United States, France, or any other major country if the crime of the century had been committed on THEIR patch.

When it happens here, there is about as much urgency as if someone had booked the Commissioner's car for illegal parking. Days pass. Leisurely Press conferences are held to keep in touch.

Mysterious figures, like the Colonel, who is supposed to be the robbery mastermind, flit through the inquiries.

The Colonel is said to have been the man behind the earlier £3 million Security Express hold-up last Easter.

HE is still at large.

ALL the £27 million gang are still at large.

There are no arrests, apparently no clues.

A massive consignment of gold has vanished as completely as a feather in a hurricane.

And it is not just major crime that is a major scandal today. Only 16 per cent of ALL cases are being solved in London.

This means that four in five criminals get away with it.

PARADISE

The nation's capital has become a paradise for every would-be burglar, mugger and sneak thief who cares to try his hand.

The buck stops at Sir Kenneth Newman, the Metropolitan Commissioner.

He is concerned about the image of his Force.

If he does not want to see public trust and confidence vanish altogether, he must act NOW.

We need better detective methods. And we certainly need better detectives.

LET'S have an end of the gentlemen police officers who cut a dashing figure at Chamber of Commerce dinners.

LET'S have in their place some old-fashioned cops who know about crooks, and where to find them.

LET'S have cops who may cuss a bit and even throw their weight around occasionally, but also actually get things done.

The joke is on Sir Kenneth Newman. What does he intend to do about it?

I've reproduced the article in full so as to demonstrate the truth of the well-known claim that policemen need to have broad shoulders. They certainly do. After all, we were only four days into the investigation when it was published.

Later that week, when Brinks-Mat felt they could allow us to use their warehouse for the purpose, and when all the six employees present at the robbery could be made available, I mounted a reconstruction of the crime at the warehouse. At the suggestion of one Squad officer, Detective Inspector Brightwell, we made a full video film recording of the reconstruction and that film proved invaluable, for it vividly demonstrated that the man Black had lied to police in the written statement he had made at Hounslow police station on the day of the robbery. In his statement he'd described how he'd dived to the floor of the Control Room as the robbers burst in, guns in hand. We had meanwhile established that he had reached the floor split seconds before another of the employees in the Control Room with him and now the reconstruction and film revealed that from his position in the Control Room on the morning of the robbery he could not have seen the robbers as he claimed, for he had been behind the Control Room door. It was our first break, and just a tiny one, but enough to justify detaining him at Hounslow police station for further questioning. And from such acorns do oak trees grow.

Black was a young dark-haired ex-serviceman, clean cut, smart and a fellow with a friendly open face, outwardly not at all a man you'd expect to throw in his lot with violent criminals. But even so, faced with the lie he'd told and his suspiciously timed visit to the toilet on the morning of the raid, he eventually admitted to Inspector Brightwell and Sergeants Benwell and Branch that he'd been involved in 'setting up' the robbery.

He'd worked briefly for Brinks-Mat before, back in 1977, and then resumed again from 1979. At one time he'd been living in East London and working at a Brinks-Mat depot nearby. His sister knew a man called Brian and as soon as this man heard where Black worked he began to show interest in his hours of work and duties and in the construction of the security vehicles his employers used. Brian was persuasive, and finally Black agreed to bring him Polaroid photographs of a Brinks-Mat security van, taken from the inside. This he did and Brian was pleased.

Black now came on to the present Brinks-Mat robbery and the account he gave was one he was to tell again many months later, as a witness at the Old Bailey. In late 1981 Black married, moved to Hounslow and asked his employer for a transfer to the nearby Brinks-Mat Green Lane depot so that he would be working close to home. Brinks-Mat agreed to this. Black soon discovered that his new job sometimes involved collecting large amounts of money and bank-notes from airline flights arriving at Heathrow, and when Brian heard of this he was immediately interested. He wanted to know what sort of amounts were left in the warehouse overnight, and asked if it was possible for someone to sneak in behind a security van as it was entering through the rear shutter doors of the warehouse late in the evening, without being seen. Black told him there wasn't a hope. He also told Brian that consignments of gold, jewels and travellers' cheques were often held overnight on Friday nights to be delivered on the Saturday morning.

Later Black met Brian and two other men after dark outside a garage at Bedfont. The men asked him a whole series of questions about the workings of the warehouse – some of these he was unable to answer, but he promised he'd find out what they needed to know in a couple of days or so. From then on these clandestine meetings became quite frequent, during which Black gave the men details of every aspect of the warehouse security systems. He also took a camera to work, so that he was able to supply them with pictures of the doors, the vault, the staircases, and everything else which would be useful. And he drew a plan of the warehouse layout.

At one of the meetings a man called Mick gave him a piece of cuttlefish and showed him how to take an impression of a key. With some difficulty Black gained possession of the warehouse keys for long enough to take impressions as he'd been shown, but when the copied keys came back from Mick they didn't fit. Soon afterwards all the locks and the alarm systems were to be changed at the warehouse anyway.

Now Brian said the best way was for Black to borrow the front-door key long enough for proper copies to be made. Black was able to lift the key from an office and hand it over to Brian and Mick in the car park of a nearby pub. They got the keys back to him within fifteen minutes. He returned the original safely to the warehouse office but wasn't able to try the copy in the door until the following day. The key didn't fit properly so he rubbed it down with emery paper until it did.

The preparations now complete, it was decided the robbery would take place at the next opportunity. The date was not decided upon until 5.30 on the afternoon of Friday 25 November 1983, when Brinks-Mat told Black to report for work next morning at 6.30. He contacted Brian at once by telephone and the four men held a final meeting that evening. Asked what would be in the vault overnight, Black said he didn't know, but when pressed for an estimate he made a guess of possibly two million pounds' worth of gold or jewellery.

I had until that time assumed that the criminals who had robbed the warehouse had known in advance what their haul would be and probably had a 'buyer' for the gold already lined up. But, if what Black was now saying was true then they had obviously stumbled upon a far bigger haul than they had been expecting, so in some ways they now had difficulties. Black went on to describe how at that Friday evening meeting it was agreed he would show himself at the warehouse door the next morning to indicate it was safe to carry out the planned robbery. The members of the gang would be waiting outside and after they'd seen him at the door inside the warehouse they'd wait another two or three minutes before entering, with the key he'd provided.

Black spent the rest of that Friday evening quietly at home with his wife. Next morning, and quite incredibly I thought, he'd genuinely overslept and had then rushed off late for work. As he arrived he saw a transit van standing at the far end of the road from the warehouse, but the light was poor and he couldn't be sure of the colour. From then on the plan had gone ahead as arranged. He'd been let into the warehouse, found an excuse to go downstairs alone and had shown himself at the front door. Then he'd returned upstairs. The robbers had burst in and from that stage treated him exactly like all the other staff members – except that when he'd been lying tied up one of the raiders had apparently whispered to him, 'We've got the lot.'

Black went on to say that although he'd been promised payment for what he'd done no precise amount had ever been mentioned. Brian and his friends had simply said he must stay in his Brinks-Mat job, and they'd fix it for him to be paid as soon as they could. One of the reasons they gave for this was that the gold had had to be buried somewhere until arrangements could be made for its safe disposal.

His interview with Brightwell took several hours. When it was over he asked to see me for he was worried about the safety of himself and his wife. I could only tell him that we'd make sure his wife was safe, but he would appear in court charged with the robbery.

At first light next morning Flying Squad officers arrested three other men. Eventually they appeared at Feltham magistrates' court and were remanded in custody. A day or so later identification parades were held and two of the men were identified by some of the Brinks-Mat employees who had been tied up and robbed. One was also recognised by his voice.

In the run-up to Christmas that year and against a relentless background of many other armed robberies in and around London, we pressed on with the case. It wasn't a time when the Flying Squad officers had much opportunity to do their Christmas shopping. I was meanwhile still looking for the gold and the vehicles used by the robbers.

Then, on New Year's Day, 1984, an officer of the uniform branch, PC McQuirns of G Division, away on the opposite side of London from the robbed warehouse, noticed a blue transit van parked in Hilborough Road, Dalston, at the junction of Albion Drive. He found that the chassis number didn't check with the registration number shown on the vehicle. According to the chassis number it should have been bearing a registration number CLO 421T but instead it bore VLO 734X. The latter number was in fact allocated to an identical blue transit van owned by a company in Leyton. This vehicle, however, now with the false numberplates on it, had been stolen several months before, during the night, from outside a house about a mile away, in Bethnal Green. Someone had chosen carefully, it seemed to me, for one of those transit vans had been in legitimate use by its lawful owners quite recently in the Hounslow area.

It is an old villain's trick. If an inquisitive policeman had by chance checked out the registration number on the stolen vehicle by radio on the day of the robbery, for example, then he'd have been told the registration number on it was allocated to a blue transit and it would all appear to be quite in order. And in fact that trick had worked in this case. Several weeks before, on the very night after the robbery, a rather less alert policeman had checked the number on that vehicle, after it had been dumped in Dalston, but had decided everything was in order. The van had stayed there ever since, whilst we on the Squad were hunting for it, not knowing what registration number to look for.

Now however, the van was examined by the Yard's forensic experts, who found that one of the tyre treads was an exact match with the tyre print we had found on the piece of paper in the loading bay of the Brinks-Mat depot on the day of the robbery. Further tests of sweepings taken from the floor in the back of the van revealed traces of sealing wax identical to that used on the boxes of stolen gold. In addition, a footprint found in the van was identical to one found in the warehouse. Clearly the van had been used to carry away the gold and probably the rest of the stolen property.

It now came to light that at about 2 a.m. on the morning after the robbery, the Sunday, a man living in Albion Drive, Dalston had seen the blue van being parked by two men who had left it and were then driven away in a saloon car by a third man. The man had reported what he'd seen to the local police but the connection was missed.

So we now had the vehicle used in the robbery. But we were still no nearer to finding the gold. Except that, since the thieves had risked driving the stolen van which had been used to move the gold all the way across London from Hounslow to Dalston, it seemed to me there was a fair chance they'd dropped off the loot somewhere in or near the Dalston area before getting rid of the van – for all the time they had that vehicle in their possession, even after removing the gold from it, they had been at risk from a routine check by police. An East London connection was therefore suggested. I was still, of course, expecting to find a link between this robbery and the Security Express vault raid back in April, because the two cases had both been major vault robberies and were very similar in the manner they had been committed, and because of the scale of the losses.

I then realised that the street in Dalston in which the van had been dumped was less than a mile or so away from the Security Express vaults in Shoreditch and that the public house which had been under observation by the Flying Squad when we'd been watching the man Hickson and his friends some months earlier in connection with the Security Express robbery, albeit simply as vague suspects, was only a few yards from where the van had been found.

With all that in mind I now conferred with Detective Chief Inspector Peter Wilton, who had been following up the Security Express vault robbery ever since Easter 1983 and whose officers had carried out the earlier public house observations in Dalston. He reminded me that the man Horsley, one of the men who'd been under observation at the public house, also ran a garage business just around the corner, in Malvern Road, also just a few yards from where the Brinks-Mat van had been found. It was clear this needed to be followed up quickly so Peter Wilton arranged for a team of officers to interview Horsley and search his garage.

The search of the garage produced some cans of oil or paint which became the subject of a police enquiry, but nothing else of significance, but then Horsley was also questioned about moneys which he'd recently come into possession of and he was detained for further questioning. Then, suddenly, Horsley blurted out that the garage of his home address in Waltham Abbey, Essex, had been used to store the money which had been stolen from the Security Express vaults.

Now, Peter Wilton quickly organised the arrest of the two other men, Perkins and Hickson, who had been seen previously with Horsley in the Albion Drive public house. Their questioning led to further arrests, those of Perkins' wife and a man named Knight.

Horsley, meanwhile, had directed Wilton to another address in Waltham Abbey, the home of an elderly relative of his, where a secret compartment was found built into the back of a cupboard. In the compartment were several box files, and bundles of banknotes which added up to £279,000. One of Wilton's men, Detective Constable Jeffery, was then given the mammoth task of collating the serial numbers on these banknotes after they'd been checked for fingerprints in an attempt to prove a connection with the Security Express robbery. Wilton also noticed a list of figures scribbled on the back of the panel which gave access to the secret compartment, apparently representing a tally of moneys already removed from the cache.

Now we were busy on two fronts. We had the van used in the Brinks-Mat robbery and had arrested several people for that robbery and now others in connection with the earlier Security Express raid.

In the Security Express case the police questioning of Horsley suggested that on the night of the Security Express vault robbery, in April 1983, two men had unloaded a number of large and heavy sacks of money into Horsley's garage in Waltham Abbey and later, a day or so, had removed them again in a white van. Wilton followed this up very quickly with his officers.

A check by the Flying Squad officers of every van-hire agency in North London produced a white van of similar description which had been hired from a firm in Palmers Green on 6 April, two days after the Shoreditch robbery, and returned the following morning. The man hiring the van had given his name as Opiola, and the connection led back to Knight and Perkins, for the address he'd given was that of M & M Bodyworks, a business with which we knew they were both connected.

Once detained, Opiola quickly admitted his involvement with the Security Express vault robbery in Shoreditch and later gave his story as a witness in court. Knight and Perkins had asked him to hire the van for them, and then they'd asked him to make sure his wife went away, leaving their address for a day or so. He persuaded her to stay with her family. That same evening Knight and Perkins had arrived at his home in the hired white van, out of which they had unloaded five or six large sacks, some too heavy to be lifted by one man. These were dragged one by one into the house and dumped upstairs in a bedroom. Opiola had already read of the robbery, but it was only now, when the sacks were opened, that he realised he was knee-deep in its spoils.

The whole evening was spent by those two men sorting and counting the money. At one point Opiola went out to buy a Chinese takeaway meal for the other two: when he left they were busy counting, and when he returned they were still counting. In fact they continued working all night, and by the morning he said one wall of the bedroom was stacked four feet high and three feet wide with banknotes, all in denominations of between five pounds and fifty.

Now, after he'd made coffee, Opiola was asked to provide suitcases, so he produced the only two he had. He was worried by now because workmen were expected at his address, by prior arrangement and any minute, to do some redecorations downstairs and he wanted Knight and Perkins out of the way. But they were unwilling to leave, so when the workmen arrived Opiola told them to work downstairs, but make as little noise as possible, explaining that he had relatives staying who were asleep. He also telephoned his wife, asking her to stay away for another night.

Later that morning Opiola was sent out to buy four more suitcases fitted with strong straps, and after dark that night and another full day of counting and sorting all six cases, crammed with the money, were taken away by Perkins and Knight. Still more money remained in Opiola's house, however, and before his wife's return he hid it in the loft. Perkins and Knight took some of it away later and the rest, some £60,000, Opiola himself 'laundered' by passing it through a number of bank accounts in North London.

Things were now going reasonably well for us and, since we'd been able to work out that the suitcases Opiola had described had probably held no more than a third at most of the total Security Express money stolen, we guessed there could still be at least four or perhaps even more robbers at liberty with their shares of the ill-gotten gains. But that took no account of the more recent Brinks-Mat robbery and the total stolen in those two crimes alone was, we knew, around £33 million in all. We had no reason to feel complacent, therefore, and our investigations remained as intensive as ever.

9

1984: GOLD

In all, bad as the robbery situation involving the use or production of firearms (the Flying Squad's special preserve) had been in 1983, it had at least been reduced that year in London by some thirty per cent or more against the Squad's case load for 1982. Obviously we would all have liked to see that downward trend continue, but I had to admit that this was highly unlikely. That was now one of my major concerns for not only were the two big robbery cases of the previous year still absorbing large numbers of Flying Squad men, but a further reorganising of the force during 1983 – designed to get more men back on the beat, an aim I couldn't altogether disagree with in one sense – was now facing me with a loss of some fifteen Flying Squad detective officers. There was also talk of a substantial reduction in the number of specially trained Flying Squad drivers attached to the Squad and I knew those two reductions could prove crippling to the Squad's efforts, for about one third of the Squad's total strength was now tied up on the two vault robberies.

There were other problems as well, for a disturbing feature emerging towards the end of 1983 had been a growth in the number of attacks upon GPO security vehicles and this had continued into 1984, so that by the end of February 1984, out of a total of forty-one armed attacks upon security vehicles in London, twelve had involved GPO vans. And attacks upon the post offices themselves were also beginning to increase again. One man in particular – who quickly became known as 'the man in black' on account of his all-black clothing and who always worked alone – had been responsible for many armed robberies upon London post offices. He had seriously injured several GPO employees, and more recently he had sought to improve his robbery technique by discharging smoke grenades to cover his getaway, and he had teamed up with a colleague.

Now however, on 11 March, he over-reached himself. Working with another man, he shot at and wounded a policeman, then took a family hostage at gunpoint and drove with them through Sussex and on into Hampshire. When he was finally cornered and arrested the gun in his possession linked him firmly with fourteen earlier 'man in black' offences, committed over a period of four years, and he was removed from society for a long time.

Meanwhile, since October 1983, because I had been unable to devote sufficient Flying Squad officers specifically to the new GPO security vehicle threat, I had enlisted the help of another of my branches at the Yard, the London Regional Crime Squad. With their sixty-plus experienced and mobile detective officers they were able to make a number of arrests in London and Essex and had carried out invaluable work in 'the man in black' case. And in January 1984, they had arrested two men for the dishonest handling of certificates of deposit, valued at £5.5 million, stolen during a bank raid in the City of London in 1983. Then, with help from the Criminal Intelligence Branch, on 20 March 1984, they not only ambushed and arrested a group of armed men as they attacked a security vehicle making a BBC payroll delivery in Duchess Street, W1, but they also managed to have the whole incident filmed. Thus the jury which finally dealt with those robbers was treated to a ring-side seat to help them reach their decision.

Film cameras were also set up when on 23 March, only three days later, one of the Flying Squad teams laid in ambush to capture robbers who had planned an armed attack as money was being delivered to a factory in Downs Park Road, Hackney, by a security vehicle crew.

In this case the thieves did good advance planning, and put in a lot of hard work. On the night before the planned attack two men and a woman cordoned off an area in the roadway directly in front of the factory with some road cones taken apparently from a local authority site. Early the next morning their plan was interfered with slightly when one of the factory employees moved some of the cones when he arrived for work, so that he could park his car. The Squad officers already in position watched this occur. Now, when the two male robbers arrived, dressed as council workmen, with picks and shovels, and a sawn-off shotgun hidden in a toolbag, they had to make do with a rather smaller area of operations. Even so, the younger man began to dig up the road and to swing his pick energetically – so much so that the factory employee, who must have seen this, returned to his car and moved it some distance down the road to what he obviously considered a safer place. And so the morning wore on, the younger robber loosening the tarmac and shovelling it neatly to one side. The Squad officers continued to watch and wait and their filming was maintained.

Quite by chance the van due to deliver the payroll that morning was unusually delayed and was already an hour late. The younger 'workman' however laboured on. Time passed and the hole in the road deepened. After a while the two men conferred together rather nonplussed and looked anxiously up and down the road for the missing security van. Then, surreptitiously, they started filling in the hole again. From then on, filmed all the while, the younger man's task was to shovel the same pile of soil in and out of the same hole.

Finally, over two hours late, the security vehicle arrived. As it drew to a halt beside the line of cones outside the factory the older thief reached for the shotgun in his toolbag. At last his patience would be rewarded. But his hand never reached the shotgun for at that moment the Flying Squad officers reached him and the weapon remained safely where it was, in the bag. So yet again the trial jury had a film to help them.

Not all crimes are so successfully prevented however. For example, in late 1983 and in early 1984 some post-office robbers were adopting a new technique which was rather harder to counter. On four occasions in 1983, in Hackney, Forest Gate, Hornsey and Hammersmith, teams of armed men had broken into post-office premises overnight, concealed themselves inside and then ambushed members of the staff when they arrived in the morning to open up. In every case men and women were held at gunpoint and forced to unlock the post-office safes. March 1984 saw two further postmasters, in East Ham and Plumstead, who lived with their families over the premises, held at gunpoint overnight until the time locks on the safes allowed them to be opened in the morning. And in May, a postmistress was attacked in a similar manner by gunmen in London and forced to open the safe.

And still the eternal round of armed robbery and shooting in London continued. Shots were fired at Flying Squad officers during a high-speed chase, men were arrested in possession of an appalling selection of revolvers, shotguns, knives, coshes and other weapons and by 12 May, in addition to all the successful ambush operations carried out and the one hundred or more arrests made, the Flying Squad had investigated attacks upon 122 security vehicles, 66 armed attacks on banks, 131 upon post offices, 170 upon building societies, 146 upon betting shops, and 411 upon other types of commercial premises – a total of 1,068 in four months, all committed in the London Metropolitan Police area and all involving the use or production of firearms.

There were many other similar robberies in London which were dealt with by the local detectives, because the Squad could not cope with the numbers of such offences being committed – and that is to say nothing of all the other violent robberies, not involving firearms, which the Squad does not deal with.

By now, in the Brinks-Mat case, the security guard Black had been brought for trial at the Old Bailey, in February 1984, found guilty of being an accomplice in the robbery, and had been sent to jail for six years. The three other men charged were awaiting trial. The Security Express case, too, was developing and a number of people were now awaiting trial: four had been charged with the robbery itself, four with dishonestly handling the proceeds, and three with conspiring to pervert the course of justice. One of these men, Opiola, pleaded guilty to dishonestly handling the proceeds, was tried on 14 May and was sent to jail for three years and three months.

In the Security Express case many of the leads pointed overseas and to Spain in particular. It was time now to follow up some of the contacts I'd made during my own visit to that country in 1983, so a small team of Flying Squad officers travelled there in an attempt to trace at least some of the stolen money. It soon became clear that several Britons resident in Spain or with interests in Portugal had recently come into large amounts of money which had been invested either in property or placed into bank deposits.

Some of their names and family connections in London we knew only too well, but there was little we could do about it for we could not have them extradited. Even so, we did eventually reckon we'd found out where at least two million pounds of the stolen Security Express money had gone.

The Flying Squad's enquiries in Spain then stirred up another, quite different storm. They provided the basis for a cover story and feature article in the Spanish magazine *Tiempo* on 2 July 1984, which mistakenly reported that the British police were at that time seeking men in Spain who had been responsible for the Brinks-Mat robbery – an error which was picked up and repeated at once by our British newspapers and TV. This raised quite a furore, and a lot of ill-informed debate about the efficiency or otherwise of the Spanish police and their lack of co-operation with the British police in dealing with those British criminals who had sought refuge in their country. Much of that criticism was totally unfounded and unfair to the Spanish police, but it did bring to official attention the lack of an extradition treaty between the two countries – and that, I suspect, led in turn to the extradition treaty which was eventually signed in 1986.

The mistaken assumption that Flying Squad men had been follow-ing up the Brinks-Mat robbery in Spain, on the other hand, didn't worry us. If the criminals really thought we'd shifted our enquiries, so much the better.

Then came June 1984, which proved to be just about the worst month of the entire two years I spent with the Squad. Wednesday 13 June that year was marked by a particularly vicious and futile killing. It was at a small general store in Enfield where a young Asian woman sitting alone behind the shop till was mercilessly shot down by a man with a shotgun.

And the motive, the contents of the till, amounted to less than thirty pounds. Detective Superintendent Ron Chapman handled the enquiry and, with very little to go on, managed to arrest the murderer a week or so later, recovered his weapon, and charged him, and eight other people with harbouring and assisting him after the murder.

And then, two days after that young woman's death, my breakfast at home was interrupted by a phone call: during an armed operation I had authorised for that morning two robbers had been shot and wounded. I went to the scene of the incident immediately.

It was a post office in Seven Sisters Road, North London. Several days before an alert woman counter clerk had reported to her super-visor that she thought the building was being watched, and the supervisor had wisely reported the matter to the local police station. They in turn called in the Flying Squad who kept watch outside the post office and agreed that there were indeed two men hanging around suspiciously. The two men even followed the counter clerk for a distance, on foot, on two successive mornings, as she made her way to work, before driving off in a motor car.

Detective Inspector McLean was in charge of the investigation. He conferred with the local Detective Inspector Craig, and they realised that the following day, Thursday, would be 'pensions day', and the post office would be holding overnight a larger amount of money than at any other time during the week. If there was to be a raid on the office, therefore, it seemed likely it would happen early on that Thursday morning.

As well as setting a police watch outside the post office it was decided to position Squad officers before the post office opened in the morning actually inside the building as well, so a flat upstairs with direct access to the post office, via an internal staircase, was made available for them. A door from this staircase opened directly into the post office itself, out

of which led two other doors, one the front door to the street and one to
a rear kitchen.

Before dawn on Thursday morning the watch began. Detective
Inspector Craig waited upstairs with a team of officers, two of whom,
Detective Sergeants May and Fry, were armed, and two further armed
policemen were deployed with other surveillance teams outside. The
firearms to be carried had been properly applied for and authorised.

Unknown to Inspector Craig, however, the would-be robbers were
in fact already on the premises. They had broken in at the back during
the night and under cover of darkness before the officers had arrived,
lifting the reinforced steel rear door off its hinges with a car-jack and
replacing it behind them so that from the outside all looked normal.
Once inside the kitchen they'd found that the further door through into
the post office itself was securely locked and bolted, so they'd decided
to wait quietly in the kitchen until post-office staff arrived and opened
the door.

At 7.55 a.m. the post-office supervisor arrived, unlocked the front
door, relocked it behind her, and went upstairs to confirm arrangements with Inspector Craig. They talked for a moment and then he
sent the two armed detective sergeants down with her to check out the
post office itself and then take up hiding places ready for when the
office opened.

She showed them round, then they stood behind her while she
unlocked the door into the rear kitchen, one of them leaning forward to
help pull back the bolts. The minute she turned the key the door was
yanked open from the other side. She described afterwards how she
saw a man appear in the open doorway, and how he immediately 'went
for the police officer'. Terrified, she turned and ran. Behind her she
remembered hearing a gunshot. In fact there were several.

The accounts given by Sergeants May and Fry shortly afterwards
agreed that as the supervisor went to open the door it was pulled out of
her hand. From their position behind and to one side of her they could
see straight through into the kitchen beyond. Two men were there who
at once rushed forward. There was a struggle in the very confined area
just outside the kitchen. One of the officers, thinking he saw the first
intruder fumbling for a gun, drew his police revolver and fired twice in
quick succession, hitting the nearest man with his second shot. When
the other policeman heard the shots he had no way of knowing in the
close quarter confusion who had fired them. He saw the second man
reaching for a hold-all which lay behind him on the kitchen floor and,
believing this to be an attempt to reach a firearm hidden in the bag, he

also fired. Silence descended. Both the would-be robbers were in-capacitated and cordite smoke drifted heavily in the air. It had all taken no more than a few seconds.

Detective Inspector Craig now burst into the post office from the flat above. Each of the robbers was suffering from a gunshot wound, but both were fully conscious. While others of his men cordoned off the whole area and calmed the supervisor, Craig took charge of the two sergeants' handguns and telephoned for an ambulance. That done, he called me at my home.

The two intruders were taken to hospital where they underwent emergency surgery. Both survived, but the more seriously injured man was partially paralysed.

They talked to me some time later in the presence of their solicitor when one admitted to the illegal entry and an intent to rob. But, as we already knew, they had been unarmed. Neither man had carried a gun, and the hold-all on the kitchen floor had contained nothing but their tools, the car-jack with which they had removed the rear door, and handcuffs they'd intended to use on the post-office staff. For once this was to have been a GPO robbery without use of firearms.

The two Squad officers' mistake was understandable however. Most GPO robberies being carried out at that time did involve the use of firearms, and there had been hundreds of these. A hold-all or toolbag is also the traditional means by which robbers conceal their sawn-off shotguns or other firearms when travelling to or from the scene of a planned robbery, so much so that a robber's hold-all is always referred to by Squad officers as 'the happy bag'. But the fact remained that two experienced police officers had shot down two unarmed men. An enquiry was mounted at once, led by the then deputy commissioner of the Metropolitan Police personally, who also visited the scene of the incident on the day it occurred.

Detective Sergeants May and Fry were eventually exonerated but the shooting had left them in deep shock and traumatised for a long time. Yet even when the public outcry which resulted was at its height I remember thinking to myself how very few people outside the police service itself had actually thought to ask me about them, or how they might be feeling.

When they want to, some newspapers have long memories. All the details of the 1983 Waldorf shooting were immediately rehashed, together with the all too familiar accusations that the London Metro-politan Police were 'cowboys', and too ill-trained and ill-equipped to carry firearms. On the other hand there was no mention whatever of the huge number of other successful and bloodless police operations involving the carrying of police firearms which had been and were being carried out, day after day, by the Flying Squad against armed criminals. Neither was it remembered that the two officers in question both had long records of similar but mistake-free and successful operations and that they had both in fact taken part in the Islington operations in January 1983 when none of the police weapons being carried had been fired, even when a colleague, Detective Sergeant Kelly, had been shot at by a criminal and injured. But then perhaps the press had not been aware of all those other police operations?

It was the National Federation of Sub-postmasters which stood up to support police. In the July 1984 edition of its official journal, *The Sub-Postmaster*, the editor wrote:

> The gunsmoke had hardly settled at the scene of the unfortunate incident at the Sub-post office in Seven Sisters Road, North London, before some politicians took it upon themselves to put the verbal boot into the body of the police force in general. The police have a dangerous, difficult job which is not made any easier by politicians who appear to relish undermining the credibility of the forces of law and order.
>
> Making political capital out of misfortune, whether it results from criminal action or from an accident, is obnoxious. If the politicians have no regard for all those policemen who protect them at the palace of Westminster they should release them for duty on the streets of the metropolis. The Sub-postmasters, shopkeepers and tradespeople of London would welcome the additional protection they would afford. Those at the sharp end of the crime wave know and appreciate the value of the man in blue. He is human, he can make mistakes, he can be good and he can be bad. But only he and the law stand between us and criminal anarchy.

Another example of just such criminal anarchy was to occur exactly seven days after those shootings in the Tottenham post office, on Thursday, 21 June. The scene was a large office block on the Great West Road in Brentford, at ten o'clock in the morning. A Securicor armoured vehicle arrived outside the block's main entrance to make a substantial delivery. The two men in its crew left the vehicle and walked into the foyer through the open glass front doors, one man escorting the other who was carrying the money. They crossed the reception area, rang for a lift, and waited. Suddenly, behind them a man armed with a pistol and wearing a motorcycle crash helmet (now a favoured method of disguise) rushed in through the doors and shouted at them. Then, just as the lift doors opened and the Securicor men ducked into the lift, he fired at them, the bullet striking one side of the lift doorframe. Seeing that the lift doors were about to close he then pushed his way in and threatened the Securicor men with his gun. One of the guards struggled with him in the close confines of the lift cage. In the course of the struggle the gun discharged, mortally wounding the guard. At this point his companion intervened and their attacker, now without his gun, tried to escape back across the foyer but the uninjured guard pursued him, grappling with him so that the two men staggered away from the main entrance doors and towards a smaller glass side door which was locked.

Meanwhile, outside the block a second man, also armed and wearing a crash helmet, had been waiting, sitting astride a powerful motorbike, revving the engine. He now came to his accomplice's aid. Moving along the outside of the building until he could see through the glass door, he took careful aim and shot the second Securicor guard in the leg, disabling him. As bystanders looked on helplessly the first gunman then made his escape out through the front doors and the two men roared off together on the motorbike, leaving one guard dying and the other very seriously injured.

One of the motorcyclists was wearing a courier's tabard as part of his disguise and witnesses described it. That was traced by the investigating officers back to a shop in Brentford and that in turn led to a robber who had hurriedly left for a 'holiday' in Spain. We traced him there, watched and waited for him and when he came back he and his fellow robber were arrested and later convicted.

But that month of June 1984 still held other things in store for us and only a day or so later an armed robber held up a bank only a few yards away from Scotland Yard in busy Victoria Street.

Brandishing a gun he held the bank staff at bay and demanded money. An alert member of the staff had managed to inform police by way of a 999 call and that was responded to by a police radio vehicle which was close to the bank. It was crewed by a sergeant and four constables of the Yard's Diplomatic Protection Group, all armed as part of their normal duties.

The sergeant, in uniform, called for the robber to drop his gun. Then he repeated the command. Instead the robber turned towards the sergeant, only a few feet away, and raised his gun. The sergeant fired one shot and the robber fell to the ground.

That robber was lucky. The one shot had hit him dead centre and passed through his body without striking any vital organs or bones.

Within a few days he had recovered in hospital and was later convicted. That case had to be dealt with by my Chief Superintendent on the Regional Crime Squad for by the end of that month of June we had run out of senior Flying Squad officers. Every one was committed to a major investigation.

At about this time developments occurred in the continuing Security Express investigation. Enquiries made in Spain, Portugal and here in London had come up with the names of a number of Englishmen who had gone to live in Spain, one only a few weeks before the first arrests had been made, in January 1984, including a man who had been the licensee of yet another pub in Dalston.

Those Spanish residents now became of more than passing interest to the Flying Squad and warrants were eventually obtained for their arrest. At that time however we were without an extradition treaty between Spain and Britain and when in 1986 a treaty was signed it was not made retrospective, so events occurring in this country in 1983 and 1984 could still not be made the subject of an extradition application.

It was all very frustrating, but there it is. I dare say those warrants are still in existence and one day those named on them may discover the Yard has a long memory.

Now, in September 1984, a personal decision which had been niggling at the back of my mind for some time suddenly had to be faced. I was approached from outside the force and offered a security post in industry. I was a Commander in the Metropolitan Police and in every other police force (save the City of London which also has the commander rank) that is the equivalent to an assistant chief constable, a rank which carries with it a compulsory retirement age of sixty. But in the Metropolitan Police the retirement age is fifty-seven for commanders and, although admittedly it does offer the same pension as that due to an assistant chief constable at the age of sixty, no allowance is made in the Metropolitan force for the man who feels that at fifty-seven he isn't quite ready to retire.

In fact the force in no way encourages an officer to stay after he has served his basic thirty pensionable years, which in my case had come way back in 1982: at that point his retirement pension reaches its maximum and from then on, although he continues paying into the pension fund, he notches up no further pension advantages. In effect, therefore, his salary decreases after thirty years of service quite dramatically, for if he chose to do so he could now be retired and drawing a pension of two-thirds his salary anyway. It is a policy which keeps the force young, I suppose, and perhaps admirably free from elderly reactionaries at the top. Some of course may like the idea of retiring at fifty-seven, but it left me with a difficult decision to make.

I enjoyed police work, I was in the middle of several important cases and I was holding one of the top operational posts at the Yard. The regulations allowed me another two years of service, if I chose, but, on the other hand, at fifty-five I had another ten years to offer a civilian employer, and I had received an excellent job offer of a type which might not be repeated. I talked it over with Bridget who was now asking me to leave the force anyway, because of the November 1983 *Sun* newspaper article which had really upset her, so I decided to accept the outside job offered to me and I immediately informed the assistant commissioner of this decision. It was now September 1984 and, because the Brinks-Mat robbery trial at the Old Bailey was due to begin in October and likely to be lengthy, I told both the assistant commissioner and my future employers that I would remain in the force until that trial was concluded. Allowing two full months for the trial, I fixed January 1985 for the date of my resignation.

Then, just as the Brinks-Mat robbery trial was about to begin, another major investigation overtook the Squad: a robbery that was to have some pretty devious complications, caused by criminals who tried to discredit the police.

On Monday, 1 October 1984, two men armed with automatic handguns raided the Abbey National Building Society office on Church Road in Stanmore, Middlesex. They held up the staff, and took away more than £13,000 in cash, stuffed into a bag. But as they ran for their waiting getaway car they were tackled by a passer-by, George Davey, who'd seen the robbery through the office window. A violent struggle developed. One of the robbers fired at Davey, missed, and fired again – but the gun jammed so he hit Davey over the head with its butt. This caused the gun to go off, the bullet luckily ricocheting harmlessly away across the pavement. But the blow to Davey's head had enabled the two robbers to break free and make off again – their car, a Ford Granada, had been parked some yards away.

Davey refused to give up. He pursued them again, tried to grab at them, and the bag containing the money was torn open, spilling the cash out across the roadway. One of the robbers again threatened Davey with his gun, but he still persisted. As a further shot was fired, again missing Davey, a second member of the public came to his assistance. A young RAC patrol officer, Terry Tomkins, joined Davey in wrestling with the gunmen and chased them into an alleyway where the two turned at bay. More shots were fired, one grazing Davey's thigh, and finally the gunmen made it as far as their car, scrambled in, and started the engine.

Now Tomkins ran to his own car and was able to use it to block their getaway. But the gunmen snatched another nearby motorist and threatened him with death if the roadblock wasn't removed, so reluctantly Tomkins backed up out of the way and the two thieves drove off. His and Davey's courageous delaying tactics had given someone time to make an emergency 999 call however and a police car roared up just as the robbers were making off. Tomkins pointed wildly at the getaway car and the police driver responded at once, setting off in pursuit.

The driver, PC Jones, and his radio operator, PC Horswood, chased the Ford Granada up Stanmore Hill at speeds of up to a hundred miles an hour. The gunman in the Ford's passenger seat leaned out of the side window and fired shots at the police – six in all, none of which hit the police car. Then, in Bushey High Street, dense traffic brought the car chase to a sudden halt. As the Granada stopped and the police car drew up behind it both the gunmen leapt out and strode back, ordering the two policemen out into the street at gunpoint. Jones got out warily. Horswood made as if to comply, but then flung his car door violently open, unbalancing the gunman who was standing by it. He grappled with the robber and was struck twice viciously across the head with the gun. Jones meanwhile had evaded the robber on his side of the car and had run round to help Horswood. A general mêlée followed, in which Jones too was struck over the head with a gun butt. Tomkins had caught up by now in his own car, and he joined in the fight, helping to bring the two gunmen, still struggling, to the ground.

At this point another pedestrian, a fifty-five-year-old woman, Mrs Joanne Wakefield-Smith, took a hand. First she lashed out with her shopping bag at one of the robbers, then she actually managed to prise the gun out of the hand of the other man as he fought and struggled in the roadway. She took the gun and threw it out of reach. Other passers-by then joined in and, despite two more shots being fired, the gunmen were eventually overpowered and arrested.

They were taken to Harrow police station, where they gave their names. They were later charged with armed robbery and locked in a cell to await magistrates' court proceedings.

The following night, at shortly after twelve, when the station sergeant at Harrow police station made a routine visit to the two men in their cell, he was jumped upon and knocked unconscious. The police station was lightly staffed at that time of night, and the two men were able to use the sergeant's keys to leave him locked inside their cell. Then they gained the yard at the rear of the station and climbed over a wall to escape.

In due course the station sergeant was rescued, and the Flying Squad was alerted. I asked Chief Superintendent Brown to head the enquiry to recapture those men using Flying Squad and Regional Crime Squad officers to do so. But several weeks then passed without any trace of them being discovered, until Don Brown heard about a party which had been held in a Middlesex pub on 13 October by various friends of the escaped robbers at which a telephone call was said to have been received from them, reputedly from Spain – and indeed the *News of the World* soon published a report of that party, complete with photographs – but no other firm evidence was discovered until 19 November.

On that day four postcards signed by the missing men and post-marked Lloret de Mar, Spain, arrived in London. Three were addressed to friends of theirs who had been at the public-house party, and who obligingly passed them on to us. The fourth was addressed to the Chief Superintendent in charge of Harrow police station. It too was signed by the wanted men and bore one of their fingerprints. The message on the card claimed that the Flying Squad officers who had dealt with them at Harrow police station after their arrest had taken a bribe of £2,000 to allow them to escape.

This was of course a very serious accusation. I knew it to be false however for – although the detective inspector named on the card was admittedly now a member of the team hunting the robbers – during the time of their arrest, charging, and two-day detention at Harrow police station he'd been nowhere near the place: he was in fact a Regional Crime Squad officer from Scotland Yard. But of course the card was passed onto the Police Complaints Investigation Branch.

While they were looking into it we stepped up our search for the missing men. This wasn't the first time we'd received postcards from abroad intended to put us off the scent, and we had a strong suspicion that these two robbers were still in Britain.

Next day the corruption accusation received what appeared to be a carefully timed boost. Certain information – I have to be careful here for fear of libelling the presumed innocent – certain information led police officers to an address in Hayes where they found what appeared to be a written statement made by a woman known to one of the two wanted men. In it she described how, on 2 October, while he was in custody at Harrow police station, he had telephoned her and asked for £2,000 to be brought to him at the police station in cash, saying that he needed it to pay his solicitor. She had obtained the money and placed it, together with a note to him, in an envelope which she had given to a detective of the Flying Squad as soon as she reached the police station. This detective had read the note, had seen the money, and had allowed her to deliver it to the prisoner.

In fact the detective concerned had already reported the woman's visit to Superintendent Brown. He reported he had been shown an envelope and the note inside it, which had been innocuous, there'd been no money, and he'd allowed both to be taken into the prisoner.

The statement went off to join the postcard with the Police Complaints Investigation Branch and the enquiry continued.

By now, of course, the Brinks-Mat robbery trial was under way and taking up a great deal of time, as was the continued search for the missing gold. And the Harrow escapees, too, were still missing.

On 4 December 1984, a Sunday, a jury at the Old Bailey found two of the three men who had been tried for the Brinks-Mat robbery guilty. It was apparently the first time ever that an Old Bailey jury had brought in a verdict on a Sunday and it was the next day, the Monday, when the two men found guilty were each sentenced to twenty-five years' imprisonment.

It was also early in December that the corruption allegation made in the escapees' case received another purported injection of authenticity when two articles were published in the popular press, one claiming that a reporter had actually met them both in a Spanish holiday apartment. A tape-recorded conversation with one of the wanted men was said to have taken place and the article stated that in it the allegations against Flying Squad officers were repeated, the date of the conversation in Spain being given as 30 November. This tape, too, ended up with the Police Complaints Investigation Branch. Its contents were undeniably what the article had claimed they were, but its provenance was more doubtful.

By now, in December 1984, my retirement from the force was fairly imminent, and I had agreed to commence my new employment outside the force early in the New Year. My actual retirement date from the force would be 31 January 1985 and I had intended to follow the traditional pattern of taking one month of leave, which was due to me anyway, prior to my retirement. But then other events interceded.

Don Brown, the Flying Squad Chief Superintendent, who had

joined the Flying Squad as its Chief Superintendent on the same day as myself in January 1983, and who had been a tower of strength throughout the two years since, now told me that he too intended to retire from the force, a month later than myself.

That meant of course the Squad would now be losing both its Commander and its Chief Superintendent at almost the same time. I brought that to the notice of the assistant commissioner straight away.

Meanwhile, while the Brinks-Mat robbery trial had been going on at the Old Bailey, we had been following up yet another line of enquiry in connection with the missing Brinks-Mat gold.

We had discovered that a man named Kenneth Noye had, in about mid-1984, purchased eleven one-kilo bars of gold from a bank in Jersey and paid for them partly in cash. That was checked out and it was established he had also received documentation which would confirm his ownership of those eleven bars of gold.

I knew of course that a great deal of the stolen Brinks-Mat gold had been in bars of one kilo in weight so I was immediately interested in the Jersey transaction.

Further enquiries revealed that Noye lived in a large house set in its own grounds of several acres at West Kingsdown in the countryside of Kent and that only served to increase my interest, for in January 1984, after the initial scientific examination of the transit van used by the Brinks-Mat robbers to remove the gold had been carried out, I had requested that it also be examined by a geologist, in particular the underside of the vehicle. His examinations had some time later indicated that the transit van had recently been 'out in the country'.

That vehicle had been stolen three months before the robbery so it had probably remained hidden or 'laid down' somewhere by the robbers, throughout the intervening three-month period, only to be actually used on the day of 'the job', a quite common tactic used by professional robbers.

That being so the findings of the geologist as to the vehicle's more recent movements had been significant.

We had also known throughout the case that disposal of the Brinks-Mat gold was not going to be an easy matter for the villains. Somewhere they had in their possession more than six thousand bars of what is known as 'four nines gold', which means pure gold, containing 999.9 parts of gold to the 1000, and every bar so stamped into the metal. Each bar was also stamped with its own individual serial number, an assay mark and its weight, all of which meant every single bar was identifiable.

None of the gold bars could therefore be disposed of through legitimate gold markets while in their present form without police becoming aware of it, so clearly the gold would have to be disguised in some way before it could be disposed of. And even then those who had it would only be able to do so a little at a time, for any sudden influx on to the gold market in this country of the three tons of gold which had been stolen would immediately come to notice.

One alternative might be to smuggle it abroad in some way and have it smelted and doctored there, stamped with some other refinery markings, then fed back on to the world gold market in that way. I thought this most unlikely myself for that would have to involve a recognised refinery and assay markings.

But there was one other way the gold might be dealt with. That would be to smelt it here in England, a little at a time, thus disposing of the identifying markings, then further disguising it by adding some other metal, possibly brass or copper. With the right connections it could then be disposed of little by little as 'scrap gold' of which there is a great deal of trading in most countries, quite legitimately. That, I suspected, was what would most probably happen. So, in 1984, so far as we on the Squad were concerned, it had all been a question of simply seeking, or waiting, for some sign that this was being done.

That sign was the Jersey transaction by Noye. Black had told us the gold was to lie buried 'until the heat was off', and the Jersey transaction had taken place some six months after the robbery, so when we later heard of it we realised it could be just what we had been waiting for. On the other hand, of course, it might have nothing to do with the Brinks-Mat case at all.

There was only one way to find out and that was to take a close look at Noye. That task fell to Chief Inspector Ken John and Detective Inspectors Tony Brightwell and John Walsh, assisted by their officers, all of whom had been with the Brinks-Mat investigations from the outset way back in 1983. They set about keeping surveillance upon Noye and his address.

The Harrow escapees' enquiry had meanwhile been progressing slowly but surely and now we were quite sure they were in England.

We were now into early January 1985 and because of the Noye matter I had decided to forgo part of my pre-retirement leave and instead had arranged to hold my farewell gathering at the Yard on the evening of Friday 18 January which would now be my last day of duty, although I would remain the Commander of the Squad until midnight on 31 January 1985, my actual retirement date. I was to start work in my new employment on 4 February.

I had believed, and with reason, that by 18 January both the Harrow escape and the Noye enquiries would be resolved, but as things turned out I was only partially correct.

I was right insofar as the two escaped robbers were concerned for, helped by officers from the Flying Squad and Regional Crime Squad, Chief Superintendent Don Brown had persisted with his search in Britain for the two missing men, and on Monday, 14 January 1985, their determination was rewarded. Their enquiries led to an armed operation by them, with officers of the Thames Valley police, upon a house on the London Road in Langley, Buckinghamshire. There at dawn detectives forced an entry and, after a struggle, the two robbers were re-arrested.

One of them made a statement to officers of another force soon afterwards, admitting that since their escape from Harrow police station they'd been hiding with friends in various parts of Britain and hadn't been out of the country.

Now Superintendent Brown was able to detain quite a few of these 'friends', the charge being harbouring and assisting wanted criminals, and more arrests were to follow. Among these were individuals who had actually arranged for the postcards from Spain to be sent, in order to confuse the police. Trials subsequently followed. Convictions and some substantial sentences were passed.

Before those arrests however, and earlier in January, the surveillance upon Noye and his address had also paid dividends when a man, who it was to appear was a fairly regular visitor to Noye's address in Kent, was seen to meet with other men in Central London, after he had been seen collecting a briefcase from Noye.

The two men he met were then seen to make their way to Paddington Station and to be in possession of a briefcase the contents of which were obviously very heavy. There they boarded a train to Swindon in Wiltshire where they met two other men in a Jaguar car.

The briefcase was passed to those two men and they in turn were tailed by officers. It transpired one of the men in the Jaguar was in fact the Managing Director of a bullion company in Bristol.

The two men who had travelled by train to Swindon returned to London the same day and were then seen to meet Noye's visitor again, that evening, in an hotel in London, where they handed another briefcase to him.

Those three men had now been seen to meet together three times in a three-day period and one of them had visited Noye's address on three occasions over the same three-day period. Briefcases had been very much in evidence and one of them, obviously very heavy, had been passed to a Bristol bullion dealer.

It was fair to assume, I thought, that what had been seen being carried in the heavy briefcase was probably gold and if so the manner in which it had been transported and transferred was unusual, to say the least.

Those meetings had taken place in mid-week and strongly suggested a transfer from Noye's visitor to Bristol and we had reason to believe Noye had documentation which would prove him to be the lawful owner of eleven one-kilo bars of gold. Thus, if what had been seen carried in the briefcase was gold, up to a total of eleven kilos in weight, then if Noye were challenged about it he could produce genuine documentation suggesting that he was the owner of that gold.

Furthermore, even if it was gold in the briefcase, unless it was identifiable there was no way of knowing whether or not it was part of the stolen Brinks-Mat gold. The apparent secrecy with which the briefcase transaction had been carried out might be accounted for by other reasons, perhaps some other type of criminal enterprise.

What we needed to establish, of course, was whether or not this was Brinks-Mat gold and, if so, where the rest of it was hidden. That was not going to be easy.

I also had another problem. I now knew that Don Brown, the Squad's Chief Superintendent, and I were both about to leave the force and if this Noye business could not be resolved quickly then I would have to involve yet another senior officer for purposes of continuity – for if it should prove to be the Brinks-Mat gold then a lot of long-term follow up work would have to be done.

I therefore consulted at that stage with the assistant commissioner, told him of the Noye matter and said what I thought needed to be done. He agreed and appointed Detective Superintendent Brian Boyce, from another branch at the Yard, to join the Brinks-Mat enquiry team. Brian Boyce was awaiting fairly imminent promotion to Chief Superintendent rank and it was decided that when promoted he would be appointed to the Flying Squad to replace Don Brown upon his retirement. Meanwhile, Boyce would supervise the Noye surveillance operation and in doing so would also seek the assistance of officers of the Yard's Criminal Intelligence Branch, a branch in which he had served previously himself. That agreed, I briefed Brian Boyce myself.

The transfer of the briefcases which had been observed had left me upon the horns of dilemma. It was reasonable to suppose that if we continued the surveillance upon Noye and those other persons we now knew of, then further similar transactions might be witnessed.

If so, we could then step in to check out what was being carried in the briefcases. If it was gold, then that might lead us to the rest of the missing Brinks-Mat gold. But then again, it might not. There was nothing to say it would be identifiable, and if we could not identify it and there was eleven kilos or less in the briefcase, we probably wouldn't even be able to prove whether or not it was Noye's own property.

We could search his house and its grounds, together with the addresses of those other persons who we now knew had been involved in the earlier briefcase transaction. But there was nothing to say that we would find any other gold, and if we didn't then all we would achieve would be to alert everyone that we had been watching Noye and his activities. Then, we would have simply blown our line of enquiry, and all for nothing.

The next step therefore was quite obvious. The surveillance operation had to be continued, its terms of reference to establish if possible the source of whatever it was which was being carried in the briefcases. And to do that we had to wait for another transaction to occur.

There followed however a week or more, during which time no further movement was observed and the mid-week briefcase transaction of the week before was not repeated.

So I entered what I had intended to be my last week of actual police service on duty and, by Wednesday 16 January, there had still been no development in the Noye matter. I called a further meeting with Superintendent Boyce. By now his team of officers had found out that the grounds of Noye's house had apparently been used as part of a government establishment either during the war years or since, and they were believed to contain several disused underground bunkers. If that were true then it presented all sorts of possibilities. That information was all rather vague, however, and the exact locations of the bunkers, if they did exist, were unknown.

One way or another however I now had to make a decision – whether to have Noye's house and grounds searched straightaway, together with the addresses of all the other people who had been involved with the earlier briefcase transactions, before I went on leave that coming weekend, or, alternatively, to tell Brian Boyce and his officers to keep the surveillance operation going in the hope that another briefcase transaction might yet occur.

There really wasn't a choice. The surveillance had to be continued, and I had to hope that Noye and his associates hadn't already become suspicious, aware of the police observations which were being kept upon them.

That decided, I asked to be kept informed of any developments which occurred up to the date of my own retirement from the force, and at the same time I pointed out that if another transaction did not occur within a reasonable time then police should move in anyway to conduct searches.

On the Friday of that week, 18 January, with no further news about Noye forthcoming, I held my farewell party as planned at the Yard, and went off for two weeks of leave at home, prior to my retirement at the end of the month.

I heard nothing more about the Noye operation and I assumed there had been no further developments. But then nine days later, on Sunday morning, 27 January, I opened up a Sunday newspaper.

It reported that during the evening before, Saturday 26 January, a detective officer from the Yard had been stabbed to death in the grounds of a house in Kent.

I guessed the connection immediately and telephoned the Flying Squad communications room at the Yard. The duty officer confirmed my suspicions.

After telephoning both the assistant commissioner and the deputy assistant commissioner at their homes, I contacted my own Flying Squad driver, telling him to pick me up at once.

We drove to the Kent police station nearest the Noye address to find numbers of Flying Squad and other officers gathered there. I discovered that the death of the Metropolitan police officer – Detective John Fordham – was being dealt with by Kent police, because it had occurred within their policing jurisdiction, and on account of that investigation Metropolitan police officers were now excluded from the grounds of the Noye address.

Noye and another man had apparently been detained by police the evening before and were now being held at a police station elsewhere.

Later that day I again spoke with my assistant commissioner and the deputy assistant commissioner when they too arrived at that Kent police station. I had meanwhile talked with a senior detective officer of Kent police, from whom I had gathered that a search for gold had not yet been carried out in the grounds of Noye's address.

The Assistant Commissioner, John Dellow, and I then made our way together to the Noye address. By now it was after 4 p.m. on the Sunday afternoon and as we arrived a search of the grounds was just being carried out in the close vicinity of the house itself, by uniformed officers of Kent police, led by an inspector.

Just as we arrived we heard one of those officers shout out that he had found something. We walked forward with the Inspector, to see what it was.

He had found a cloth-covered bundle hidden beneath an empty and upturned five-litre paint can which was positioned close alongside the wall of a garage just a few yards from the house itself. Wrapped in the bundle were what appeared to be eleven one-kilo bars of gold, all of which appeared to me to have been recently smelted and roughly cast.

The follow-up operation by the Flying Squad, which I had originally intended should take place immediately we moved in upon Noye, that of questioning and searching the addresses of those other persons who we knew to have been involved in the earlier briefcase transaction, had not yet been carried out.

The publicity already given to the events of the Saturday evening and to the present police investigations at the Noye address did not suggest to me that we would now have the element of surprise on our side, but clearly it was of importance that those searches and interviews be carried out as soon as possible. Otherwise a great deal of evidence might be lost.

I discussed this with Mr Dellow and a senior officer of Kent police that evening and it was arranged that early the next morning a further meeting would be held at the Yard to resolve the co-ordination of the two separate investigations – that by the Kent police into Detective Fordham's death and the other by the Yard into the Brinks-Mat gold robbery.

The meeting at the Yard took place as arranged on the following morning, the Monday. A number of senior officers of both forces attended, including myself, and it was agreed that I should co-ordinate those two enquiries, at least, up to the date of my retirement on the Thursday of that week. The Kent police would continue, in liaison with Superintendent Boyce, to deal with investigations into Detective Fordham's death whilst with assistance from Commander Phil Corbett of the Yard's C11 Criminal Intelligence Branch, of which Detective Fordham had been a member, I would myself have the follow-up Brinks-Mat gold enquiries carried out.

I made my plans that afternoon and at six the next morning, Tuesday 29 January, a whole series of police raids were carried out in London, the West Country and elsewhere, by numbers of officers drawn from several different branches of the Yard, including the

Flying Squad and the Regional Crime Squad, with assistance from officers from other forces. That day, and the next, some twenty-six people in all were detained and questioned, including a man named Chappell, a director of the Bristol Bullion Company, and another man, Constantinou, in connection with whom we quickly established evidence of false documentation which purported to account for a series of transactions involving some eight or nine millions of pounds' worth of gold, between October 1984 and January 1985.

It was Thursday evening, 31 January 1985, the very last day of my service with the force, before those immediate follow-up enquiries had been completed. Then at 8.30 p.m. I put on my coat and went home.

Up to this present time, as far as I know, the rest of the Brinks-Mat gold has never been found. But on 24 July 1986, some eighteen months after my retirement from the force, Noye and three other men, Reader, Chappell and Constantinou, were convicted at the Old Bailey. Found guilty of conspiring to dishonestly handle stolen gold, Noye was sentenced to fourteen years' imprisonment and fined £500,000, Chappell to ten years' imprisonment with a £200,000 fine, and Reader to nine years' imprisonment. Constantinou received a two-year suspended prison sentence for VAT fraud in connection with dealings in gold. Noye was ordered to pay £200,000 towards the costs of the prosecution, and Chappell £75,000. The total cost of the trial had apparently amounted to a million and a half pounds. Society pays dearly in its pursuit of justice.

Twelve months or so before that, on 10 June 1985, at the Old Bailey, a number of men had also been brought to trial and sentenced to long terms of imprisonment for the earlier Security Express vault robbery itself, or for dishonestly handling the proceeds of that robbery. They had been rather unlucky. They'd been caught simply because the blue Ford transit van used by other criminals for a completely different crime, the Brinks-Mat robbery, had been dumped on Horsley's doorstep. I'd suspected a possible connection between the two crimes – when in truth, as we all now know, there'd never been one. It had been a pure coincidence.

There had remained one other outstanding matter, however, and that wasn't resolved until February 1988. Four years and three months after they had published their critical editorial in November 1983, the *Sun* newspaper apologised to me and the officers of the Flying Squad in the High Court in London. So now my police career really was behind me.

But back in January 1985 the tragic death of John Fordham in connection with my last ever case with the force had greatly saddened me. That was uppermost in my mind when I had walked out through the Back Hall at New Scotland Yard, at 8.30 p.m. on 31 January 1985, for the last time as a serving police officer.

John Fordham was one of those fine men who are numbered among the officers of the London Metropolitan Police Force, men with whom I had been proud to serve for almost thirty-three years. It was another of those officers, a PC on duty in the Back Hall, who wished me goodnight as I walked away from the Yard, that January evening. I wish him and all the serving officers of the force today every good fortune. They need it, and they deserve it.

POSTSCRIPT

THE FUTURE?

Over the thirty-odd years since I joined the Metropolitan Police Force, its training, equipment and technology have all been improved enormously. There have also been vast improvements in manning levels. So why is it then that London today is a far more dangerous, violent and crime-ridden city than it was way back in 1952? Why is it that in many areas old people live in fear of attack, women are afraid to venture out alone after dark, and all around us the twin problems of crime and violence are steadily worsening?

Those are questions which many people ask. And if they are like me they don't come up with a simple single answer. The crime rate in London really began to accelerate far too long ago – at the height of the prosperous Macmillan era, in fact – for the recent high levels of unemployment, or the gap between the so-called haves and have-nots in today's divided society to be the cause, as I have often heard suggested. It wasn't only the young who were swinging back in London's Sixties: the criminals too were moving with the times, increasing in number and expanding their activities.

No simple answers, therefore. And no complicated answers either, if the inconclusive results of many years of expert sociological research are to be trusted. In fact, no answers at all: society at large now seems to accept that crimes of violence are widespread in our cities, that the situation is likely to worsen, and that the police can do no more than fight a rearguard action.

I find this a shocking conclusion: it demonstrates in society a smug callousness and flippant denigration of its police, exactly those dangerous attitudes which have helped to bring the present situation about. Here I believe are two factors that go right to the root of our troubles: one, a newly resigned acceptance of violent crime, and the other, a newly ambivalent attitude towards the police.

Acceptance of crime creates a vicious circle: every time we fail to be shocked by a violent crime so that it ceases to be newsworthy, we make things easier for the criminal next time round. Our courts and legislators too, in their more recently expressed sensitivity, have in my opinion made criminality easier by refusing to disclose the names of young offenders convicted of violent crime, thus, in many cases, protecting an increasingly violent section of our society from precisely that ostracism and social stigma which in earlier times acted as a powerful deterrent. After all, at the age of eighteen, young people can sit as jurors, yet up to the age of seventeen they are protected by anonymity in the courts. Similarly when adult offenders are brought to trial the cases are so seldom reported that even neighbours living in the same street may remain unaware of it, which removes much of the local pressure which once acted so powerfully against any tendency towards criminal behaviour.

Resigned acceptance also influences sentencing levels, it seems to me. Shorter sentences, it appears, are often proposed simply as a response to prison overcrowding, and remission of sentence for good behaviour and parole seem to be encouraged for the same reason, so much so that a sort of discount now operates for the professional criminal in relation to his business affairs, which of course he takes into account when planning a crime and assessing the risks: certainly this must help prison administration, but the public, or the victims, who presumably approved the original prison sentence, are not informed of the reduction. They presumably know that something of the sort goes on, but just shrug resignedly.

Which is not to suggest that all crimes are the result of inadequate deterrent sentencing. Drug-related crime, for example, is more often than not an uncalculating response to the mindless urges induced by drugs. But here again social acceptance has helped to create the situation of which people now seem to despair. Today's young are the children of parents who grew up in the permissive society of the Sixties, when traditional values were recklessly challenged – I say recklessly, since nothing was put in their place – resulting in a basic indiscipline the tragic results of which can so often be seen all about us. And, with those challenges to values in the 1960s there came challenges to those whose role it was to uphold those values – churchmen, teachers, and in particular the police. The Sixties made protest respectable – including mass protest on the streets, which for the first time actually involved many ordinary citizens in violent confrontation with the police. Back in 1952 the police constable had been universally seen as the ordinary citizen's friend. Now, the ordinary citizen, when given to public protest, all too often sees the constable as his enemy – a situation which was so tragically highlighted only a few years ago, at the time of the coal miners' strike and on other notable occasions since.

To all of this, the permissiveness of the 1960s has had few answers. It had no answers, either, to the wave of terrorist violence which began in Northern Ireland in the late 1960s and later spread to this country. Instead society's response, in the main, has been a sort of stunned acceptance. That same acceptance covers the increasing use of firearms by the criminal fraternity in this country in recent years.

Possibly 'permissiveness' is an unfortunate word, loaded and emotive. 'Tolerance' might be more apt, and it might surely be said that any society should be judged by the breadth of its tolerance. Yet tolerance is one thing, while indifference is quite another. It seems to me that today society's capacity for shock has been dulled – and it's there, too, that perhaps casual displays of bloody violence in the media may well have played a part, not so much by inflaming imaginations as by dulling the traditionally British law-abiding sense of outrage.

In Britain, as in any other democracy, the law and its administration by the courts can only, in the final analysis, reflect the attitudes and opinions of the people they serve. Thus, with all the changing attitudes of the Sixties, it's perhaps not surprising that our laws and their administration by the courts quickly began to reflect those changes. In fact, between 1965 and 1970 more changes were effected in the criminal law legislations of this country than, I suspect, any other previous five-year period in our history, save perhaps during the 1860s. They included the final abolition of capital punishment, the introduction of the Theft Act and the Criminal Law Act, both in 1968, and the Criminal Justice Act of 1967.

All these measures represented genuine and no doubt well-meant liberalisations, but unfortunately they were introduced precisely at a time when crime and violence in this country were rapidly increasing. They were therefore, in my opinion, liberalisations we could ill afford. And in addition, much of the new legislation – which seemed to me, as a policeman, to have been designed at least partly to ease the work of the overloaded courts – resulted in enormous amounts of additional administrative paperwork being thrust on to the police instead, and particularly on to the CID. Thus it was that the men kept longer at their desks as a result were exactly those already overworked officers who were desperately needed out on the streets where it mattered most, to combat increasing levels of crime.

It was not a recipe for success. And yet, by dint of hard work and high morale, for a while the police held their own. Indeed, in 1967, for the first time in many years, the London crime rate actually began to drop.

But then, in the early 1970s, came the *Times* Enquiry exposing corruption in the London police force. I've already referred to this, and its very serious repercussions, at some length. It's worth repeating, however, that although corruption undeniably existed, and indeed a number of police officers, including two very senior men, were prosecuted to conviction, the true extent of that corruption was grossly exaggerated in the media, and – perhaps in consequence – the reaction to it was in my opinion hasty, ill-judged, and excessive.

The resultant damage came in two parts. First, and most importantly, the public image of the Metropolitan Police as a whole was unfairly tarnished. Policemen became fair game for every kind of insinuation. Many defence counsels leapt on the bandwagon, so much so that CID officers in giving evidence in court have become liable ever since to the most insulting allegations and insinuations, almost as a matter of course. Portrayals of the 'bent cop' are so commonplace in the media these days as to be positively predictable and, fiction being so much more exciting than fact, the beating-up of persons under questioning is quite simply assumed to be widespread. Racial prejudice is virtually a part of every copper's official equipment, according to some television programmes, and harassment a part of his stock in trade.

Such assumptions are nonsensical. Equally they do a major disservice to society at large, for they can only serve to undermine fundamentally the morale and the day-to-day effectiveness of the only body of men and women willing and able to protect society from its own criminal elements.

I have what I believe to be powerful evidence of the effects of the erroneous 'bent cop' image in Britain, and I propose to offer this later, for it grows out of yet another response brought about by the corruption scandals of the Seventies.

In what I think was a major general over-reaction, officialdom in the 1970s appeared to perceive the London Metropolitan CID as rotten in root and branch, and it therefore set about a course of action which eventually resulted in that department's virtual dismemberment. And the method chosen in effect dismantled the previously recognised career structure of CID officers in such a way that, I suspect, had it occurred in any other kind of employment, they could almost certainly have claimed as individuals to have been the victims of a serious breach of contract by their employer.

That was the true effect of the system of 'interchange' introduced in 1972, for it devalued CID officers' specialist training and frequently made them subordinate to men of far less experience. Career prospects within the force, outside the CID, became more attractive than those within, and for many of those who chose to stay in the CID, simply because they believed it provided a job well worth doing, their prospects for promotion were diminished and frustrated. Even so, the interchange system was continued for many years in the face of constant warnings within the force of its damaging effects and, although it was finally discontinued in that form in 1987, by then the CID, as it had existed before, had to all intents and purposes ceased to exist anyway.

So it was that a constantly increasing rate of violent crime in London came to be met by a police force in quite serious disarray. And meanwhile, the setting up of the Metropolitan Police Complaints Branch, initially known as A10 Branch and on the face of things an excellent provision, was in fact to place a further handicap upon the force. Introduced to satisfy a need for an independent investigative body of men at New Scotland Yard, A10 Branch was formed to deal with all allegations of crime or serious complaint made against Metropolitan police officers, and in such a way that no accusations of cover-up could be made.

To do this a large number of very senior operational detective officers were deployed to A10 Branch from elsewhere in London, together with an equal number of senior uniformed branch officers and with the addition of an equal number of sergeants, making a total of some one hundred men in all, plus clerical support staff.

This group then investigated, and still does so today, all allegations of crime or other serious misconduct made against London policemen, and in the most searching and detailed manner possible.

The findings of all these valuable and highly experienced police officers have been all too predictable: a very high percentage indeed of all such allegations are proved to be unfounded, unwarranted or made falsely and sometimes maliciously. In 1982, for example, and according to the Commissioner's own annual report, out of 2,496 complaints of crime levelled against officers (including traffic offences), only thirty-six were substantiated, and twenty-seven of those were traffic offences. Of the other nine substantiated complaints eight involved allegations of assault but the Director of Public Prosecutions, to whom all such cases are referred, obviously decided not to bring criminal charges. Not one of those substantiated claims in 1982 therefore involved corruption or so-called 'bent cops'. In other words the Metropolitan Police Complaints Branch, which by 1982 had grown to number 266 full-time officers and civil staff, at a cost to the public purse that year of £6.7 million, laboured long and hard in 1982, in order to reveal crime offences which resulted in the criminal conviction of eight policemen of the London force for traffic offences.

The figures speak for themselves: 2,496 allegations of crime, eight traffic convictions as a result of complaints from the public. And yet, thanks to the 'bent cop' image that persists, not only is a large body of experienced police officers in the Complaints Branch kept from doing their more normal job of crime prevention and detection because of public misapprehension, but their findings still go unnoticed. Every policeman feels this loss of public trust. He lives with it and suffers its injustice. And yet he is still expected to perform his duties with courage and determination, even in the face of steadily increasing physical hazards – and indeed, amazingly, he still does so.

In 1982, again, 3,141 police officers of the Metropolitan force were injured in assaults during their duties. Forty-five officers (men and women) were so seriously injured on duty that they were retired from the force that year. And in 1981 the figures were even worse, with 4,444 officers injured. In a force of less than 27,000 men and women in all that is surely unacceptable.

It is a constant source of surprise to me that so few people today seem to realise just how vitally important is the role performed by the police officer in our society or even understand what that role is. It is that of ensuring that the laws which our democratically elected representatives in Parliament bring into being for our society's protection are upheld. Police officers do not make the laws, they simply have a duty to uphold them. And if society at large fails to respect those officers and their ability to do their job, then eventually law itself becomes meaningless and falls into disrepute. Then society itself goes unprotected.

And it is precisely to that situation that we in London are now perilously close. The statistics are clear: over the last thirty years there has been at least a ten-fold increase in crime and violence. If that rate continues it is sobering indeed to visualise the quality of life for those who will live and work in the metropolis in 1998.

So what is to be done?

First, as I hope I've demonstrated, radical changes have to occur in public attitudes, both towards criminals and to the police, and here I'm optimistic. Over more recent years I've detected a new awareness within our society of the seriousness of the present situation and a willingness to look for fresh solutions. Neighbourhood crime watch schemes which work in full co-operation with the police are a good beginning and an intelligent response.

Random inspections of police stations, organised by the Howard League, are another, providing their visits and findings are given full publicity, demonstrating as they do that such places are positively not centres of racial oppression and illegal interrogation as so often presented in certain sections of the press and TV. Magistrates are more fully recognising their responsibilities, and a nationwide movement is underway for more rational and consistent sentencing policies. In short, I see encouraging signs in many directions that the nation's conscience is at last waking to the realisation that acceptance of crime is fatally dangerous, that tolerance can be taken too far, and that to understand is not necessarily to excuse.

Secondly, I believe there is also a growing awareness of the need for a co-ordinated and specialist approach to crime, headed perhaps by a minister with a government-sponsored committee of specialists drawn from all the relevant professions. Certainly there is a need for some authoritative body to formulate and recommend policies and pro-cedures which are designed in the national interest rather than disproportionate minority considerations, or interests, which can actually impede or obstruct true justice being applied with common sense.

In 1962, a Royal Commission report upon a review of the police service in this country highlighted the contemporary increases in crime which even then prevailed and some of its members strongly advised a highly specialist approach to criminal investigation – a recommen-dation which, along with an urgent need for improved CID enlistment, was warmly endorsed by many within the police service itself.

In the event, however, neither of those findings was followed up. Very soon afterwards, as I have described, the London Metropolitan Police in fact took an opposite course to enlarging its department of specialist detectives, and actually began later to dismantle the CID. I suggest that we have since seen, in London, the dire results of that policy.

Today, therefore, almost thirty years later, perhaps what is needed by the police service, and in particular the London Metropolitan force, is the appointment of yet another Royal Commission, with a brief to report upon the mistakes of the past thirty years, the current law enforcement needs of British society, and the best ways in which our police service can be helped to satisfy those needs. In particular, I would suggest, a high priority should be set upon creating a new, far more truthful and realistic public image of that service and what it does, because it is only when justice is seen to be done and the police have fully regained the public's trust that any real progress can be made. And if I'm optimistic about what could be achieved by such a Royal Commission, it's because I believe British citizens, as a whole, are basically fair-minded and law-abiding. I believe the public would now need very little encouragement before returning to the happier and far more constructive situation in which the ordinary copper is regarded as a friend and helper against forces of violence and disorder, which in truth he has always been.

INDEX